I0755869

THE Khalistan Conspiracy

THE Khalistan Conspiracy

A FORMER R&AW OFFICER UNRAVELS THE PATH TO 1984

G.B.S. Sidhu

HarperCollins *Publishers* India

First published in hardback in India by
HarperCollins *Publishers* in 2020
Building No 10, Tower A, 4th Floor, DLF Cyber City, Phase II,
Gurugram – 122002
www.harpercollins.co.in

2 4 6 8 10 9 7 5 3 1

P-ISBN: 978-93-9032-772-0
E-ISBN: 978-93-9032-773-7

Typeset in 11.5/15.7 Bembo (T1) at
Manipal Technologies Limited, Manipal

Dedicated to my father-in-law, late Sardar Swaran Singh, whose service to the nation in various capacities is yet to be fully documented and appreciated

Contents

Preface

MY TWO and a half years' tenure at Gangtok, Sikkim, as station head of India's external intelligence agency, the Research & Analysis Wing (R&AW) of the cabinet secretariat, was rather hectic. I was there from August 1973 to February 1976. In addition to covering trans-border intelligence on Tibet and China, we were entrusted with a highly sensitive and landmark operation relating to Sikkim's merger with India. The operation was undertaken upon personal instructions from Prime Minister Indira Gandhi to the founding chief of the R&AW, R.N. Kao. On the ground, it was carried out by a specially created three-man top-secret cell, headed by me.

The sophistication of that operation may be judged by the fact that even its main target – the former Chogyal – whom I met at frequent intervals to brief him on matters related to Tibet–China, did not know about my link to it. Till the end, he and his family members continued to blame the Intelligence Bureau (IB) for their troubles. As a result of that operation, Sikkim became the twenty-second state of the Union of India through the Thirty-sixth Constitutional Amendment in May 1975. I wrote about the details of that operation in my book *Sikkim: Dawn of Democracy, The Truth Behind the Merger with India* (PenguinRandom House India, 2018).

With the post-merger issues sorted out, I left Gangtok in February 1976 for New Delhi to prepare myself for my next posting as first secretary at the High Commission of India in Ottawa, Canada. I was expected to reach Ottawa by June 1976, but for reasons explained in chapter 1, I could join my new post only in September. I was in Canada for three years and returned to New Delhi in October 1979. During my time in Canada I visited almost all the major cities from east to west, an expanse of over 5,000 km with six different time zones, some more than once. I took one month's leave in July 1978 and travelled from Ottawa to Vancouver across the prairies, and then drove southwards along the west coast of the US to Yuba City, San Francisco, Sacramento, Los Angeles, and down to San Diego and back to Ottawa by re-entering the prairies at Winnipeg. During those trips I met several old friends and relatives and developed new friends and contacts, with whom I remained in touch even after my return to New Delhi.

During that period the Indian community in Canada, comprising mostly Sikhs, were a satisfied lot and were earnestly involved in trying to improve their socio-economic status. In the process, they were contributing their bit to the development of a multicultural society in the country they had chosen as their new home. Other than the normal jostling for the management of gurudwaras in the two major cities of Vancouver and Toronto, for an average Sikh the concept of Khalistan was a non-issue – if not a bit of a joke – not worthy of attention.

Fate sometimes brings you face to face with falsehood wrapped in layers of obfuscation. For an average and casual observer, in awe of the reputation and status of the creator of the falsehood, it is difficult to see through the outer layers and identify the bare bones of the hidden skeleton of falsehood. In that context, I am perhaps no exception.

The falsehood I refer to was designed to make the people of India believe that a fairly large number of the Sikh diaspora from Canada, the US and the UK nursed pro-Khalistan sentiments. Which started to surface 1981 onwards; that soon such feelings started to rub off on a certain segment of the Sikh population in Punjab; that differences between Jarnail Singh Bhindranwale and the moderate Akali Dal leadership led by Harchand Singh Longowal were the outcomes of their differing religious/ideological perceptions, with which the Congress party had nothing to do; that the law and order situation in Punjab resulted from these differences and from Bhindranwale-inspired extremist activities alone; that the Central government under Indira Gandhi and the Punjab government under Darbara Singh up till 5 October 1983 and thereafter under governor's rule did everything possible to restore peace in the state; that Prime Minister Gandhi and her government sincerely wanted a peaceful solution to the Punjab problem through negotiations with the Akali Dal leadership but it was the unhelpful, adamant and uncooperative attitude of the Akali leaders that caused the talks to fail; and that finally, with no other option left to restore normalcy in Punjab, Indira Gandhi was compelled to approve Operation Blue Star.

The reality, in my perspective, was the opposite. The genesis of the falsehoods can be traced to 1978 , when former chief minister of Punjab Giani Zail Singh advised Indira Gandhi's younger son, Sanjay Gandhi, that the Akali Dal-Janata Party coalition government in Punjab could be destabilized if the moderate policies followed by the senior Akali Dal leadership, comprising Harchand Singh Longowal, Shiromani Gurudwara Parbandhak Committee (SGPC) chairman G.S. Tohra and Chief Minister Parkash Singh Badal, could come under constant attack by a suitable Sikh sant.[1] If a forceful hard-line Sikh leader emerged as their rival, the moderate Akali leaders would be forced to adopt an uncompromising stance on issues of Sikh interest to retain their following. Any significant shift in the policies of the moderate Akali Dal leaders would naturally not be to the liking of Janata Party leaders, who represented mainly urban Hindu business interests.

With Indira Gandhi's approval sought and Sanjay's ally Kamal Nath on board,[2] Sant Jarnail Singh Bhindranwale of Gurudwara Darshan Prakash at Chowk Mehta was chosen as the sant who would do their bidding in Punjab. Even though the demand for Khalistan was attributed to Bhindranwale to make his anti-moderate Akali leadership campaign more effective, nothing significant was achieved through this part of the operation till January 1980, when Indira Gandhi returned to power as prime minister. The general elections for the eighth Lok Sabha were due before January 1985, and in preparation for them the Congress decided to focus on the Bhindranwale-Khalistan issue. The details of this two-phase special operation are given in this book. For clarity's sake I have named the two phases of this operation as Op-1 and Op-2. I refer to the Punjab-centric operation as Op-1, and the one which started after January 1980 and ended with Operation Blue Star in June 1984 as Op-2.

As Op-2 progressed, the bitter pill of falsehood had to be repeatedly sugar-coated by its creators before it could be administered in the form of Operation Blue Star to a large number of 'suffering' potential voters to relieve them of their 'fear', 'apprehension', 'pain', 'mental agony' and 'hatred', and earn their gratitude and their votes.

The characters running Op-1 have already been mentioned above. For Op-2, after January 1980, Makhan Lal Fotedar, political assistant to Prime Minister Gandhi, Arun Nehru, Sanjay's cousin and MP from Rae Bareli, and later Arun Singh from the Kapurthala family were added to this group. After Sanjay's death in June 1980, his elder brother Rajiv Gandhi took his place. Sanjay was the main driving force behind Op- 2. After his death, Rajiv depended heavily on Arun Nehru, M.L. Fotedar and Arun Singh, even much after his mother's assassination on 31 October 1984.

As all the decisions pertaining to Op- 2 were taken at 1 Akbar Road, '1 Akbar Road group' has been used in the book to refer to those responsible for certain actions taken in connection with Op 2. Further, during that period, decisions in the various ministries at the Centre and in the Punjab government that had a bearing on Op-2 was informally taken over by the 1 Akbar Road group or the senior bureaucrats working with them. Besides running various errands, Arun Nehru and Arun Singh were also attending meetings either alone or along with Rajiv Gandhi. Two such meetings have been mentioned in Chapter 9.

In view of the developments mentioned above, while performing a small role in furtherance of the main purpose of that operation, I initially felt I was doing what was routine work for a member of a pliant intelligence agency to help its mentor score brownie points against political rivals. However, I had successive opportunities to look at the bare bones of the wrapped skeleton, and soon developed a feeling that I was being used, in howsoever limited a manner, to further the interests of one political party, one person, and one family, in a manner totally at variance with the larger interests of the nation. It was becoming extremely difficult for me to internalize that. My conscience would not allow me to compromise with that and I had to take a decision, sooner rather than later.

A person in my position had limited options to deal with such a dilemma. There was no question of silencing my conscience for the sake of my job. I could not have acted as a whistleblower either. The leaked information could have easily been traced back to me, leading to my summary dismissal, possibly with a trumped-up charge of being an Inter-Services Intelligence (ISI) agent or a Khalistan activist. It would have been my word against theirs. The ever-obliging media would have torn me apart. Second, I could have resigned from service and joined a political party. But I had seen what had happened to my father-in-law, Sardar Swaran Singh, former external affairs minister and a close confidant of Indira Gandhi. He was made to resign from her cabinet in November 1975 because of his opposition to the imposition of National Emergency in June that year. I was small fry compared to him.

The third option for me was to resign from service and return to teaching, which I still loved. But pay scales, the main reason I had switched careers to the Indian Police Service (IPS) in 1964, had not improved much over the years. So I opted for the only sensible and safe choice available to me. I quietly delinked myself from the said activities and moved over to an analysis division within the R&AW, where my job was confined to reading and writing papers/reports, conducting research work, and developing short- to long-term strategic analysis.

And that was what I did on my return from my third operational visit to the US in the first week of October 1983. I shared my views on the matter with Director G.C. (Gary) Saxena, my highly understanding boss, who listened to me patiently, but incredulously, at my frank expression of views. In the end he agreed to my request to relieve me of the charge of the two highly sensitive divisions I was handling and additional operational work related to Punjab.

Those who have had to face a similar dilemma in their lives will realize how difficult it is to live with it without sharing some of your thoughts with someone whom you can trust. Fortunately for me there were a number of such persons. My late wife Iqbal (Bali to family and friends), being her father's daughter, was extremely discreet and understanding. She would listen to me patiently and lighten my burden with the most understanding and consoling words. Sometimes, when my in-laws visited us or stayed with us, I would discuss the situation with my father-in-law. Initially he did not believe me. At one stage he tried to disprove what I was telling him. He was a political leader from the old school, always protective of his party's policies, both in private and in public. But after some time I could observe his frustration with the situation in Punjab and the government's indifference towards it.

Karnail Singh, my batchmate from the IAS (1964, Uttar Pradesh) on deputation to the Government of India, was living in one of the D-I flats in Chanakyapuri, close to where I was. A man of few words, Karnail acted as a good sounding board for me as I grappled with these matters. In the evenings after office hours I would sometimes walk over to his flat and discuss what was happening in Punjab, without disclosing my connection with some of the R&AW operations.

From February 1982 to May 1985 we had a car pool arrangement among four officers working in the R&AW – S.C. Mishra (1959 Odisha), Amar Bhushan (IPS 1967 Madhya Pradesh), J.K. Sinha (IPS 1967 Bihar) and I. We all lived in the Chanakyapuri Satya Marg flats and would travel together in a car for about twenty minutes each in the mornings and evenings. This provided us with some relaxed time to discuss issues of common interest. As a Sikh officer from Punjab, I would share my views on the developing situation in Punjab. To their surprise most of my observations and predictions would come true. My three car pool friends and Karnail Singh are retired now. All four still remember what I used to tell them about Punjab, though not in detail. Amar Bhushan even remembers my listening in on the Delhi police wireless network during the anti-Sikh pogrom on those four fateful days and nights from 31 October to 3 November 1984.

Later, while posted at Tokyo in the early 1990s as one of the ministers in the Indian Embassy, I used to share during our lunch-time walks some of my thoughts on this subject with minister (economic) S.C. Tripathi (IAS 1968 Uttar Pradesh, who later retired as petroleum secretary). I continued exchanging my views on this and other subjects of common interest with him, whenever we played golf at the Delhi Golf Club. I had similar chats with former secretary, R&AW, Vikram Sood, who, like me, had settled in Gurgaon after his retirement.

Based on my twenty-six years' experience of working in the 'Department' (a term normally used for the R&AW by insiders), I decided to write two books on subjects of significant national importance. Because of a number of reasons – both official and personal – I could not undertake these projects earlier. When the time came for writing the first book on Sikkim, May 2011 onwards, my wife's leiomyosarcoma was detected, and my time and energy were entirely devoted to her treatment. After the initial positive response, the cancer resurfaced. She faced the ailment boldly and there was no regret or pain on her face till the last moment, which came in January 2017.

With the book on Sikkim published in 2018, it was time to think about the next one. Initially, I had apprehensions as to how the average Indian would react to the contents of such a book. Most of the people I knew, including some close friends, were unwilling to look beyond Bhindranwale in pinning the blame for Operation Blue Star, without caring to know who had created that monster and most importantly, for what purpose. Efforts were also being made to describe the anti-Sikh pogrom of Delhi and elsewhere as a natural consequence of Indira Gandhi's assassination by her two Sikh security guards. However, certain developments that came to my notice 2017 onwards led me to think that in so far as informed public opinion about the 1984 anti-Sikh pogrom was concerned, things were changing for the better. The subject was being actively discussed on various television channels, and major newspapers carried editorials and lead articles critical of the role played by some Congress politicians and the Delhi police in the massacre of innocent Sikhs.

In the last week of December 2018, I observed that a website with a membership comprising IPS officers, both serving and retired, of which I happened to be a member, had taken up for discussion the topic: 'After Sajjan Kumar, Time to Hold the Police Accountable for their Role in 1984 Massacre'. One member significantly remarked, 'When people were killed in front of officers; when pleas for assistance were cynically turned down; when evidence was deliberately destroyed, it was not by design of the organization.... These were rogue and criminal personnel unfit to wear khaki and have any responsible position... We need to introspect how to weed out such elements from the police – for they exist even today.'

Further, out of the 147 police personnel indicted by the Kusum Lata Mittal Committee of 1987 and the Justice J.D. Jain and D.K. Aggarwal (a former director general of police [DGP]) Committee of 1990, ultimately none were brought to justice. On the contrary, one senior IPS officer against whom there were serious charges got promoted as DGP of a state as early as in 1987.

In his post, dated 27 December 2018 on the same website, former DGP of Uttar Pradesh, and subsequently DGP Border Security Force, Prakash Singh (IPS 1959 Uttar Pradesh) – who had filed a public interest litigation (PIL) in 1996 and obtained in 2006 a highly favourable landmark judgment from the Supreme Court on the yet-to-be-fully implemented police reforms – noted,

> Police reforms are necessary, but their absence cannot be the excuse, much less justification, for the near total abdication of responsibility of the police of the kind we witnessed in 1984. I have always held that we do not require any order to uphold the Rule of Law, and we are under no obligation to carry out any unlawful orders. The point is, are we prepared to pay the price? The majority are not, and that is where the trouble starts.

I also attended, incognito, a public meeting of the Sikh Forum held at the Constitution Club of India in New Delhi in November 2017 to mark the thirty-third anniversary of the anti-Sikh pogrom of 1984. I deliberately reached late and sat in the last row. After senior journalist Saba Naqvi and journalist, editor and academic

Siddharth Varadarajan had spoken, founder-member of the Forum, Professor Amarjit Singh Narang, made a significant observation in his concluding remarks. He said that if it was somehow not possible to punish those guilty of the 1984 pogrom despite the plethora of evidence against them, it was better not to prolong the agony of the concerned family members and the overall Sikh community. He said Sikhs were prepared to forget and forgive the Congress party, if the party apologized for its role in abetting and organizing that massacre. But for that, leaders of the Congress party insisted on evidence in support of the charge.

'Where from should we produce that evidence?' lamented Professor Narang. I left the meeting at that point. While driving home it struck me that I actually have the requisite knowledge about how it all started in 1980, how the operation was carried out and who were the persons responsible for what followed. I had been carrying this burden for almost forty years. It was time to transfer it into a book, in the hope that it might somehow help bring closure to one of the darkest chapters of post-independent India's history.

Acknowledgements

NORMALLY, IT is difficult to remember events that took place some forty years ago. If you somehow remember them, it is even more difficult to place them within a precise timeframe. But when the events happen to be of great national importance, they get embedded in your memory and don't leave it easily. In fact, with the passage of time, the burden of memories of those events compels you to unload it in one form or the other, without further delay. For me, writing a book about the events described here was the most suitable choice to unburden myself.

The contents of this book revolve around a two-phased, top-secret operation, which I name 'Operation Bhindranwale-Khalistan'. It was initiated and managed by some senior and influential Congress leaders operating from the prime minister's residential office at 1 Akbar Road, New Delhi. Normally, no records are kept of such operations, and everything is decided verbally. However, as that operation had some external ramifications, the

R&AW became involved in one form or the other. It was in that context that I had my own personal experiences and insights related to the operation, and they form the core of this book.

However, additional information was required to fill in some gaps. Most newspapers, journals and the other media, suitably 'managed' by the Government of India's officers and agencies concerned, gave coloured, if not distorted, views of the developments. The rest could not grasp the true nature of the operation and got carried away by the meticulously managed flow of events. Even so, some publications like *India Today* and the *Indian Express* among others, provided useful information. Credit for such articles and news items quoted from these publications has been provided.

Certain books proved very useful in clearing some doubts about the jigsaw puzzle that the operation was. Others corroborated some of the information that had come to my attention while in service. Some of these books were written by senior government officials who held crucial posts at that time. These include: *From Poona to Prime Minister's Office* by B.G Deshmukh, former cabinet secretary, *Through the Corridors of Power* by P.C. Alexander, then principal secretary to the PM, and *Kaoboys of R&AW: Down Memory Lane* by B. Raman, former additional secretary, R&AW. Some others that I have relied on were written by well-known journalists – for instance, *Amritsar: Mrs Gandhi's Last Battle* by Mark Tully and Satish Jacob; *Beyond the Lines: An Autobiography* by Kuldip Nayar, and *Bloodshed in Punjab: Untold Saga of Deceit and Sabotage* by G.S. Chawla. *1984: Anti-Sikh Violence,* an eyewitness account of the anti-Sikh pogrom in Delhi by Sanjay Suri, who was at the time a young reporter with the *Indian Express,* was an eye-opener on two counts – it made plain the role of some Congress leaders in the 1984 pogrom and the inaction and even connivance of some Delhi police officials; and it corroborated what I had heard on the Delhi police wireless network, which I monitored on my personal radio for three days from 1–3 November 1984. My special thanks to all these authors.

Soon after the manuscript of my previous book on Sikkim's merger with India was given to the publishers in early 2018, I started preparing handwritten notes about the events described in this book. After the release of *Sikkim: Dawn of Democracy*, I started dictating the contents of those notes to my daughter, Harmeeta, and they came in handy for inclusion in this book. She continued to help me by taking dictation as and when I needed it. My son Gagan helped me locate relevant material on the internet and also in reading the draft manuscript at the pre-editing and editing stages, making some important suggestions, which have been incorporated. I am grateful to both for their help.

My special thanks to R.T. Nagrani, former director general, security, for sharing very useful information regarding the aborted heliborne commando operation, which I have written about in Chapter 8. He also let me see his family album, from which I was able to take a couple of good photographs for use in the book. For this, I am very grateful to him. I am also grateful to Prakash Singh, former DGP UP and DG BSF, for having permitted me to quote one of his posts, details of which appears in the Preface.

G.S. Chawla, former senior correspondent of the *Indian Express,* shared with me some of his experiences to help me better understand what had been happening on the ground. I am grateful to G.S. Pandher, former DG BPR&D and DIG of BSF at Amritsar when Operation Blue Star was launched, and to M.P.S. Aulakh, former DGP Punjab, who held the crucial post of assistant director, Intelligence Bureau, Amritsar, from 1982 to 1985, for the information provided by them.

Special thanks are due to my friend and IPS batchmate Ratan Sahgal for being very helpful during Indira Gandhi's two visits to the US in 1982 and 1983. I am also grateful to my IPS batchmate Chaman Lal who provided me with some very useful information about the functioning of the Punjab Police during the two-year period he was posted as DIG BSF (Border) and Punjab Police. Another of my IPS batchmates, P.S. Bawa, helped me understand the functioning of the Delhi police and their role in the November 1984 anti-Sikh pogrom. My special thanks also to Dr Mohinder Singh, director, Bhai Veer Singh Sahitya Sadan (BVSS), New Delhi, for lending me books from his personal library, which proved useful in writing some portions of Chapter 1. He also procured some very useful photographs which have been included in this book. Ambassador K.C. Singh (Retd), who still remembered my brief conversation with him in September 1983 in New York, has kindly shared with me crucial information that came to his knowledge while he was posted as deputy secretary in the President's secretariat in November 1984. My gratitude to him for it.

Last, but not the least, my special thanks to the very energetic Swati Chopra, executive editor at HarperCollins, without whose enthusiastic support this project would not have taken off, to begin with. She was a great support throughout the writing process and made many valuable suggestions at the editing stage.

1

Introduction

AN OBJECTIVE assessment by future historians of Indira Gandhi's role as prime minister of India would not be complete without a closer scrutiny of two of her most controversial decisions – promulgation of National Emergency (26 June 1975 to 21 January 1977) and Operation Blue Star (4 to 8 June 1984). The circumstances under which these decisions were taken and their implications for the nation will be discussed and debated for a long time to come. A couple of things are common between the two – both were taken by Indira Gandhi to retain power, without much concern about their short- to long-term implications for the country, and the government machinery was misused for furthering her personal/family and party interests. But one significant difference between the two was that while the decision to implement the Emergency was taken at short notice, Operation Blue Star was the tragic culmination of a decision taken years before the event, in early 1980.

The purpose of this book is to unravel the truth behind the developments leading to Operation Blue Star and its aftermath. However, it is also pertinent to briefly share some of the hitherto unknown facts about events immediately preceding the imposition of National Emergency on 26 June 1975, which came to my knowledge.

On 12 June 1975, Justice Jagmohan Sinha of Allahabad High Court countermanded Indira Gandhi's election from Rae Bareli Lok Sabha constituency on grounds of misuse of government machinery and debarred her from contesting elections for the next six years. She challenged the verdict in the Supreme Court. On 24 June, Justice V.R. Krishna Iyer granted her a partial stay on the high court's order till her appeal was finally decided. She was allowed to remain as prime minster, but the order stated, 'she will neither participate in the proceedings in the Lok Sabha nor vote nor draw remuneration in her capacity as Member of the Lok Sabha'.

Though Indira Gandhi had won the fifth Lok Sabha elections held in March 1971 with two-thirds majority on the '*garibi hatao*' (remove poverty) plank, by 1974 signs of discontent had started manifesting in some states of India. Jayaprakash Narayan also known as JP or '*Loknayak*' (peoples leader), who had already given a call for a 'total revolution' at a rally in Patna, Bihar, on 4 June 1974, was increasingly putting pressure on Prime Minister Indira Gandhi to resign. Keeping that in view, West Bengal chief minister Siddhartha Shankar (S.S.) Ray, an old family friend of hers, in a handwritten letter dated 8 January 1975,[1] had suggested mass arrest of political leaders and suspension of fundamental rights as a measure to handle the deteriorating situation. She did not pay much heed to his advice all the time. In fact, she told Pranab Mukherjee (who, many years later, became president of

India), one of her cabinet colleagues, that she was not even aware that constitutional provisions allowed for the declaration of a state of emergency on grounds of internal disturbance. According to Mukherjee, it was S.S. Ray who finally led her into taking that controversial and much reviled decision.[2]

As per information revealed to me by a close friend who was working in the office of the Chief of the Army Staff (COAS) at the time, COAS General T.N. Raina departed for a three day-tour of Bikaner on the morning of 25 June 1975. Gen. Raina had just finished his lunch at the local Army Mess in Bikaner when he received a call from New Delhi requesting him to return to headquarters immediately. He returned around 4.30 p.m. and attended a meeting at 1 Akbar Road (presumably with the prime minister) at 6.30 p.m. It is not known what actually transpired in that meeting. It appears that rattled by the prospect of an adverse outcome from JP's speech at a rally scheduled for later that same evening and coupled with the impact of the Supreme Court's order of the previous day, Indira Gandhi may have asked Gen. Raina to keep the army ready to aid the civil administration, should there be any need for the same.

Addressing that rally at Ram Lila Maidan in Delhi, JP called for a nationwide satyagraha demanding Prime Minister Gandhi's resignation. He also exhorted the army, police and civil service personnel not to obey the 'illegal and immoral orders' of the government.

Almost coinciding with the end of JP's rally that evening, members of the Political Affairs Committee (PAC) – Indira Gandhi and her three senior cabinet colleagues, Babu Jagjivan Ram, Sardar Swaran Singh and Y.B. Chavan – met to discuss the implications of the Supreme Court order. After due deliberation, it was decided that the following morning (26 June), she would resign and Sardar

Swaran Singh would take over as interim prime minister. As it was believed that Sinha's judgment was based on flimsy grounds, it was expected that his order would be reversed by the Supreme Court in three months' time, when Indira Gandhi could return as PM with her position legally vindicated.

Sanjay Gandhi, who came to know about the PAC decision, immediately consulted Bansi Lal, the chief minister of Haryana, who told him that his mother was mistaken if she thought Swaran Singh would hand over the PM's post to her even after the Supreme Court decided the case in her favour. The other senior Congress leaders could gang up against her to prevent her from returning to power. Consequently, Sanjay consulted Siddhartha Shankar Ray, on whose advice a letter was written by the prime minister to the president, requesting him to sign the proclamation of National Emergency on the grounds of imminent threat to the security of India from internal disturbances. A compliant President Fakhruddin Ali Ahmad signed the proclamation minutes before the midnight of 25 June, leading to the imposition of Emergency with effect from 26 June. The rest is history.

Though Sanjay Gandhi had been influencing his mother following her victory at the March 1971 national elections, it was the declaration of National Emergency at his behest that marked the beginning of Indira Gandhi's policy of 'family before nation'. Emboldened by his enhanced clout, Sanjay started influencing his mother's political decisions also. Soon after the declaration of Emergency, Sanjay Gandhi started approaching Swaran Singh's senior private secretary, Z.S. Bains, with recommendations for the grant of defence ministry-related contracts. Swaran Singh told Bains to convey to Sanjay that such recommendations should be routed through Sanjay's mother, which never happened.

Swaran Singh resigned from Indira Gandhi's cabinet in November 1975, after having served a record uninterrupted twenty-three years as cabinet minister under three prime ministers. Interestingly, Singh was replaced by Bansi Lal as defence minister. Given the changed political environment, an insecure Indira started leaning heavily for support on Sanjay, and after his death in July 1980, on her elder son Rajiv and some of his friends, all extra-constitutional entities.

While I was in Canada, the Congress lost the Punjab state elections in 1977 to the Akali Dal-Janata Party coalition led by Parkash Singh Badal. Soon after this, some sketchy details reached me about former chief minister Giani Zail Singh and Sanjay Gandhi trying to destabilize the Akali Dal-led coalition government by enlisting the support of Sant Jarnail Singh Bhindranwale of Chowk Mehta gurudwara. Efforts were also being made to plant pro-Khalistan ideas in the minds of Sikhs in Punjab and to link that demand to Bhindranwale.

Further details came to my attention on my return to headquarters in October 1979. I realized that what was happening in Punjab since 1978 was a sort of special operation launched by Sanjay Gandhi and Giani Zail Singh, the details of which have been mentioned in the Preface. That was also the time when Sanjay Gandhi and Kamal Nath were trying to topple Prime Minister Morarji Desai's government at the Centre by working on the disgruntled Janata Party leader Raj Narain. They were able to achieve this objective in July 1979.

Prime Minister Charan Singh's government then came to power, backed by the Congress, but could last only twenty-three days as Indira Gandhi withdrew her party's support. Parliament was dissolved and mid-term elections to the seventh Lok Sabha were held in January 1980, in which Indira Gandhi and the Congress returned to power. For his loyalty to Sanjay Gandhi, Kamal Nath, originally from Kanpur in Uttar Pradesh, was rewarded with a 'safe' parliamentary seat at Chhindwara in Madhya Pradesh, which he easily won in those elections.

Emboldened by his success in manipulating political developments at the national level, Sanjay Gandhi, along with the others, launched Op-2. However, Giani Zail Singh, who was rewarded by Indira Gandhi in July 1982 with the country's highest post, that of president, was gradually sidelined by her, despite his continued interest in Punjab politics.

In March-April 1982, a trusted family friend (name withheld on request) from Patiala came to meet me in New Delhi and shared with me some interesting information he had gathered from Rashtriya Swayamsevak Sangh (RSS) members in Patiala. The information went that sometime after the return of the Congress party to power in January 1980, the prime minister had taken a decision, as advised by Sanjay Gandhi, to win the next general elections by using the services of Bhindranwale to create a serious Hindu-Sikh divide and plant the fear of Khalistan in the minds of the majority community. With a majority baying for strongest possible action against Bhindranwale and his men, Indira Gandhi would in the end emerge as a 'strong leader' who saved the country from a 'monster' (which she herself had created). That would in turn help her party garner votes from grateful members of the majority community. When my friend asked the RSS members whether they had received the information from their headquarters or from Pawan Kumar Sharma, the Patiala based head of the Hindu Surakhsha Samiti, who had been rather active lately in creating a Hindu–Sikh divide, they parried his query.

Insofar as the Research and Analysis Wing's (R&AW's) involvement in Op-2 was concerned, things started changing towards the end of 1980 when a new division headed by Deputy Director B. Raman was created, to 'collect intelligence about the activities of the Sikh extremist elements abroad and their links with the ISI'[3] of Pakistan. In early 1981, director (R&AW), in short director (R), N.F. Suntook asked me to send proposals to the Ministry of External Affairs (MEA) for the positioning of seven new R&AW stations in some Indian missions located in west Europe and North America.

Sometime in the middle of 1981, I was asked by Suntook to brief the R&AW officers, of and above the rank of deputy director posted at headquarters, on the concept of Khalistan and the type of information they should be looking for. On his appointment as senior advisor in August 1981, R.N. Kao also started using the R&AW's resources to further the cause of certain aspects of Op-2. It was in that context that I was asked by the director (R) to visit Canada and the US thrice between December 1981 and September 1983.

Sometime in February-March 1990, B. Raman prepared the R&AW's white paper on 'Khalistan and Sikh Extremism'. With the approval of Secretary (R) A.K. Verma, Raman decided to present it to a select group of senior R&AW officers and some invitees from sister organizations dealing with security-related matters, which included the Intelligence Bureau. The invitees also included some Delhi police officers who were on duty during the November

1984 pogrom. Air Commodore Jasjit Singh (Retd), director of the Institute of Defence Studies and Analysis (IDSA) and a Sikh, was invited to chair the meeting at the R&AW's plush auditorium.

Raman approached the lectern and started addressing the audience with the 'white paper' in his hand. He said the Sikhs had never forgotten the prestige and eminence of the Sikh empire (1709–1848) established by Maharaja Ranjit Singh and wanted to recreate that era in one form or the other. He also gave some details of the activities of Jagjit Singh Chauhan and Sikh extremist organizations. He linked their activities to the lingering desire on the part of the Sikhs to secure an independent Sikh state called Khalistan, thereby laying the entire blame for what had happened in Punjab since 1980 solely on Sikh extremists.

Raman's glossing over of the activities of the Congress leaders involved in Op-2, made me feel that whatever he was saying should not be allowed to go unchallenged, even though it would mean criticizing my own department's white paper in front of outsiders. I also had sufficient knowledge of Sikh history as before joining the IPS in 1964, I had worked for two years as a lecturer of history at Government Ripudaman College, Nabha, Punjab. I was, therefore, conversant enough on the subject to challenge the historical contextualization that Raman was seeking to make.

No sooner had Raman finished his presentation than I stood up and said, 'Mr Raman, your white paper is full of white lies.' For a few seconds there was pin-drop silence in the auditorium. Thereafter, I started demolishing Raman's assertions one by one. About Ranjit Singh, I told him that he was one of the most secular rulers India had ever seen. He had donated the same amount of gold to the Kashi Vishwanath temple in Varanasi as he had to the Harmandir Sahib at Amritsar. He sent a special military expedition to Ghazni to retrieve the doors of the Dwarka temple which

Mahmud of Ghazni had carried back as a trophy of his exploits in India. What I did not know at that time was that before his death, Ranjit Singh had also expressed a desire to offer the invaluable Kohinoor to Lord Jagannath at Puri.[4]

With reference to Raman attributing to the Sikhs ambitions of an independent state of Khalistan, I told him that barring a brief pre-Independence period, and that too due to the policy of 'divide and rule' followed by the British, there was no such demand from Sikhs in the post-independence period that I knew of. Renowned martyrs and freedom fighters such as Bhagat Singh, Udham Singh and Kartar Singh Sarabha did not give their lives for Khalistan. As a Sikh born and brought up in Punjab, I knew of only one person – other than a couple of Sikhs who held pro-Khalistan views in their personal capacity in the pre-1980 period – and that was Jagjit Singh Chauhan – who was actively propagating pro-Khalistan views. Even in his case, it was widely believed that his activities were being financed and sponsored by the ISI of Pakistan and some Republican leaders from the US.

I asked Raman whether he had made efforts to ascertain the real reason behind the sudden spurt in pro-Khalistan activities in Punjab and abroad only after the Congress came to power in January 1980. As he had nothing to say, I pointedly told him that the real reason was a conscious decision taken by some senior Congress leaders, soon after Indira Gandhi returned to power in January 1980, to win the next elections (due before January 1985) by first creating and then solving the Khalistan issue through the use of Bhindranwale. I also suggested to him that since the Congress was not in power then (V.P. Singh had become the prime minister on 2 December 1989), he should revise his white paper, thereby exposing the true nature of the conspiracy.

I concluded by saying that the situation that had been created would be taken advantage of by Pakistan and some Western countries for a long time to come. When Raman asked me how, I told him that the ISI would continue to bolster the pro-Khalistan movement using every possible means to avenge its loss of East Pakistan (now Bangladesh) in December 1971. Some of the Western countries would use it as an instrument to further their respective geopolitical, commercial and economic interests in their dealings with India.

Jasjit Singh fully agreed with my views. There was no intervention from the audience and the meeting ended soon after, with the white paper being consigned to the vaults of the Department for future reference. It is obvious that my dissenting view had not been placed in the concerned folder as it would have reflected poorly on the credibility of the Department. Is there not a need for revision of this white paper or the Central government's white paper on Punjab released in July 1984 or, for that matter, similar white papers produced by other ministries or departments? It is for the authorities concerned to consider. The author has done his part of the job by writing this book.

Why did I say what I said to Raman, who continued to be a very good friend even after our retirement, though we never discussed this issue again? Why and how was Bhindranwale's support enlisted by a select group of Congress party leaders for Op-1? How did Op-1 get converted to Op-2? Why were Bhindranwale and his men used to encourage extremism, leading to a Hindu-Sikh divide in Punjab? How did the concept of Khalistan gain credibility amongst the Sikh diaspora in the West from 1981 onwards?

What was the final solution to the Punjab/Khalistan problem that the 1 Akbar Road group wanted? Was it to ensure maximum impact on their potential voters in the next general elections? Why was the hope of a negotiated settlement with moderate Akali Dal leaders kept dangling till the very end of May 1984, a few days before Operation Blue Star was launched? Why was R.N Kao recalled from retirement, and how did the R&AW, for which Sikh extremism and Khalistan were non-issues till the end of 1979, suddenly get involved in related activities from the end of 1980? Why were other comparatively less harmful solutions to capture Bhindranwale from the Golden Temple complex overruled?

All this, as well as my own experiences in the days following Operation Blue Star – during and after the November 1984 anti-Sikh pogrom in Delhi and other cities of India – has been narrated in this book in as dispassionate a manner as possible. This book is a painful revelation of a high-level conspiracy that resulted in the death of thousands of innocent persons and created a gigantic problem out of a hitherto non-existent issue – that of Khalistan.

2

Canada and the Sikh Diaspora in the Late 1970s

TOWARDS THE end of November 1975, I was told by my bosses that I should be ready to move from Gangtok to New Delhi by end February 1976 and start preparing for a posting as first secretary in the high commission of India in Ottawa, Canada. In the normal course, after the completion of various formalities, I should have reached Ottawa by early June 1976. But my predecessor Shamsher Singh (IPS 1957 Rajasthan) had other plans. He wanted to prolong his stay at Ottawa and had secured some minor assignment in the Montreal Summer Olympics (17 July to 1 August 1976). So I had to cool my heels in New Delhi till after he had finished with the Olympics. While I was waiting to depart for Ottawa in order to take charge from Shamsher over there, he suddenly landed in New Delhi.

Within a week or so of his arrival Shamsher Singh submitted his resignation from the service, foregoing the pension to which he would have been entitled had he put in one more year of service to complete the minimum qualifying service of twenty years. Within a few days of resigning he returned to Canada. Everybody was surprised as to which passport he had used for his return to Ottawa as he had already surrendered his diplomatic passport. Inquiries made by the MEA revealed that he had returned to Ottawa on an ordinary passport issued by the high commission of India at Ottawa, which he had obtained some months before his transfer, with the approval of High Commissioner Uma Shankar Bajpai (elder brother of K.S. Bajpai, political officer in Gangtok during my posting there), on the plea that a separate ordinary passport would provide him with a better cover to meet with his operational contacts in the San Francisco and Los Angeles areas.

The high commissioner was obviously asked by the MEA to explain the reason behind the issue of an ordinary passport to Shamsher without their approval. Little did Bajpai know that Shamsher had other plans to use that passport. After surrendering his diplomatic passport Shamsher had apparently obtained an immigration visa on his ordinary passport at the Canadian high commission at New Delhi. This is something Shamsher would have already arranged for with the concerned Royal Canadian Mounted Police (which at the time did the work now being done by the Canadian Security Intelligence Service) or Canadian immigration authorities at Ottawa before his departure for New Delhi. It can be safely assumed that in return for such a big favour Shamsher had compromised his position and shared some crucial information about the Department (R&AW) with the RCMP.

Upon my arrival at the Montreal-Mirabel International airport I was subjected to an 'interview' by the head of the immigration unit, despite the fact that my family and I held diplomatic passports, despite the fact that I was coming to join as a diplomat at the

Indian high commission, and also despite a middle-level officer from the Indian high commission having come to receive us. I can only surmise that this interview was meant to probe and assess if I too could be a potential asset, willing to follow in Shamsher's footsteps. We had to wait for about half an hour before we were finally cleared. The next morning when I called on the high commissioner, he was aware of the incident, and a note verbale was sent to the Canadian foreign office protesting the treatment meted out to me and my family at Mirabel airport.

In the aftermath of the Shamsher Singh incident, the behaviour of the high commissioner and some of the senior officers was a bit cool towards me. I, however, tried my best to improve relations with them, but as long as Bajpai remained the high commissioner I could not fully gain his trust, so very essential for the smooth functioning of the R&AW officers abroad. Things changed significantly when he was succeeded by a very cultured Mahbub Ahmad (a former staff officer to Netaji Subhash Chandra Bose in Burma as an Indian National Army officer) and later by the very thorough and meticulous General T.N. Raina, former chief of the army staff.

As far as my operational work was concerned, I was conscious of the fact that the nature of Shamsher's job and his operational contacts had been fully compromised. Therefore, I preferred to lie low for some time and cut off all links with Shamsher's contacts.

The first Sikh settlers

Before I go on to the period I was posted at Ottawa (September 1976 to September 1979), it would be useful to briefly note the history of Sikh immigration to Canada over the years.

Kesar Singh, a risaldar major in British Indian Army's Sikh Lancers and Infantry Regiment, is considered to be the first Sikh settler in Canada. He was among a group of Sikh officers who were taking the Pacific route, and therefore transiting through Canada on the way back to India after participating in Queen Victoria's diamond jubilee celebration in London in 1897. Sikhs settled in Singapore and Hong Kong and their friends and relatives back home started moving to Canada, first to Vancouver and its suburbs – mainly due to Vancouver's comparatively milder climate and easy accessibility through the Pacific Ocean – and soon from there to the Yuba City, San Francisco and Sacramento areas of the US. Most of them found jobs in farming and lumber (especially in and around Vancouver).

Gradually, they moved on to other professions also. As the British Columbia authorities were busy controlling the Japanese and Chinese influx into their state, the Sikhs arriving in smaller numbers faced no problems in the beginning. As a result, between 1903 and 1908, around 6,000 Sikhs entered Canada, half of them moving southwards to the US. Very soon, they began facing problems with the Canadian civil authorities and Canadian labour of European origin.[1]

The Canadian government decided to curtail this influx with a series of laws aimed at limiting the entry of south Asians into the country and restricting the political rights of those already there. The Punjabi community, especially the Sikhs, had hitherto been a loyal force of the British empire, and they naturally expected equal treatment and rights from the British and Commonwealth governments as extended to British and other white immigrants.

'The continuous passage' (reaching Canada without break of journey from place of origin) law and other discriminatory measures restricting immigration of south Asians to Canada led to discontent, protests, and anti-colonial and nationalistic sentiments within the Sikh community. As a result, it began organizing itself into political groups. It was during this period that Tarak Nath Das published an edition of *Free Hindustan* from Vancouver, which provoked a reaction from the British government when it was published in India.[2]

In 1907, the Khalsa Diwan Society was set up in Vancouver. Though its objectives were religious, educational and philanthropic, it also took note of problems connected to immigration and racism. The Gursikh temple at 1866, Second Avenue, West Vancouver, was established on 26 February 1911. Sikhs and non-Sikhs from British Columbia attended the ceremony, and a local newspaper reported on the event. It was the first gurudwara not only in North America but in the world outside south Asia. Soon the gurudwara management wing of the Khalsa Diwan Society built some other gurudwaras in Vancouver, Victoria, Surrey and neighbouring areas, which became centres of Sikh socio-religious and political activities. The Sikh population in British Columbia and the west coast of the US, however, got depleted during the Ghadar movement, when thousands of Sikhs sold their properties and moved back to India to participate in the freedom movement against the British.

The door to Canada was firmly shut against the Sikhs by the Canadian government in 1908. A small community of Sikh workers had been established in the Pacific coast states of the US and in the British Columbia by 1910. During the period 1919–47, generally referred to as 'quiet years' in the Canadian Sikh history, the Sikh population dwindled in size. It is hard to tell how many Sikhs left British Columbia during these quiet years. Some shifted southwards to the US and others returned to Punjab. The population dropped from its peak of 6,000 around the First World War to about one 1,100 only, just before the Second World War.[3]

As per the 1951 census Canada's Sikhs numbered 2,148. The Canadian government amended its immigration laws in 1951 and instituted a quota of one hundred and fifty citizens (over and above the blood relations and spouses) a year from India which was increased to 300 in 1957. With further relaxation in the immigration laws, Canada's Punjabi population rose twenty times between 1961 and 1976.[4] From the mid-1950s onwards, tens of thousands of skilled Sikhs, some highly educated, settled in Canada, especially in the urban corridor from Toronto to Windsor. As their numbers grew, they established temporary gurudwaras in every major city eastward to Montreal, with the first gurudwara in eastern Canada being made in 1965. During my stay in Canada, there were a little over 90,000 Sikhs there, a majority of whom were living in the province of British Columbia (Vancouver area) followed by Ontario (Toronto), Alberta (Calgary and Edmonton), Manitoba (Winnipeg) and Quebec (Montreal) provinces. The capital city of Ottawa had about 2,500 Sikhs.

From a total of 94,803 as per the 1981 census, the Sikh population in Canada grew by 103.2 per cent to 192,608 in the 1991 census and by 66 per cent to 319,802 in the 2001 census. The sudden increase in the growth of Sikh population in the 1980s appear to be related to political instability in Punjab, which some took advantage of by posing as political asylum seekers. As per 2011 Census (next one due in 2021), the Sikh population in Canada was 468,670, which was 1.4 per cent of the total population of Canada and 1.96 per cent of the total population of Sikhs worldwide. Even if we take an increase of 30 per cent in the Sikh population in Canada after the 2011 Census, the present population of the Sikhs in Canada should be over 600,000.

In the last Canadian parliamentary elections held in October 2019, twenty Indo-Canadians were elected to the 338-member House of Commons. Of these, nineteen are of Punjabi origin and eighteen are Sikhs. Of the eighteen Sikhs, thirteen were elected from the ruling Liberal Party, four from the Conservative Party and one from the New Democratic Party. Ten Sikh MPs are from Ontario province, four from British Columbia, three from Alberta and one from Quebec. Out of the thirty-seven members of Prime Minister Justin Trudeau's cabinet, four are of Punjabi origin – three Sikhs and one Hindu (Anita Anand). Three Sikhs had been members of Trudeau's previous cabinet, including Defence Minister Harjit Singh Sajjan. This time, Trudeau's Liberal Party could get only 157 seats, thirteen short of an absolute majority, and the main opposition Conservative Party won 121 seats. The fourth largest party, the New Democratic Party, led by Jagmeet Singh, a Sikh lawyer, secured twenty-four seats.

Ghadar Party and Komagata Maru

Two developments of the early twentieth century – the founding of the Ghadar (rebellion) Party in San Francisco in 1913 and the Komagata Maru incident of 1914 – require special mention here because of their respective roles in India's freedom movement and in addressing some of the problems faced by contemporary Punjabi/Sikh settlers in Canada.

The Ghadar Party, initially called the Pacific Coast Hindustan Association, was formed in 1913 in the US at Yughantar Ashram, San Francisco, with Sohan Singh Bhakna as its president. The members of the party were largely Sikhs, including some from Vancouver. Some of its members were also students at the University of California at Berkeley, including Har Dayal, Tarak Nath Das, Maulvi Barkatullah, Harnam Singh Tundilat and V.G.

Pingle. The party quickly gained support from Indian expatriates, especially in the US, Canada, east Africa and Asia.

The movement was built around the weekly journal *Ghadar*, first edited by Lala Hardayal and later by seventeen-year-old Kartar Singh Sarabha. Its first issue dated 1 November 1913 was in Urdu. The one in Punjabi started from 9 December in the same year. The *Ghadar* of 11 August 1914 gave on its title page, the following audacious call of urgency to fellow Ghadarites 'Wanted – Fearless, Courageous Soldiers for spreading Mutiny in India; Salary – Death; Award – Martyrdom & Freedom; Place – The Battlefield India'.[5] The ideology of the party was secular. In the words of Sohan Singh Bhakna, they were neither Sikh nor Punjabi. Their religion was patriotism.

Ghadar Party's ultimate goal was to overthrow British colonial rule in India by means of an armed revolution through the incitement of mutiny within the Indian army. It viewed the Congress-led mainstream movement for dominion status for India modest, and its constitutional methods soft. The mutiny was planned to start in Punjab, followed by Bengal and the rest of India.

Influenced by the Ghadar Party, around 3,000 Indian residents from the US and Canada, mostly Sikhs, sold their land, properties, businesses and homes and moved back to Punjab to participate in India's freedom struggle. Sohan Singh Bhakna (1870–1968) sailed to India at the outbreak of the First World War to organize and direct the rebellion. British intelligence was keeping a close watch on the revolutionary conspiracy and the movements of its leaders. The planned uprising in 1915 failed, and a number of revolutionaries were arrested and were subsequently tried. At Lahore, a special tribunal was constituted under the Defence of India Act 1915, and a total of 291 revolutionaries were put on trial. Of these, forty-two (including Sohna Singh Bhakna and Kartar

Singh Sarabha) were awarded the death sentence, 114 sentenced to life imprisonment and ninety-three awarded varying terms of imprisonment. A number of these (including Bhakna, whose death sentence was commuted to life imprisonment and who was later released after serving sixteen years) were sent to the Cellular Jail in the Andaman. Forty-two defendants in the trial were acquitted.

In May 1917, eight members of the Ghadar Party were indicted by a federal grand jury on a charge of conspiracy to form a military enterprise against the United Kingdom. Their trial began in the district court of San Francisco and lasted from 20 November 1917 to 24 April 1918. The British authorities hoped the conviction would result in their deportation from the United States to India. However, strong local public support prevented the US Department of Justice from doing so.

The participation of thousands of Canada/US-returned Sikhs in the movement against British rule 'left a widespread mark in Punjab, its history and society and political evolution, even though as a story within India's nationalistic movement, the Ghadar movement still remains a footnote.'[6] Also, 'moving beyond the objective of liberating the country, they (Ghadarites) dreamed of creating in India a new social and political order (*nawan roop rachna Hind de samaj da*): secular, democratic and egalitarian. Their imagination of *deshbhakti* appeared to be different from the prevailing narrative of nationalism.'7

In 1914, Gurdit Singh, a Sikh businessman from Singapore, 'chartered on a time lease basis a Japanese ship Komagata Maru with the intention of becoming the first Sikh businessman operating what he visualized as Guru Nanak Steamship Company'.[8] His was partly a business venture, partly a mission to help 340 Sikhs, twenty-four Muslims and twelve Hindus immigrate to Canada and test the limits of Canadian exclusion laws, which prohibited the settlement of south Asians in Canada. Tickets were priced at a high of $100, but those who could not pay in advance were also taken on board with the promise that their relatives would pay for them on their arrival at Vancouver. The ship was renamed 'Guru Nanak Jahaz', and it flew the flag of Shri Guru Nanak Steamship Company.

When it berthed at the Vancouver harbour on 21 May 1914, the passengers, dressed in their best suits and ties, waited to disembark. But the conservative premier of British Columbia, Richard McBride, issued a categorical statement that they would not be allowed to disembark. On 7 July, the full bench of the Supreme Court of Canada gave a unanimous judgment that it had no powers to interfere in the decisions of the Department of Immigration and Colonization. Following this the Canadian government ordered the harbour tug Sea Lion to push the ship out on its homeward journey. Komagata Maru arrived in Calcutta on 26 September but was diverted to Buj Buj (27 km away from Calcutta, where the British intended to put the passengers on a train to Punjab).

The passengers held demonstrations in Calcutta but were forced to return to Buj Buj and re-board the ship. When the passengers protested, with some refusing to re-board, police opened fire, killing twenty and wounding nine. Gurdit Singh managed to escape and lived in hiding till 1922. He was persuaded by Mahatma Gandhi to give himself up as a true patriot, which he did, resulting in his imprisonment for five years. 'The return of Komagata Maru passengers (to Punjab) became a cause of concern of the traditional Sikh leadership known for its loyalty to the British Empire. It became increasingly difficult to defend this loyalty. The British administration could not be the guarantor of Sikh interests abroad.'[9]

Addressing the House of Commons in Ottawa on 18 May 2016, Canadian Prime Minister Justin Trudeau formally apologized for the Komagata Maru incident:

> Canada's government was without question responsible for the laws that prevented these passengers from immigrating peacefully and securely. For that, and for every regrettable consequence that followed, we are sorry ... first and foremost, to the victims of the incident. No words can erase the pain and suffering they experienced.
>
> Regrettably, the passage of time means that none are alive to hear our apology today. Still, we offer it, fully and sincerely. For our indifference to your plight. For our failure to recognize all that you had to offer. For the laws that discriminated against you so senselessly. And for not apologizing sooner. For all these things, we are truly sorry.

Trudeau also apologized directly to the passengers' relatives and descendants, some of whom, he noted, were present in the House of Commons' visitors' gallery to hear the apology. 'We can never know what your lives would have been like had your relatives been welcome to Canada... The ways in which your lives would have been different. The ways in which Canada would have been enriched. Those possibilities are lost to history. For that – and to you – we apologize.' He said that Canada must commit itself to positive action, to learning from mistakes, and make sure that the errors of the past were never repeated. Interim Conservative leader of the Opposition Rona Ambrose and NDP leader Tom Mulcair endorsed Trudeau's apology and also apologized on their respective parties' behalf.[10]

Establishing a network

During my posting at Ottawa, India's consular and visa services in Canada were handled by two Indian consulates (Vancouver and Toronto) and the Indian High Commission at Ottawa. The two western provinces of Alberta and British Columbia were served from Vancouver, and the provinces of Manitoba, Saskatchewan and Ontario from Toronto. The city of Ottawa, which was otherwise part of the Ontario province, and the four eastern provinces of Quebec, New Brunswick, Nova Scotia, and Newfoundland and Labrador, were served directly from Ottawa. Besides being in charge of these services at the high commission, I also coordinated consular work of the two consulates on behalf of the high commissioner.

As first secretary in charge of consular and visa services at the mission, I started contacting (on the phone and through personal meetings wherever feasible) my relatives, friends and contacts spread over various parts of Canada and the west coast of the US. Soon I was able to build a fairly large 'information bank' about the kinds of problems that persons of Indian origin, especially those from Punjab (mainly Sikhs), were facing in Canada and in the west coast of the US. I also noted the external influences on the community.

In July 1978 my in-laws came to visit us for a month and a half. I took one month's leave and drove them and my family across the prairies from Ottawa to Vancouver via Edmonton. Then we travelled southwards, from Vancouver to Yuba City, San Francisco, Stockton, Sacramento, Los Angeles and San Diego, and back to Ottawa via Las Vegas, the Grand Canyon, Yellowstone Park,

Calgary, and so on. At many of these places (other than those of tourist interest) we met several people of Punjabi origin. At the Yuba City and Stockton gurudwaras, several Sikhs turned up to meet my father-in-law Sardar Swaran Singh. A few of them who had been members of the Ghadar Party were now in their eighties and known as '*Ghadari Baba*' (revolutionary elders).

The knowledge and contact bank I built during this trip came in handy while discharging my consular duties in Ottawa and also during my three operational visits to Canada and the US, in 1981, 1982 and 1983, after I returned to Delhi. These details appear in this book at appropriate junctures.

Within a few months of my arrival in Ottawa I noticed that although some of the representational officers from the three Indian missions in Canada did interact at a personal level with prominent Sikh residents, there was hardly any interaction at the official level between them and the Sikh organizations or institutions whose activities revolved around the local gurudwaras.

In March 1977, the Congress had lost the general elections as a fallout of the Emergency and was replaced by the Morarji Desai-led Janata Party government. The Akali Dal was a member of the coalition government.

Though the Morarji Desai government was considered pro-US, in the Cold War environment India was still perceived to be closer to the Soviet Union because of the continued relevance of the Indo-Soviet Treaty of Friendship and Cooperation of 1971. Incidentally, it was signed at Moscow on 6 August 1971 between Sardar Swaran Singh as India's external affairs minister and A.A. Gromyko, his Soviet counterpart. As a result, bilateral relations between India and Canada lacked warmth and were at best correct, if not cold. Normally, such a relationship rubs off on persons of Indian origin settled in the host country, and Canada was no exception. In view of that, the local Sikhs were always conscious of the fact that any unwarranted institutional contact with the Indian missions in Canada may not be appreciated by Canadian authorities. As such, the change in government in India, despite having a pro-US prime minister, and the Akali Dal as a coalition partner, resulted in no perceptible change in the attitude of Sikhs in Canada towards the Indian missions.

While Vancouver and its suburbs had a number of gurudwaras, the main one was Khalsa Diwan Society Sikh Temple on 8000 Ross Street, Vancouver. In other cities both in central and eastern Canada, gurudwaras were still functioning from residential buildings, school complexes, and so on. Although a number of gurudwaras had come up in smaller towns around Toronto, the main gurudwara was run out of a building at 269, Pape Avenue, off Gerard Street, purchased in 1968 by the Shiromani Sikh Society.

The managements of gurudwaras in Canada were typical of the managements of gurudwaras in Punjab. The functioning of gurudwaras in the smaller cities faced no problems. But the growth of the community's population resulted in factionalism, rivalries, assertion of supremacy and feelings of revenge amongst groups in the more prominent gurudwaras. There was a joke doing the rounds amongst the local Sikhs that it was difficult to build the first gurudwara but the second one came soon thereafter. This meant that the faction that was not able to control a particular gurudwara would soon build another one in the same city. Older gurudwaras such as the Ross Street one in Vancouver were gradually shedding their traditional liberalism and were moving towards orthodoxy. From being venues of weekly or monthly jormelas (social gatherings) of Hindus and Sikhs, they were gradually exclusively catering to Sikh religious orthodoxy, thereby discouraging Hindus from participating in such gatherings.

With the establishment of gurudwaras came granthis (readers of sacred scriptures), ragis (singers of sacred hymns) and sewadars (caretakers) from India, courtesy of some senior Akali Dal leaders or members of the SGPC. They carried their convictions and prejudices with them, which started rubbing off on some Sikhs, especially of the older generation. But two things were common to all gurudwaras in Canada till the end of 1979: the idea of Khalistan was totally alien to them, and Bhindranwale was a complete nonentity.

Pape Avenue Gurudwara in Toronto had its own problems related to the election of its management committee. There were no fixed electoral rolls. Anybody from the neighbouring areas could come and cast his or her vote. There were several groups among the community. At one end of the spectrum were the Viveki Sikhs – the righteous or the puritans – and at the other were members of the Hardial Bains-led Communist Party of Canada (Marxist-Leninist) – a recognized political party at the federal level – who also wanted a say, directly or indirectly, over gurudwara affairs to further their interests. In the March 1975 elections, the CPC(ML) lent its support to Kuldip Singh Samra for the president's post. Having lost, Samra filed an appeal in a local court. When he lost the case there too he opened fire in court, killing one and wounding another.[11]

Given the above environment, I started building my contacts with important persons from the local Sikh (about half the population of about 5,000 persons of Indian origin) community in Ottawa. Fortunately, the president of the local gurudwara committee, Sardar Ganda Singh, was an old family friend from India. In Ottawa, a monthly function was held at the Memorial High School on Viewmont Drive. The religious ceremony was followed by Shabad Kirtan by Sikh children. Depending on the importance of the occasion, in the end a short speech on a relevant subject was made by someone from the local Sikh community. Ganda Singh, who knew about my knowledge of Punjab affairs and Sikh history, would often ask me to speak. This would happen every three to four months. I soon started getting invitations from prominent members of the local Sikh community to attend functions and social get-togethers at their homes.

My local Punjabi friends, both Sikhs and Hindus, were first-generation immigrants. They were educated and worked as professionals or federal government employees. At social get-togethers, I noticed that they tended to be aware of developments taking place in Punjab and, as was the case back home, they held divergent views on the happenings in Punjab or India. Due to my speeches at the local gurudwara, quite a few Sikh/Punjabi drivers from the local ABC taxi service came to know me rather well. Travelling in their taxis provided me with greater insight about their views on what was happening in Punjab. They would normally refuse to accept payment at the end of the journey but would finally relent when I told them I was being paid by the government for that journey. I also attended a couple of marriage receptions hosted by them.

During one of my visits to Toronto I had a detailed discussion with our consul general M.L. Suri, an experienced officer. We decided that, to start with, we should visit the Pape Avenue Gurudwara and meet members of its management committee. I talked to the president of the local Sikh gurudwara committee on the phone and fixed a meeting with him and other members in the gurudwara office for around noon. He welcomed the idea on the phone, but to our surprise, when we reached the gurudwara there was no trace of the management committee or the president. The two sewadars who met us pretended to have no clue about their whereabouts. From their behaviour it appeared that we were not welcome and they wanted us to leave as soon as possible, lest our presence on the premises should be noticed. In view of that, after paying obeisance to the Guru Granth Sahib we returned to the consulate, disappointed.

Similarly, when the president of the Montreal gurudwara committee came to the high commission at Ottawa for some consular service, I inquired about the welfare of the Sikh community there and asked him if I should visit Montreal on any of the Sundays when they had their functions in the gurudwara. Though outwardly enthusiastic, he never followed it up with an invitation.

The two pro-Khalistan men

During the course of my interaction with Sikhs of diverse backgrounds, I discovered that there were only two persons in Canada who either professed or propagated pro-Khalistan views. One of them was Toronto-based Kuldip Singh Sodhi, self-styled consul general of Khalistan, who represented Jagjit Singh Chauhan's outfit. The other was Professor Uday Singh of Sudbury.

Jagjit Singh Chauhan, a medical doctor by profession, was first elected to the Punjab assembly in 1967 and became its deputy speaker when the Akali Dal-led coalition government took office in Punjab. Later he served as finance minister in Lachman Singh Gill's cabinet. In 1971 he shifted to the United Kingdom. The same year he went to Guru Nanak's birth place, Nankana Sahib in Pakistan, in an attempt to establish a Sikh government in exile. He then visited the US at the invitation of some Republican party members. On 13 October 1971, he placed a full-page advertisement in the *New York Times* proclaiming the creation of an independent Sikh state named Khalistan.

When the Janata Party government was formed in 1977, Chauhan returned to India, but went back to Britain in 1979 before Indira Gandhi's return to power. There he established an organization called Khalistan National Council. In reaction to Operation Blue Star, Chauhan announced a government of Khalistan in exile in London on 13 June 1984. Remarkably, the Rajiv Gandhi government allowed Chauhan to enter India in 1989, hoist the Khalistan flag at Anandpur Sahib, and return to the UK. It was only after his return to the UK that his Indian passport was cancelled on 24 April 1989 by the Indian high commission. Later on the Indian government protested when the same Chauhan was allowed to enter the US using the invalid passport.

In June 2001, the Government of India decided to overlook Chauhan's past activities, softened its stance towards him and allowed him to return to India. On his return, in an interview, Chauhan said he would keep the Khalistan movement alive 'democratically', and claimed that he had always been against violence. He died on 4 April 2007 at his native village Tanda in Punjab's Hoshiarpur district at the age of seventy-eight.

In the 1970s, Canada's Sikh community was in general of the view that Jagjit Singh Chauhan was in the pay of the ISI. His representative in Canada, Kuldip Singh Sodhi, was a bit of an oddball whom the community avoided. But occasionally some would buy the so-called Khalistani passports, postage stamps or currency notes from him out of curiosity. The sphere of his and Chauhan's influence was extremely limited. The western provinces of British Columbia (Vancouver area) and Alberta remained generally immune to such activities. Rather, the Sikhs of British Columbia still fondly remembered the contribution made by some of their elders to the freedom movement of India as members of the Ghadar Party. The Sikhs of Ottawa and Quebec province were busy pursuing their professional and business interests and had no time for divisive activities.

Professor Uday Singh was a deeply religious man and a follower of Bhai Randhir Singh, whom he assisted in Amrit Parchar (baptism) for sixteen years in Punjab before migrating to Canada in 1961. He took the job of a mathematics professor at Laurentian University in Ontario near Toronto. Unlike Kuldip Singh Sodhi, for whom propagating pro-Khalistan views was a full-time paid job, Uday Singh was an ideologue, who kept his views limited to discussions with persons who came in contact with him.

After his retirement, Uday Singh started devoting time and attention to teaching Gurmukhi to Sikh children and spent most of his pension on Sikh charitable causes. After Operation Blue Star and the 1984 pogrom, he came out openly in support of Khalistan and wrote a book, *The Waning and Waxing of Khalistan*. He also provided financial help to the families of Ajaib Singh Bagri and Inderjit Singh Reyat, the two accused facing trial in the Air-India Kanishka bombing case. He was of the opinion that no Sikh was guilty of the conspiracy and believed that 'the Hindu government got it done'.[12] He died on 23 November 2013.

That there was no public support in Canada in the 1970s for Khalistan would be evident from the following incident. A Sikh conference was held on 24-25 March 1979 at Hotel Inn on the Park in Toronto. I was one of the people invited to address the gathering of about 300 to 400 Sikhs. While I was delivering my speech on my favourite theme – that Sikhs in Canada should take advantage of the Canadian government's policy of multiculturalism and prepare their next generation to play the role of responsible Canadian citizens rather than worry about what was happening in Punjab or India – Kuldip Singh Sodhi, who was sitting in the audience, stood up and began to speak loudly.

'Mr Singh is an agent of Morarji Desai's Hindu government,' he said, 'and is trying to mislead the Sikhs in Canada. He should rather explain the discrimination faced by the Sikhs in India.' No sooner had Sodhi started uttering these words than he was picked up and forcibly escorted out of the venue by four young Sikh men from the audience. Soon after that, I resumed my speech, which was well received by the audience. After the function Sodhi met me in the hotel lobby, and in a bit of an apologetic tone told me that there was nothing personal in his criticism. 'I was doing my job and you were doing yours,' he said. I met Sodhi for the second and last time in New York on 1 August 1982, outside Richmond Hill Gurudwara in New York, the details of which are given in Chapter 5.

The fact that the R&AW had no interest in Sikh activities or in Sodhi's quixotic pro-Khalistan agenda in Canada till the end of my tenure in September 1979 would be evident from a letter I received in July-August 1979 from my joint director. In it he informed me that the Department was not interested in the 'gurudwara politics' of Canada and I should not waste my time reporting on it. Incidentally, on my return to headquarters, when Suntook asked me in the middle of 1981 to brief the R&AW officers of and above the rank of deputy director on Khalistan, I specifically asked that same joint director as to what had led to the Department's sudden interest in pro-Khalistan activities. His reply was that things had changed considerably in the meanwhile. However, he did not elaborate what brought about the change within the one and a half years' time since my return from Canada.

How did things start changing in Canada after Indira Gandhi's return to power as prime minister in January 1980; how the

R&AW, which was not interested in 'gurudwara politics' till the end of 1979 suddenly made a 180-degree turnaround under the new government; and how the land which gave birth to the Ghadar movement started hosting pro-Khalistan activities, are dealt with in the subsequent chapters.

3

Punjab in the Late 1970s and My Return to Headquarters

FOLLOWING ITS loss in the sixth Lok Sabha elections in March 1977, the Congress also lost the 1977 elections in Punjab to the Shiromani Akali Dal (SAD) and Janata Party coalition. The newly elected Punjab government under Chief Minister Parkash Singh Badal put some Congress workers and leaders in jail for their activities during the Emergency. Having lost power in the state, former Congress chief minister of Punjab (1972–77) Giani Zail Singh advised Sanjay Gandhi to launch what I have described as Op-1[1]

The Congress meddling in the affairs of the Akali Dal was nothing new to Punjab. It was done in the early sixties by Congress chief minister Pratap Singh Kairon, who played Master Tara Singh and Sant Fateh Singh against each other to retain his influence over the SGPC. Zail Singh, who after his religious studies at the Sikh Missionary College in Amritsar had started his career as a preacher, used this approach successfully as chief minister by building a 577-km road called Guru Gobind Singh Marg. The road followed the route taken by Guru Gobind Singh, the tenth Sikh guru, during his retreat in AD 1705 from Anandpur Sahib to Talwandi Sabo (Damdama Sahib). Zail Singh inaugurated the road on 10 April 1973 with great fanfare, and led a religious procession on it, stopping on the way at all the major gurudwaras that the road connected.

In order to select a Sikh religious leader who could further the cause of Op-1, Zail Singh, in consultation with his confidants, shortlisted the names of two Sikh sants for approval by Sanjay Gandhi. One of them was Bhindranwale, who had become the fourteenth head of the Damdami Taksal Gurudwara Darshan Prakash at Chowk Mehta near Amritsar in 1977 following the death, in an accident, of the previous head, Sant Kartar Singh.

The word 'taksal' (literally a mint to manufacture coins) in Punjabi refers to an educational institute or community of students who associate with a particular sant or prominent spiritual leader. According to one school of thought, Damdami Taksal was founded by Guru Gobind Singh in 1706 at Talwandi Sabo (Damdama Sahib) and was later headed by Baba Deep Singh, who gave his life fighting the Afghan army to liberate the Golden Temple at Amritsar from their hold. Keeping in view Jarnail Singh Bhindranwale's dedication and accomplishments, the thirteenth head of Damdami Taksal, Sant Kartar Singh, had anointed him as his successor instead of his own son Amrik Singh.

The process of selecting a suitable sant for the above purpose has been described by the renowned journalist Kuldip Nayar in his book *Beyond the Lines, An Autobiography*: 'As Sanjay's friend, Kamal Nath, a Member of Parliament, recalled: "The first one (sant) we interviewed did not look a 'courageous type'. Bhindranwale, strong in tone and tenor, seemed to fit the bill. We would give him money off and on, but we never thought he would turn into a terrorist."'

Nayar adds: 'Little did they realize at that time that they were creating a Frankenstein. Zail Singh too maintained contacts with Bhindranwale, although he denied it after he became president.'[2]

Whether Kamal Nath or other members of the 1 Akbar Road group were actually surprised at Bhindranwale's turning into a 'terrorist' will become clear from the contents of the succeeding chapters.

Sikh–Nirankari violence

Bhindranwale was originally a religious preacher, and in his sermons he would warn his audience about the growing tendency among some of the Sikhs to adopt Hindu religious practices, such as idol worship, pilgrimage to religious places and observation of Brahminical rituals. He would object to Sikhs cutting their hair or trimming their beards, drinking alcohol and smoking. But Sanjay Gandhi and Zail Singh were not concerned with his dharam prachar (religious preaching). He had to be groomed to take up political causes that would appeal to the Sikh masses and embarrass the moderate Akali Dal leadership, thereby building pressure on them to either adopt a harder line or lose their Sikh following.

An opportunity to test Bhindranwale's political mettle presented itself on 13 April 1978, when the Akali Dal government in Punjab allowed the Nirankari sect to hold its convention in Amritsar. This was done to please a group of Hindu traders in Amritsar who were supporters of the Janata Party, a coalition partner in the state's Akali Dal government. A large congregation of Sikhs present at the Golden Temple on the occasion of Baisakhi protested, since the Sikhs consider the Nirankaris to be heretics.

Addressing the gathering, Bhindranwale strongly objected to the Nirankari convention in Amritsar and exhorted the audience to march to the convention site and disrupt it. Fauja Singh, an agriculture inspector in the Punjab government, led the Sikh procession, shouting slogans against the Nirankaris. On reaching the site of the convention, Fauja Singh drew his sword and tried to kill the sect's head, Gurbachan Singh. But before he could do so Gurbachan Singh's bodyguards shot Fauja Singh dead. In the battle that followed, thirteen Sikhs and three Nirankaris lost their lives.[3]

The Sikhs who were killed became martyrs, and 1 Akbar Road had a cause for which Bhindranwale could be encouraged to fight. The state government prosecuted sixty-four Nirankaris, including its head, Gurbachan Singh, in the case. But the trial was shifted to the sessions court in Karnal in Haryana, and the accused were acquitted in 1980. Following the Nirankari convention incident, Bhindranwale became extremely critical of the Akali Dal leadership. Soon after the incident he attended an Akali Dal conference at Ludhiana, where he criticized a senior Akali Dal leader (Jathedar Jagdev Singh Talwandi) in his presence but without naming him.

According to Fauja Singh's widow Bibi Amarjit Kaur, Bhindranwale had slipped away from the procession early on and had returned to the Golden Temple. Amarjit Kaur never forgave Bhindranwale; she formed a group called Akhand Kirtani Jatha, which continued to be a thorn in Bhindranwale's flesh till the very end. She was one of the very few who had the courage to openly criticize Bhindranwale from inside the Golden Temple complex for his cowardice.

While the Congress in Punjab did everything to give credit to Bhindranwale for his defence of Sikh beliefs, the Akali Dal leadership, due to its coalition compulsions, did not do anything to support the anti-Nirankari agitation. On the other hand, the Sikh leadership in Delhi, especially those linked to the Delhi Sikh Gurudwara Management Committee (DSGMC), openly supported the anti-Nirankari agitation, possibly because of the Congress party's control over its affairs.

The Nirankari movement had started with the teachings of Baba Dyal Singh in the early nineteenth century. Agra-based Baba Dyal Singh emphasized the importance of a living guru, while mainstream Sikhism accepts the Guru Granth Sahib as the final guru of the faith. In 1929, one segment of the Nirankaris led by Baba Buta Singh, now known as the Sant Nirankari Mission which has its headquarters in Delhi, disassociated itself from the original Nirankari movement as well as from mainstream Sikhism and became an independent sect. The Amritsar convention was held by this group. Due to its belief in a living guru as well as its significant differences in other practices, the Nirankari movement is considered heretic to Sikhism by Sikhs in general.

Dal Khalsa

Whenever Bhindranwale was asked by reporters or others about Khalistan, he would say that he would not refuse the offer of Khalistan if made by the government. Because he would not make Khalistan his core demand, which was central to the Op-1 strategy, the 1 Akbar Road group, specially Zail Singh, came up with the novel idea of floating an organization that would openly demand Khalistan and simultaneously support Bhindranwale. The hope was that by doing so the demand for Khalistan would gradually stick to Bhindranwale, as he would neither contradict nor counter it.

The radical Sikh organization that was thus floated soon after the 13 April 1978 attack on the Nirankari convention was called the Dal Khalsa, 'army of the pure'. Its first meeting was held at

Chandigarh in Hotel Aroma, and the bill of Rs 600 was paid by Zail Singh.[4] According to Kuldip Nayar, 'The inaugural function of the organisation pledged in a resolution "to preserve and keep alive the concept of the distinct and independent identity of the 'Sikh Panth'". The political goal spelt out was the "pre-eminence of the Khalsa".'[5]

In his 2016 book, *Bloodshed in Punjab: Untold Saga of Deceit and Sabotage*, senior journalist G.S. Chawla wrote,

> The president-elect of Dal Khalsa had earlier worked as a stenographer with a former Congress MP from Chandigarh. In a press conference held in Gurudwara Akal Garh, Sector 35 Chandigarh, on August 6, 1978, it was announced that the main objective of setting up Dal Khalsa was to secure the establishment of an independent Sikh state. Next day many Punjab newspapers had published reports that the bill for the expenses at the press conference was also paid by Punjab Congress leaders.[6]

The Dal Khalsa continued to enjoy the patronage of Zail Singh, who became home minister at the Centre in January 1980, and thereafter president of India in July 1982. He would reportedly ring up journalists from Chandigarh and ask them to publish news related to the Dal Khalsa on the front pages of their newspapers. Satish Jacob and Mark Tully wrote in their 2006 book, *Amritsar: Mrs Gandhi's Last Battle,* 'Bhindranwale was never openly associated with the Dal Khalsa. Until his death he maintained that he was a man of religion, not a politician; but the Dal Khalsa was always known as Bhindranwale's party.'[7]

Despite the Congress's support, when elections to the 140-member influential Shiromani Gurudwara Parbhandhak

Committee (SGPC) were held in 1979, only four persons supported by Bhindranwale were elected. None of the candidates supported by the Dal Khalsa were elected.

'No Sign of Militancy'

That Op-1 could not bring about any significant change on the ground till the end of 1979 is evident from the description of Punjab at the time by a highly regarded Indian Civil Service officer, B.G. Deshmukh, who retired as cabinet secretary. He wrote about it in his book, *From Poona to the Prime Minister's Office: A Cabinet Secretary Looks Back*.

Deshmukh was posted as additional secretary in the Ministry of Home Affairs (MHA) from May 1978 to early 1981, with police and law and order as his major charge. Sometime in the middle of 1979, Deshmukh travelled by road to Amritsar and met SGPC officials, visitors to the Golden Temple complex, farmers and villagers.

At Amritsar he found that the main concern of a senior official of the SGPC and some of his colleagues was that Punjab's prosperity had spoilt Sikh youth, who spent their time enjoying themselves and did not want to visit gurudwaras. Deshmukh found that the visitors to the Golden Temple complex, especially those from rural areas, showed 'no sign at all of any militancy' and had no interest in Bhindranwale's militant approach, even though 'he was moving vigorously and widely in the region'.[8]

Deshmukh's planned meeting with Bhindranwale, however, did not materialize. On his way to and from Amritsar, he met residents of small towns and roadside villages, and also stopped and spoke with people working in the fields, mainly Sikhs. 'They were a happy lot and offered genuine hospitality and the whole region seemed a haven of prosperity and peace,' was his observation. Deshmukh also visited Ludhiana, the industrial and trading hub of Punjab. There he met a number of prosperous traders and manufacturers (mostly Hindus), and again found no sign of any anxiety or violence in that city.[9]

On his return from Amritsar, Deshmukh conveyed his impression of the visit to his joint secretary (internal security), an IPS officer, Jyotish Pandey, who mentioned that the outward calm was deceptive and there were undercurrents that were causing anxiety in the home ministry. Pandey's concern mainly emanated from the Congress party's activities following their loss of power in Punjab. According to Deshmukh, 'The reading in the Home Ministry was that the Congress was creating a monster who would one day devour the Congress itself.'[10]

Unfortunately, Punjab was not to remain a 'haven of prosperity and peace' for long. Political opportunism and short-term electoral gains overtook considerations of national interest and the need to maintain religious harmony, peace, prosperity and stability. A community that had played a significant part in India's freedom struggle and in providing food security through the Green Revolution, in addition to giving the country some of its best soldiers and sportspersons and was on its way to a significant industrial growth, became a victim of cold-blooded political calculations.

The developments in Punjab after January 1980 also adversely impacted the activities of the Sikh diaspora.

My Return to Headquarters

On my return to headquarters in October 1979, as per normal practice for the R&AW officers returning from foreign assignments, I reported to Gauri Shankar Bajpai (1953 IPS Uttar Pradesh), who was responsible for manning and managing the

R&AW's foreign stations and sensitive operational work. Bajpai had already been earmarked to join the ministry of external affairs on promotion as joint secretary (personnel) to look after security and vigilance-related matters of the MEA, including those of Indian missions abroad.

Soon after completion of the formalities related to my return to headquarters, Bajpai told me that Suntook wanted me to take charge of Bajpai's post the same day in order to enable him to join the MEA. This came as somewhat of a pleasant surprise to me. Bajpai was eleven years senior to me and his post had normally been held by the senior-most deputy director until that point. I was not yet even a deputy director, and in fact it took me another six months to be promoted to that rank. It appeared that my one and a half years' association with Suntook as assistant director (personnel division) in 1972-73, before my posting to Gangtok as Officer on Special Duty (police) when Suntook was joint director (establishment), had created a favourable impression, which had led him to take that unusual decision. It took me some time to settle in the new job, which also required liaising with the MEA at a suitable level (normally with the director, establishment).

Emergence of Bhindranwale

As mentioned earlier, during the nearly two years ending January 1980 when Indira Gandhi returned to power, nothing significant was achieved in Punjab by the 1 Akbar Road gang through Op-1. However, during the general elections, Bhindranwale actively campaigned for three Congress candidates – Punjab State Congress party chief R.L. Bhatia from Amritsar, Sukhbans Kaur Bhinder (wife of Pritam Singh Bhinder, a senior IPS officer who played a controversial role during the Emergency and was later appointed DGP, Punjab) from Gurdaspur, and former speaker (1969–1971,

1971–1975) of Lok Sabha, Gurdial Singh Dhillon, from Tarn Taran. The fact that Bhindranwale had by then become a well-known figure in Punjab would be evident from the fact that two Congress candidates contesting the elections had specifically mentioned in their election posters: 'Bhindranwale supports me'.[11]

It appears that Indira Gandhi never met Bhindranwale alone. However, Janata Party candidate Pran Nath Lekhi, who contested the 1980 elections against Sukhbans Kaur Bhinder from the Gurdaspur constituency, alleged that 'Mrs Gandhi herself actually appeared on the same platform as Bhindranwale in the election campaign'.[12]

In their book *Amritsar: Mrs Gandhi's Last Battle,* Mark Tully and Satish Jacob write:'Following the official denial after Bhindranwale's death that Mrs Gandhi or the Congress Party had any links with the Sant, the Janata Party candidate wrote a letter to the Prime Minister in which he said: "Bhindranwale was accompanying you during your election tour of Gurdaspur constituency during the general elections to the seventh Lok Sabha (Parliament) held in January 1980."'[13]

The authors write that the nearest Indira Gandhi ever came to admitting any connection between Bhindranwale and her party was in an interview with the BBC current affairs programme, 'Panorama'. In that interview she was asked whether her party had helped the preacher come to prominence. She replied, 'Certainly not. I did not know him. I never knew him.' But she did say, 'Mr Bhindranwale did go and speak for one of our candidates in the elections. I don't know which candidate it was. I don't know whether he knew him personally or he was annoyed with the local Akalis.'[14]

As a result of the encouragement and support extended by the 1 Akbar Road gang, Bhindranwale emerged from the relative obscurity of being a simple rural Sikh religious preacher to an influential Sikh political force capable of taking on the established Sikh leadership in Punjab. He liked the attention that he and his Taksal were getting from the media, and he enjoyed exposing the vulnerabilities of the senior Akali Dal leadership, which helped him build his own leadership and stature amongst the Sikh masses.

This was the one tangible result that the 1 Akbar Road group had derived from their support to Bhindranwale during Op-1. He had bitten their bait and was now ready for a much bigger role in helping his political mentors achieve their goal. And that occasion was not too far off in the future.

4

The Rise of Bhindranwale (1980–81)

WITH BHINDRANWALE'S capability and willingness to deliver results already tested at the state level, following the Congress party's return to power at the Centre in 1980, it was decided that the Congress would deploy him and the issue of Khalistan – which had by then stuck to him because of his refusal or inability to rebut it – in order to win the eighth Lok Sabha elections that were due before January 1985. This would mark the beginning of the Op-2 phase. Based on my operational experience of working in the Department, certain decisions that came to my notice and developments as they unfolded, the idea behind Op-2 can be summed up as follows:

Create a climate of communal mistrust between Hindus and Sikhs in Punjab and the neighbouring state of Haryana, first by encouraging and then by overlooking acts of violence and extremism attributed to Bhindranwale. This would be accompanied by coverage of related incidents by an obliging media, specially the vernacular press. Also, an impression would be created amongst Hindus that pro-Khalistan feelings were catching the imagination of all Sikhs, both in Punjab and abroad, which had the potential of endangering the integrity of the nation.

In such a vitiated atmosphere, Hindus were expected to feel hurt, victimized and threatened by the acts of the Sikh community, whose interests could easily be ignored as they comprised less than 2 per cent of the country's population. Prolonged and unhindered but carefully controlled discontent among members of the majority community was expected to generate emotional hysteria and the belief that the nation's integrity was in danger from proponents of Khalistan who were conspiring against the state, with or without the support of foreign elements. The combined impact of the above-mentioned factors was bound to create a mood of vengeance amongst Hindus, leading to demands for strongest possible action to protect national integrity and the interests of the majority community from anti-national, divisive, communal and criminal forces bent on disturbing the peace, harmony and unity of the nation.

On the other hand it was also important to keep the pot boiling in Punjab and to allow Bhindranwale to operate unhindered till the situation was ripe for final action, it was essential to initiate dialogue with the moderate Akali Dal leaders and give them the impression that Prime Minister Gandhi was sympathetic to the resolution of their demands, for which they had been agitating for some time. But in actual fact, the talks would be prolonged on one pretext or the other, because if the demands were accepted, normalcy would return prematurely to Punjab. That would leave no scope for Bhindranwale to operate. Also, if moderate Akali leaders somehow lost all hopes of a solution and decided to suspend or withdraw their agitation before the time chosen by the

1 Akbar Road group, Bhindanwale would have been left with little justification to stay put in the Golden Temple complex. He would have come under pressure from all sides to vacate the premises and go back to his Mehta Chowk gurudwara. That was also not acceptable to the 1 Akbar Road group.

With the Opposition parties left twiddling their thumbs and compelled to endorse public demands for strong action and the 1 Akbar Road group having highjacked the agendas of some of these parties, suitable conditions would have been created for Indira Gandhi to take strong action to put an end to the above-mentioned anti-Hindu and anti-national activities of Sikh extremists and emerge as a strong, decisive leader. The only problem in this plan was that such an action had to be well timed keeping in view the next national elections, as any significant lapse of time between the two might fritter away the political gains arising out of it.

Bhindranwale's growing influence

In 1980, the Shiromani Akali Dal (SAD)-Janata Party coalition government in Punjab led by Parkash Singh Badal was dismissed, resulting in fresh elections to the state assembly. In these elections the Congress returned to power. Indira Gandhi appointed Zail Singh's arch rival Darbara Singh as chief minister of Punjab. An insecure Zail Singh, who had become home minster at the Centre, now had to protect his own turf in Punjab while staying on as an active member of the 1 Akbar Road group. In addition to the personal political rivalry between the two Sikh Congress leaders from Punjab, there was a clear clash of ideology as well. Darbara Singh, a member of the old Congress school of thought, was secular in his politics, while Zail Singh not only tolerated communal forces but also compromised with them. He had no qualms about adopting a communal agenda to further both his own and the Congress party's interests in Punjab.

The change in governments at the Centre and in Punjab were followed by a significant increase in violence in the state. Pro-Khalistan activities started getting noticed. According to reports in early April 1980, while visiting village Jandua Bhimshah in tehsil Fazilka, Bhindranwale had announced that 'Bacha' (Gurbachan Singh, head of the Nirankaris) had killed twenty-five persons while he had killed only three. Therefore, he would kill twenty-two Nirankaris more. On 24 April 1980, Gurbachan Singh was shot dead in his house in New Delhi.

Bhindranwale's name figured as one of the suspects in the case. Fearing arrest, he sought refuge in Guru Nanak Niwas (an SGPC-managed guesthouse adjoining the Golden Temple complex) and did not come out till Zail Singh made a statement in parliament that Bhindranwale had nothing to do with Gurbachan Singh's murder.[1] Bhindranwale thereafter announced that Gurbachan Singh's killers deserved to be honoured by the jathedar (head priest) of the Akal Takht. He also said he would himself weigh the killers in gold, if they came to meet him.

In the middle of March 1981, a Sikh educational conference was organized at Chandigarh by Chief Khalsa Diwan, a non-political organization meant to promote Sikh educational institutions in Punjab. It was presided over by a US national, Ganga Singh Dhillon, head of the Washington DC-based Guru Nanak Foundation. Though a comparatively unknown entity in Punjab till then, Ganga Singh Dhillon was close to some influential US senators and congressmen as well as to Pakistan's President Zia-ul-Haq.

During the proceedings of the Chandigarh conference, it was declared that 'Sikhs are a separate nation'. Dhillon himself moved a resolution stating, 'Sikhs be admitted as an associate member of the UN as they are not a part of Hindu mainstream and had a separate identity.' Following Dhillon's visit, senior BJP leader Atal Bihari Vajpayee, participating in a debate in the Lok Sabha, quoted Punjab Chief Minster Darbara Singh as having said that Zail Singh had met Ganga Singh Dhillon at Karnal.[2]

As late as on 10 August 1981, Indira Gandhi had said in a press conference at New Delhi, 'So far, Khalistan existed only in Canada and perhaps in the USA also, but it does not mean that we would lower our guards and not exercise the utmost vigilance.'[3] It would be pertinent to question – given Ganga Singh Dhillon's background – why he was allowed entry into the country to preside over such a conference in Chandigarh.

To compete with Bhindranwale's growing influence, in May 1981 the moderate Akali Dal leadership demanded a complete ban on the use of tobacco in the holy city of Amritsar. There were demonstrations and counter-demonstrations in support of and against this demand. Akalis even shouted some provocative slogans against the Hindu Suraksha Samiti (HSS) led by Patiala-based Pawan Kumar Sharma, who had organized demonstrations against this demand.

Pawan Kumar was reportedly close to Amarinder Singh and Haryana chief minster Bhajan Lal. Lala Jagat Narain and a section of Congress leaders had also supported the HSS on that issue. After the anti-tobacco demonstrations of 31 May 1981 at Amritsar, the Punjab government asked people to surrender their licensed arms. Bhindranwale, addressing a congregation at Sector 11, Gurudwara Chandigarh, was adamant that his men would not surrender their arms.

On 9 September 1981 Lala Jagat Narain, proprietor of a chain of newspapers published from Jalandhar, was shot dead near Ludhiana. Jagat Narain's influential daily *Punjab Kesari* had been critical of Bhindranwale, and Narain, who had been present at the clash between the Sikhs and Nirankaris, had testified in court against Bhindranwale. *Punjab Kesari* was accused of taking a pro-Nirankari stand. According to Mark Tully and Satish Jacob, 'Narain's partisan attitude was typical. In fact, the whole of the Punjab press was divided on communal lines.'[4]

On the day Lala Jagat Narain was killed, Bhindranwale was on a preaching mission at village Chando Kalan in Hisar district in Haryana. He, along with two associates, was named in the FIR filed after the murder. A Punjab police team headed by Deputy Inspector General (DIG) of police D.S. Mangat, was sent with warrants to Chando Kalan under instructions from Chief Minister Darbara Singh to arrest Bhindranwale. Tipped off suitably, Bhindranwale had already left Chando Kalan with some of his supporters and had headed for his headquarters, Gurudwara Darshan Prakash, Chowk Mehta.

He travelled over 300 km through Haryana and Punjab and reached Chowk Mehta in the night of 13-14 September 1981. According to Kuldip Nayar, Zail Singh himself telephoned Haryana chief minister Bhajan Lal and told him not to arrest Bhindranwale and not get involved in the case. 'A senior police officer told Satish Jacob that the Haryana chief minister went as far as to send an official car to Chando Kalan to drive Bhindranwale back to his gurudwara.'[5]

My batchmate Diwakar Das Gupta (IPS 1964 Madhya Pradesh), who was DIG at BSF headquarters in New Delhi had told me at that time that their force tried to stop Bhindranwale at each of their check posts but he received instructions from the home minister's office to let Bhindranwale pass unhindered. As Bhindranwale left in a great hurry, carefully maintained transcripts of all his sermons were left behind. They were reportedly set on fire in anger by the raiding Punjab police party.

Who will arrest Bhindranwale?

Lieutenant General S.K. Sinha was the GOC-in-C of the Western Command during that period. Within a couple of days of Bhindranwale's return to Chowk Mehta, the chief secretary of Punjab requested him to arrest Bhindranwale. When General Sinha told him that it was not the job of the army, the chief secretary reportedly requested him to lend army tanks to help the Punjab police to carry out the task. That odd request was obviously refused. A personal request to Lt Gen. Sinha by Chief Minister Darbara Singh in that respect also did not work.

Two days later, General Sinha's chief of staff received orders from the prime minister's office that the army had to arrest Bhindranwale and detailed a Gurkha battalion to carry out the task. When General Sinha came to know about it, he told his chief of staff to put the operation on hold. He then called Defence Minister R. Venkataraman and requested that he be allowed to discuss the matter with the prime minster before the orders were carried out. The next day General Sinha was informed by the defence minister that the army should stand down and the task would be assigned to the local police.[6]

Gurudwara Chowk Mehta was surrounded by Punjab police. Darbara Singh had sent three senior police officers to negotiate with Bhindranwale, who agreed to surrender on the afternoon of 20 September. Santokh Singh, a close confidante of Indira Gandhi's and president of the DSGMC, was also present at Chowk Mehta that day. He made a very provocative speech before Bhindranwale's arrest. Just before the appointed time Bhindranwale also made a speech, which was highly critical of the Punjab government. That led to firing by his followers soon after his arrest. In the exchange of fire that followed, seven persons were killed. Santokh Singh's presence and his provocative speech at Gurudwara Chowk Mehta were brought to the notice of Prime Minister Gandhi by Parkash Singh Badal on 22 September when she visited Chandigarh to address an all-party meeting.[7]

Bhindranwale was kept in detention in Ferozepur jail for some time and was later temporarily taken to a canal rest house near Ludhiana. After spending some time in comfortable environments and after some casual and respectful interrogation (the investigation officer used the word 'janab' or 'sir', before every question),[8] Bhindranwale was released in less than a month, on 15 October 1981. Home Minster Zail Singh made a statement in parliament that as no incriminating evidence had been found against Bhindranwale, he was being released.

There was considerable evidence to suggest that Bhindranwale's release was ordered by the home minister himself.[9] However, a senior Congress politician from Punjab told Satish Jacob, 'It was Mrs Gandhi herself who actually ordered the Sant's release.' This was confirmed by a family member of the president of the DSGMC, who told Mark Tully, 'Santokh Singh himself went and pleaded with Mrs Gandhi for Bhindranwale's release, threatening that it would not be possible to keep the Delhi Gurudwara Management committee loyal to the Congress if Bhindranwale was not set free.' Tully and Jacob wrote: 'By surrendering justice to petty political gains, the government itself created the ogre who was to dominate the last years of Mrs Gandhi and to shadow her until her death.'[10]

Bhindranwale's arrest from Chowk Mehta and his subsequent release in fact helped raise his profile as an important leader of the Sikh community in Punjab and granted him the status of a hero. Bhindranwale himself said after his release that the government had done more for him through his arrest than he could have achieved in years.

On the day Bhindranwale was arrested, three Sikhs on a motorcycle fired at Hindus in a marketplace in Jalandhar, killing four and injuring twelve. The next day one Hindu was killed and thirteen people injured in a similar incident in Tarn Taran near Amritsar. Five days later a goods train was derailed near Amritsar. Two other attempts were made to derail trains by tampering with the tracks.

On 29 September 1981, five members of the Dal Khalsa, including its newly elected head Gajinder Singh, hijacked Indian Airlines Flight 423 from Srinagar to Delhi and diverted it to Lahore, demanding Bhindranwale's release from jail. By now the Dal Khalsa was openly demanding the creation of Khalistan. Therefore their demand for the release of Bhindranwale created an impression that the organization which demanded Khalistan had close links with Bhindranwale.

The hijacking ended with an operation by Pakistani commandos. All the five hijackers including Gajinder Singh were tried in Pakistan and sentenced to life. Following the hijacking, the Government of India imposed a ten-year ban on the Dal Khalsa in 1982, which was lifted in 1992. After lying low for fifteen years, the Dal Khalsa staged a political comeback in Punjab in 1998, which coincided with the so-called release of the five hijackers from prison in Pakistan. Two of the five, Tejinder Pal Singh and Satnam Singh, who were deported, were finally discharged from the case by a Delhi court in 2011. Gajinder Singh, as head of Dal Khalsa International (DKI), remains in exile in Pakistan.

Santokh Singh, who had pleaded with Indira Gandhi for Bhindranwale's release, was shot dead in Delhi on 21 December 1981 in his car, allegedly by a rival Sikh politician. Santokh Singh was reportedly paying the legal fees for the killers facing trial in Gurbachan Singh's murder case. He also used to pay Rs 2,000 every month to the family of one of the accused, Ranjit Singh.[11]

Zail Singh and Rajiv Gandhi attended Santokh Singh's memorial service. A photograph from the event shows Zail Singh with Bhindranwale. However, Bhindranwale was not pleased to see the home minister. In his address to the congregation, he made an obvious reference to Zail Singh dyeing his beard, anathema to an orthodox Sikh. 'Anyone who has his face blackened and sandals hung round his neck and is made to sit backwards on a donkey is being punished because he has molested someone's sister or someone's mother. I am surprised to see that some people here have blackened their own faces. I do not know whose sister they have molested.'[12] Zail Singh apparently digested that insult as he felt Bhindranwale was still useful to him in Punjab and in furthering the cause of Op-2.

New R&AW missions

As mentioned earlier, a separate division to deal with Sikh extremism and its links with Pakistan's ISI had been created at the R&AW by end 1980. Sometime in early 1981, Director (R) Suntook asked me to prepare and send proposals to the MEA for the creation of seven R&AW stations in Indian missions (both embassies and consulates) in west Europe and North America (US and Canada). These missions were to be located in areas with a sizeable presence of Sikh immigrants. Suntook said my proposal should specifically mention that we had observed the growing extremist leanings among certain sections of the Sikh diaspora and there was every likelihood that the demand for Khalistan would gain momentum in these areas in the not-too-distant future. In view of that, the R&AW would like to post its officers in those missions to keep a close watch on the developments and to help the Government of India take suitable preventive measures in advance.

While I knew first hand that the Sikh diaspora in North America did not harbour any such sentiments till then, I prepared these one-and-a-half-page proposals, nonetheless, drawing partly on my memory of some fanciful ideas narrated to me by a pro-Khalistan ideologue who, after Operation Blue Star, came out openly in favour of Khalistan. He was soon raised by the R&AW as its source and used as a double agent to gauge the extent of the ISI's involvement in pro-Khalistan activities in Punjab. Later, the senior R&AW officer who was handling that source asked me to facilitate his surrender. Without letting the officer feel that all those years I knew about his source's connection with our department, I politely refused to get involved in a contrived operation.

I thought the proposals for the creation of seven overseas missions to keep a tab on Sikh separatists would not be accepted, on one pretext or the other, by the MEA as many other proposals, even for a single junior-level post, would usually get stuck there for a considerably longer period. To convey the importance of the proposals, I got four of them signed by Joint Director A.K. Verma (later secretary, R&AW). Contrary to my expectations and to my utter delight, all seven proposals were accepted by the MEA rather quickly. I thought I had achieved the impossible.

It subsequently occurred to me that given the Department was ultimately responsible to the prime minister, these proposals could not have been cleared so fast without a word from the PM's principal secretary to the foreign secretary. For some time to come, I continued to wonder what was so special about these posts that the PMO had intervened. Contrary to the urgency with which these posts were sanctioned, for a couple of reasons we took some time to start filling them. Firstly, the Department was still reeling from the deep cuts that Morarji Desai had inflicted on its strength. Officers who were parked safely by Suntook in sister organizations such as the Special Service Bureau (SSB) had to be recalled. Also, some new officers had to be inducted. It was also felt that at least for the posts in the US and Canada it would be better if we sent Sikh officers as far as possible, who could read the minds of the local Sikh population. Further, certain time-consuming formalities with respect to their postings on special assignments had to be completed.

Finally, by the end of 1981 we were ready to fill these posts. Officers had to be introduced to the director (establishment), MEA, before their induction into the MEA. Things went smoothly till August 1982 and a couple of posts were filled without a hitch. Then, a Sikh Indian Foreign Service officer took over as director (establishment) at the MEA. The first R&AW officer who was to be introduced to him happened to be from Maharashtra, who had little knowledge of Punjab affairs, not to speak of the Sikh diaspora and their perceived susceptibility to pro-Khalistan propaganda.

So, I personally briefed the officer before his meeting with the director (establishment). Despite my briefing him, the officer concerned didn't feel confident about his knowledge when it came to being asked anything specific on the issue of Khalistan. That was exactly what happened. At the very outset the director (establishment) asked whether the officer really believed there was a Khalistan issue that needed to be addressed in Punjab and how his posting to that particular station was going to help the Department. It was a loaded question and, as expected, my colleague did not know how to address it.

The director (establishment) then sought my views on the subject. Conscious of the fact that what the director had asked my colleague was a valid question (as to whether there was really a Khalistan issue at all), I defended my proposal. He was not convinced. Finally, I told him that the difference between the MEA and R&AW was, 'Whereas MEA comes to know about the problem when it starts appearing in the media, the R&AW becomes aware of the same at the conceptual stage itself.' Naturally, he did not appreciate my 'cheeky' answer. I told him that if he was confident there was no such problem and there was no chance of its emergence in the near future, he should write so on the file and I would gladly take my officer back.

Obviously, he could not do that as he was aware of the special circumstances under which those posts were sanctioned. Later I learnt that there was a feeling in the MEA at that time that the R&AW was creating additional posts in Indian missions abroad taking full advantage of the 'non-existent' Khalistan issue. Much later, I apologized to the officer concerned for that cheeky answer. But little did I know at that time that the fast-moving developments resulting from Op-2 would soon render my proposals prophetic.

Gauging the mood of the Sikh diaspora

Meanwhile, it appeared the 1 Akbar Road group, including Indira Gandhi, were getting anxious to know about the impact of Op-2 on the Sikh diaspora, especially in the US and Canada. As the R&AW had still not managed to fill the newly sanctioned posts, and as the few officers who were already posted there were not in a position to cover large and distant areas of the US and Canada, Suntook asked me to visit those countries for about ten days. My brief was to ascertain the diaspora's views on the developments taking place in Punjab and suggest measures to improve the situation. I left for Ottawa, on or around 15 December 1981, arrived the next day and spent couple of days there. I left for

Vancouver on 18 December before moving to Los Angeles on 22 December, from where I left for Tokyo on 24 December en route to India.

From Ottawa I called my friends and contacts in Toronto, and from Los Angeles my contacts in San Francisco, Yuba City and Sacramento areas. I met my friends, contacts and relatives wherever I went. The story was somewhat similar everywhere. Rather than being repetitive, I shall sum up my impressions of the visit towards the end of this chapter.

In Ottawa, I met some of my old Sikh friends and contacts, in addition to calling on Indian High Commissioner Gurdial Singh Dhillon, former speaker of the Lok Sabha and later minister for agriculture in Rajiv Gandhi's cabinet, at his residence. He was an old colleague of my father-in-law's and was aware of my background. Dhillon told me that developments back home were having a serious impact on the traditionally cordial relations between the Sikh and Hindu Indian immigrants settled in the country. Gurudwaras in Canada, specially from the Toronto and Vancouver areas, were becoming centres of Sikh religious orthodoxy and propaganda against the Government of India.

My friends and contacts whom I met separately also endorsed Dhillon's views, though they said that Ottawa had so far remained comparatively immune to such influences. But some of their Sikh and Hindu friends were getting confused as to what was happening in Punjab and why the ruling party (Congress) was so tolerant of Bhindranwale-led or sponsored activities. I also contacted a couple of friends from Toronto by phone. There the situation appeared to have changed significantly since I left Canada towards the end of 1979. In addition to religious activities, gurudwaras were also becoming centres of political discussions reflective of what was happening in Punjab.

It was in Vancouver that I had maximum exposure to influential members of the local Sikh community. It was the Christmas holiday season. My host and his friends were thrilled to discover that my Canadian driving licence was still valid and that I held a diplomatic passport. Over and above that I was a teetotaller. It was a godsend to them. Earlier, one of them had to abstain from drinking to drive the car, but now, with me as driver, my host and his friends could all drink as much as they wished. It being the Christmas season, we started party hopping, which gave me an opportunity to meet a large cross-section of local people of Indian origin, Sikhs as well as Hindus.

What I gathered at the end of my visit to Canada, and which was to remain valid after my interactions with friends and relatives from the west coast areas of the US, is summed up below:

1. The moderate Sikhs had gradually started losing control over the management of some of the older gurudwaras in Toronto, Vancouver and its suburbs, and in the San Francisco, Sacramento and Yuba city areas of the US to Sikh hardliners. While they were trying to regain control of those gurudwaras, the developments in Punjab had made their task difficult, if not impossible.
2. The peaceful, harmonious and friendly relations which existed between the Hindu and Sikh segments of the local Punjabi population were getting vitiated because of the communal divide taking place in Punjab, in which the Indian press, especially from Punjab, divided on communal lines, was playing a significant part. The local Indian missions were also not doing anything to improve the situation.
3. Earlier, hardly anybody would mention the word 'Khalistan' at social get-togethers. It was almost taboo. But now, some

persons were showing inquisitiveness and wanted to know why it had become a matter of debate in Punjab. Some of the more knowledgeable ones were a bit surprised at the way Bhindranwale was being patronized by some senior Congress leaders.

4. There was general concern and apprehension amongst the moderate Sikhs that if urgent corrective measures were not taken by the Government of India and by Indian missions abroad, a minuscule minority of hardliners may sideline the silent majority and carry forward their anti-India agenda.

In that connection my friends and contacts made the following suggestions:

i. Both the vernacular and national press in India needed to exercise restraint in their news coverage, which could help to maintain communal harmony in Punjab and also among the Punjabi diaspora in the US and Canada.
ii. The activities of Bhindranwale, who appeared to be enjoying political patronage, needed to be curbed and controlled.
iii. Visits by US- or Canada-based pro-Khalistan ideologues to India, and specifically to Punjab, needed to be stopped.
iv. Senior Akali Dal leaders needed to be told that granthis and sewadars coming from Punjab had to be properly screened before they were sent to the US/Canada for manning gurudwaras, to avoid spawning anti-India sentiments in those countries.
v. Some senior Congress and Akali Dal leaders needed to visit their areas, openly and not quietly, to meet local Punjabi immigrants to assure them that everything in Punjab was fine and that they would do everything possible to bring normalcy back to Punjab.

vi. Indian missions located in their respective areas needed to hold or encourage joint meetings of prominent Hindus and Sikhs, to restore mutual trust between the two communities.

A note ignored

I left Los Angeles for Tokyo on Christmas eve. After spending a day there I returned to New Delhi on 26 December 1981. Taking advantage of the long trans-Pacific flight from Los Angeles to Tokyo, I prepared a short note on my visit to the US and Canada. I met Suntook on 27 December and discussed with him the inputs I had gathered during my trip. He asked me to prepare a short one-page point-wise handwritten note and show it to Senior Advisor Kao the same afternoon.

As directed, I prepared the note and handed it to Kao at his Rashtrapati Bhavan office. After going through the note carefully, to my surprise, he asked me to meet the prime minister's principal information officer, H.Y. Sharda Prasad, and hand over the note to him. Until then I had thought that the note was actually meant for the principal secretary to the PM and that the government would finally do something to improve the situation on the ground, both in Punjab and in the US and Canada.

As desired by Kao, I called on Sharda Prasad at his office on the first floor of South Block, to the left of the corridor opposite the PM's office. He went through the note carefully but did not discuss its contents with me. All he said was, 'Hmmm...' and then, 'You can go'. Managing the press and the media to project the right image of the PM and the government was his main job. In view of that, I thought he might brief the Indian press in his own way, to exercise restraint and help restore normalcy in relations between Hindus and Sikhs in Punjab and those settled abroad.

Unfortunately, that proved to be wishful thinking on my part. Gradually, the Indian media became even more virulent in their coverage of the communal divide in Punjab. The activities of Bhindranwale and Sikh extremists started getting greater prominence and front-page coverage even in the popular national newspapers. A well-known editor of a major newspaper started writing lead articles on the editorial page blaming the Sikhs for nursing ambitions of re-establishing the 'Khalsa Raj'.

5

Negotiated Solution: A Prolonged Charade?

IN A democratic country like India, where the government is elected by the people and is supposed to be answerable to them for its performance, at least at the time of the next elections, it cannot afford to be totally oblivious to its responsibility towards the very basic needs of its electorate. These include maintenance of law and order, and peace and harmony, which in turn are so very essential for agricultural, industrial and economic progress.

The Central government needed to be seen to be doing something about the unrest in Punjab. Indira Gandhi thus expressed an interest in finding a negotiated solution to the Punjab problem. Simultaneously, she also let senior officials concerned know that if the situation called for it she would not hesitate to use the elite commando unit, the Special Frontier Force (SFF), to pick up Bhindranwale from the Golden Temple complex and place him in confinement.

Indira Gandhi and her government soon started making repeated and concerted efforts to enter into and pursue negotiations with the moderate Akali leadership led by Sant Harchand Singh Longowal. But in reality the prolonged exercise was a charade, as each round (P.C. Alexander said there were a total of twenty-six rounds) of negotiation ended without producing any results, with the 'un-cooperative', 'adamant', 'incapable' or 'powerless' moderate Akali leadership being usually blamed for its failure.

When a solution was almost worked out and was acceptable to both sides, it was sabotaged at the last moment by suitably inducing Congress chief ministers of the neighbouring two states (Haryana and Rajasthan) to object. In other instances, previously approved decisions at the highest level, which had been shared with the Akali Dal delegation, were changed by Indira Gandhi overnight without ascribing any reason for doing so. In case the moderate Akali leadership, fed up with the protracted but fruitless negotiations with the government and worried about the consequences of the Bhindranwale-inspired escalation of violence in Punjab, decided on their own to withdraw their agitation, the government would use some of its carefully cultivated senior Akali leaders to sabotage their efforts.

An interesting part of this strategy was that while the so-called search for a negotiated solution was on, the governments – both Central and state – continued to ignore, if not encourage, Bhindranwale's extremist activities, with the Punjab police totally confused if not paralysed. Those like DIG Avtar Singh Atwal who dared challenge Bhindranwale were eliminated by him, sending a signal to the rest that they had better behave to avoid a similar fate. DIG Atwal was murdered on 25 April 1983 as he emerged after paying obeisance at the Golden Temple.

From the middle of 1982, Kao was allowed to plan SFF-led commando operations to grab Bhindranwale from three different locations – Chowk Mehta, Guru Nanak Niwas and the Golden Temple complex. This gave an impression to Indian agencies, their officers and staff members that Prime Minister Gandhi was actually very serious about putting an end to the whole affair by grabbing Bhindranwale from his known hideouts. But when the SFF was finally ready to launch such an operation (in April 1984, see Chapter 8), Indira Gandhi aborted it on the plea that she could not afford the possible civilian casualties that might result. That estimated loss was a fraction of the horrific losses caused by Operation Blue Star, launched within two months of that decision.

Talks begin

While Bhindranwale was still in detention in the Lala Jagat Narain murder case, the Akali Dal leadership had, in September 1981, submitted to the government a list of forty-five demands segmented under four categories: religious, political, economic and social. The first of the many rounds of talks between the government and senior Akali Dal leaders was held on 16 October 1981, one day after Bhindranwale was exonerated of the murder charge and released from detention. Incidentally, Zail Singh made a statement on 15 October 1981 that Bhnidranwale was being released in Jagat Narain's murder case, as no incriminating evidence was found against him.[1] The meeting was held in the prime minister's office in Parliament House. The Akali Dal was represented by Harchand Singh Longowal, Parkash Singh Badal, Gurcharan Singh Tohra, Surjit Singh Barnala and Balwant Singh. Indira Gandhi was assisted by Cabinet Secretary C.R. Krishnaswamy Rao Sahib, her Principal Secretary P.C. Alexander and Home Secretary T.N. Chaturvedi.[2]

In the meanwhile, the Akalis had reduced their original forty-five demands presented to the government in September 1981 to fifteen. One of the demands was the release of Bhindranwale, which had become infructuous as he had already been released. The religious demands included permission for Sikhs to carry the kirpan (a short, curved dagger) on domestic and international flights; passing of an All India Gurudwara Act; grant of Holy City status to Amritsar; installation of a radio station at Harmandir Sahib in the Golden Temple complex for live broadcast of kirtan; and renaming of the Flying Mail (train) as Golden Temple Express.

The political and economic demands included devolution of some Central powers to Punjab, as per the provisions of the Anandpur Sahib Resolution, merger of Punjabi-speaking areas of the neighbouring states into Punjab, licence for opening a new bank under Sikh management, and remunerative prices for agricultural produce by linking them to the price index of industrial production. In addition, the transfer of Chandigarh, joint capital of Punjab and Haryana, to Punjab was a major issue.

The meeting of 16 October took up only the religious demands and the transfer of Chandigarh to Punjab. P.C. Alexander wrote in his memoirs, 'The political and economic demands were never raised at the talks and, in fact, faded out of the agenda during subsequent discussions as well. The talks were held in a cordial atmosphere and the Akali leaders were assured by Indira Gandhi that their demands, particularly the religious ones, would be given urgent consideration.'[3]

While the meeting was going on in Delhi, on 16 October Sikh militants attacked Niranjan Singh, an IAS officer of the Punjab cadre, and his brother in the Punjab Government Secretariat complex in Chandigarh. Niranjan Singh escaped with serious injuries but his brother succumbed. On 23 October, Mohinder

Pal, a Hindu sarpanch (headman) of Panchta village in Kapurthala district was shot dead. On 14 November, a bomb explosion took place in the office of the DIG, Patiala, the target being DIG D.S. Mangat, who had been sent by Chief Minster Darbara Singh to arrest Bhindranwale from the village of Chando Kalan in Haryana. On 19 November, a police party was attacked in the village of Daheru in Ludhiana district, and one inspector and a constable were killed. This marked the beginning of Bhindranwale targeting policemen or government officials who had in any way stood up to him.[4]

It was in this environment of escalating violence that Indira Gandhi held the second of three rounds of talks with Akali leaders on 26 November 1981 at her Parliament House office. The same Akali leaders who had attended the first round of talks attended this meeting too. In addition to the three senior civil servants who had attended the previous round, External Affairs Minister P.V. Narasimha Rao also attended this meeting. Replying to the demand made by the Akali delegation on 16 October, the PM explained that since pilgrimage cities such as Varanasi and Kurukshetra did not have any formal special status, no such formal recognition could be granted to Amritsar. Regarding the sale of liquor and tobacco in Amritsar, she said that rather than ban them in the whole city, limited area restrictions could be imposed by the local authorities, similar to those in Haridwar and Kurukshetra.

Referring to the demand for live broadcast of kirtan and gurbani from Harmandir Sahib, she said no private party could be given a licence for it, but arrangements could be made through All India Radio (AIR) Jalandhar, for which requisite space in the Golden Temple complex would need to be provided by the SGPC. Regarding permission to carry the kirpan on Air-India and Indian Airlines flights, she said Air-India was bound by rules applicable to all international carriers and hence no exception could be made. However, the kirpan could be carried on domestic Indian Airlines flights, provided its size was reduced.

On the demand for an All India Gurudwara Act to cover all 'historical' gurudwaras throughout India, she said that it could be considered in consultation with the management of the concerned gurudwaras outside Punjab. The Akalis, however, dropped their demand for renaming the Flying Mail, as it was pointed out that it would be impossible to stop passengers from smoking, and the notoriety of the train running mostly late would not be conducive to a name sacred to the Sikhs.

In the end, the Akalis raised the issue of revising the 'unfavourable' formula announced in 1976 for the sharing of Beas and Ravi rivers between Punjab, Haryana and Rajasthan. Indira Gandhi said that she herself was looking into the problem of equitable sharing of river waters and that discussions were already underway between the Centre and concerned state governments.

P.C. Alexander wrote,

> We got the impression that the Akalis were fairly satisfied with the assurances given by the Prime Minister and we sincerely thought that the Akali leadership would not opt for a confrontation with the government. But it soon became clear that the moderate leadership of Akali party was fast losing its grip over the agitation and the militant sections in the community were no longer under the control of the Akali triumvirate.[5]

Alexander's observation is rather interesting. On the one hand, the 1 Akbar Road group was gradually eroding the hold of the moderate Akali Dal leaders over their peaceful agitation by encouraging and overlooking Bhindranwale's extremism and violence. On the other hand, they were telling the Akali moderates to regain their hold over the agitation before their demands were accepted. It was a Catch-22 situation for the moderate Akali leadership. But they had to continue their efforts if they were to remain relevant to the political and religious scene of Punjab. From the point of view of the 1 Akbar Road group, the negotiation process was going in the right direction, meaning that a certain section of Sikhs in Punjab was gradually losing faith in the ability of the moderate Akalis to protect their interests, thereby lending credibility to Bhindranwale's propaganda that moderate Akalis were incapable of protecting Sikh interests. It was just the beginning, though.

Following the second round of talks with the Akalis, Punjab Chief Minister Darbara Singh was asked by Prime Minister Indira Gandhi to withdraw the case filed in the Supreme Court by Parkash Singh Badal's government on the sharing of river waters between Punjab, Haryana and Rajasthan. On 31 December 1981, a river-water sharing agreement was signed by the chief ministers of these states (all from the Congress) in the prime minister's office. The Akalis felt the agreement was highly unfavourable to Punjab and that Chief Minster Darbara Singh had been coerced into signing it. This gave the Akalis an issue to fight for. To carry Haryana's share, the Sutlej–Yamuna Link Canal was to be dug and it was to pass through some parts of Punjab.[6]

To avoid a confrontation with the Akalis on this issue, Indira Gandhi invited them for a third and last round of talks with her personally on 5 April 1982, which lasted for over two and a half hours. Zail Singh, still the Union home minister, attended the meeting for the first time, though he remained silent throughout. Pranab Mukherjee, the Union finance minister, was also present.

Cabinet Secretary Krishnaswamy Rao Sahib, Home Secretary T.N. Chaturvedi and P.C, Alexander were also in attendance. The Akali delegation comprised Longowal, Badal, Tohra, Balwant Singh, Bhan Singh, P.S. Oberoi and Ravi Inder Singh.[7]

As expected, the Akalis vehemently criticized the December 1981 agreement on sharing of river waters and questioned the intention of the government in withdrawing the case filed by the previous (Akali) government. The prime minister tried to assuage their feelings by promising that she would do her best to find other ways to compensate Punjab, but this failed to convince the Akalis. They raised some other issues related to discrimination against Sikhs. These included reduction of recruitment of Sikhs to the Indian Army, harassment of Sikh farmers in the Terai region of Uttar Pradesh and denial of second-language status to the Punjabi language in the states of Himachal, Haryana and Rajasthan.

The Akalis were not convinced with the facts and figures presented at the meeting to counter their allegations. Soon afterwards, they announced that the talks had failed and that they would organize a mass protest at the site on the date of inauguration of work on the Sutlej–Yamuna Link Canal by Indira Gandhi.

Armed and dangerous

Despite the ban imposed by the Punjab government on possession of arms, not only was Bhindranwale openly moving around in Punjab with a posse of armed men, he also visited Delhi in the first week of April 1982 at the invitation of Santokh Singh, president of the Congress-controlled DSGMC. Bhindranwale was accompanied by two busloads of his followers, who were seen in the capital with armed men sitting on the roof of a bus.

On that day I was to go to Connaught Place for some work. My car was stopped at Baba Kharak Singh Marg by the police as a procession led by Bhindranwale had to be made way for. To ensure that nobody missed Bhindranwale's presence in the bus, it was being announced on loudspeaker that the public could have darshan of 'Sant Bhindranwale Ji' who was sitting on the left side front seat of the bus and was clearly visible to bystanders. The procession then proceeded towards the inner circle of Connaught Place. Given his notoriety, it seemed that this was being done to build his stature among Sikhs and instil fear in the minds of Hindus in Delhi.

By the end of that month the situation in Punjab had deteriorated to such an extent that parliament passed a resolution expressing 'deep anguish and concern'. Participating in the debate in the Rajya Sabha, Sikh member and senior leader of the CPI(M), Harkishan Singh Surjeet, accused the Congress of organizing Bhindranwale's visit to Delhi. 'I want to tell the House that he [Bhindranwale] gets protection from both the Akali Dal and the Congress ... I want to tell you that if these political parties, for their narrow interests, allow these persons to poison the whole atmosphere, you cannot keep communal peace in the state.'[8]

The date of 8 April 1982 was fixed for inauguration of work on the Sutlej–Yamuna Link Canal by the prime minister. To avert any untoward incident, the ceremony was held at the village of Karpoori at 11 a.m., four hours ahead of the scheduled time. As a result, it passed off peacefully. Following that, the Akalis launched their Nahar Roko Morcha (stop the canal agitation) on 24 April 1982, in Karpoori.

Two days later, on 26 April, two severed heads of cows were found hanging in two different temples in Amritsar. The Dal Khalsa claimed responsibility. Though the intention was to instigate Hindu-Sikh clashes, it did not have the desired effect as the cow is as sacred to the Sikhs (specially to those in rural areas) as to the Hindus. The only difference is that Sikhs don't consider the cow an object of worship. It appears this operation was planned by someone sitting in New Delhi who did not truly understand the Sikh psyche and executed through an organization originally raised by Zail Singh and others. However, on 1 May 1982 the government declared the Dal Khalsa and Jagjit Singh Chauhan's National Council of Khalistan unlawful. Was this done to publicly distance the Congress from the embarrassing misdeeds of its own creation, the Dal Khalsa?

After this declaration, four persons were killed and several injured when four Sikh militants opened fire in the main bazaar in the town of Patti near Amritsar. This was followed by two incidents on 27 June. In the first, three Sikh militants riding a motorcycle fired on three Hindus in Amritsar. In the second, the propaganda secretary of the Nirankari Mandal, Joginder Singh Sant, was fired upon and injured at Dhabuji village in Amritsar district. On 19 July, the police arrested the president of All India Sikh Students Federation, Amrik Singh (son of Bhindranwale's guru and predecessor Kartar Singh) and Thara Singh, who was Bhindranwale's second-in-command. On 21 July, a rickshaw puller was killed and five others were injured in Moga when Sikh militants hurled a bomb in the main bazaar.

On the day Amrik Singh and Thara Singh were arrested, Bhindranwale shifted to the safety of Guru Nanak Niwas to avoid arrest. He also launched a morcha for their release. Meanwhile, the Nahar Roko Morcha was receiving a lukewarm response from the Sikh masses as it was not launched from a gurudwara. So, the morcha was renamed Dharam Yudh (religious war) Morcha and shifted to the Golden Temple. To attract wider attention to his demand, Bhindranwale merged his own morcha with the Dharam Yudh Morcha.

Dharam Yudh Morcha

The Dharam Yudh Morcha was officially launched on 4 August 1982, with Badal leading the first batch of 300 satyagrahis. They were arrested soon after they left the Golden Temple complex. That morcha was conducted in a very civilized manner, and it became a daily routine for the next two and half months.[9]

Moderate Akalis were still in control of the situation, and Harchand Singh Longowal never missed an opportunity to chide anyone who raised slogans in favour of demands not on the Akali Dal agenda. Kuldip Nayar, in his autobiography, writes that he '... attended one of these congregations. When a slogan was raised for Khalistan, Longowal not only condemned it but also said that those who raised the slogan were "agents of the Congress party" and that Akalis were strongly opposed to it.'[10]

Within a period of two months, 30,000 satyagrahis were arrested. The jails were full and makeshift arrangements had to be made. On 11 September, when the police were escorting some detainees to jail, thirty-four of the detainees died when the bus carrying them ran into a train. 'The morcha had caught the imagination of the Sikh peasantry and there was no dearth of Satyagrahis,' according to Kuldip Nayar.[11] But the senior Akali leaders were getting worried that the religious frenzy generated by the morcha might encourage Bhindranwale to take control of it and change its direction towards extremism.

Very soon, differences arose between Longowal and Bhindranwale over the nature and scope of the morcha. Bhindranwale wanted to target the Central government but Longowal was opposed to that. The Akalis realized that Bhindranwale's style of functioning as well as his approach were dangerous to their cause. But they did not have the courage to take a stand against him openly. In order to remain relevant to the Punjab scene and retain their support among the Sikhs, the Akali Dal leadership were being forced to adopt a more aggressive stance on various issues, which they actually did not like. Worried that Bhidranwale would highjack their peaceful programme, the Akalis decided that their next programme would be announced from the Golden Temple on 4 November 1982.

It was mainly due to the predicament the Akalis found themselves in vis-à-vis Bhindranwale that Longowal sent a personal messenger to Sardar Swaran Singh sometime towards the end of September 1982, seeking his help in getting them out of the sticky situation they were in. They wanted Swaran Singh to use his well-known negotiating skills to work out a face-saving formula, which could help them withdraw their morcha and in turn build pressure on Bhindranwale to leave the Golden Temple complex and return to his gurudwara at Chowk Mehta.

Swaran Singh's intervention

After getting his M.Sc. Physics and law degrees from Punjab University, Lahore, and after a brief stint as lecturer in Lyallpur Khalsa College, Jalandhar, Swaran Singh joined Khizr Hayat Khan's cabinet in Punjab in 1946 as food and civil supplies minister. Post-Independence, he served as home minister in Gopi Chand Bhargava's cabinet in Punjab. After practising law for three years (1949–1952) at Punjab High Court, he joined Bhimsen Sachar's cabinet in 1952 as minister in charge of capital projects and electricity. Soon after that, on Prime Minister Nehru's invitation, he joined the Union cabinet as works, housing and supplies minister (1952–1957). He also served as minister in charge of steel, mines and fuel, railways, food and agriculture, and industries.

Nehru was his own foreign minister and therefore needed assistance at a political level. Because of Swaran Singh's well-known negotiating skills, Nehru started utilizing his services, for some important MEA-related assignments, including negotiations with China, Pakistan and other neighbouring countries. Most notable among these assignments were the several rounds of talks which Swaran Singh held with the then Pakistani foreign minister Zulfiqar Ali Bhutto in 1962–63 even though he (Swaran Singh) was minister for railways at the time. Lal Bahadur Shastri later appointed Swaran Singh as external affairs minister, which portfolio he handled in two spells, interspersed by two spells as defence minister.

In the parliamentary elections of 1977, the Congress had faced a complete rout in the north as a result of the anti-Emergency wave. My father-in-law Sardar Swaran Singh was no exception and lost his Jalandhar parliamentary seat. After serving as a cabinet minister for an unbroken spell of twenty-three years, followed by one and a half years as an MP, he vacated his official residence, 7 Krishna Menon Marg in New Delhi and, within the stipulated period of one month, shifted to his own house at 11 Link Road, Jalandhar.

Despite moving back to Jalandhar, he would visit New Delhi occasionally and stay with one of his four daughters. During the period October–November 1982, he mostly stayed with us at my officially allotted flat at Satya Marg in Chanakyapuri. Otherwise a man of few words and known for his discretion, it was mainly due to his stay with us that I came to know about developments related to an attempt at finding a negotiated peaceful settlement with the Akalis, in which he played a significant role.

Upon the request of the Akalis, Swaran Singh met Indira Gandhi in the first week of October 1982, soon after her return from a state visit to the US and apprised her of the message he had received from them. He impressed upon her the need to work out a face-saving formula for the Akalis to help them out of their predicament. She agreed to his suggestion and asked him to go ahead with his plan.

At the time, other than Longowal, most senior Akali leaders were in preventive detention in various jails because of ongoing Dharam Yudh Morcha. Badal was in Ludhiana jail, and the others, including Tohra, were in Ferozepur jail. Travelling in his personal car mostly in the dead of the night, Swaran Singh met all the senior Akali leaders in jail as well as Longowal, who was directing the morcha from the Golden Temple, more than once. While trying to ascertain their views on the minimum acceptable demands, which could help them take a decision to withdraw the morcha, Swaran Singh advised them to agree to a reasonably acceptable solution.

As a first step towards facilitating Swaran Singh's talks with the Akali leaders as a group, all the leaders were released from jail on 15 October 1982. Following this, Swaran Singh had several meetings with them and discussed their demands, some of which were quite mundane. 'The Anandpur Sahib Resolution was the principal snag. Swaran Singh told the Akalis he could only discuss with them matters concerning Centre-state relations and nothing beyond.'[12]

The Akalis held several meetings among themselves and watered down their demands for devolution of power to the states, as compared to what was mentioned in the Anandpur Sahib Resolution. Swaran Singh was finally able to convince the Akalis that the matter should be left to Indira Gandhi, who could consider appointing a committee to examine the Anandpur Sahib Resolution.

As no solution would have been possible without taking Bhindranwale on board, Swaran Singh went to meet him at Guru Nanak Niwas. When Swaran Singh walked into Bhindranwale's room, he found journalist Kuldip Nayar there. Nayar has described that meeting in his autobiography.[13]

> Once I caught up with Bhindranwale in his very untidy room and I asked him why he was surrounded by so many armed men toting rifles and Sten guns. His reply, in rustic Punjabi, was to ask why the police carried guns. I told him police represented authority; to which he retorted, 'Let them ever challenge me, and I shall show them who has the authority.' While I was with Bhindranwale, (former) Central Minister Swaran Singh barged in. As I was sitting on the only chair in the room, he squatted on the floor. Before I could offer him the chair, he remarked that he preferred to sit on the floor in the presence of the Sant.

Obviously, Nayar did not know the real purpose behind Swaran Singh's visit that day. Swaran Singh's words were meant to massage Bhindranwale's ego, as Singh was about to seek a favour from him as soon as everyone in the room left. About a year before Nayar passed away in 2018, in an executive committee meeting of the Bhai Veer Singh Sahitya Sadan (of which both of us were members), I told Nayar about the real purpose of Singh's visit that day. Nayar, who knew Swaran Singh very well, said that from Swaran Singh's behaviour that day he could not gauge the real importance of that visit.

When everyone in that room had left, Swaran Singh, on Bhindranwale's request, moved to the chair. He then told Bhindranwale that as one of his well-wishers he had come to discuss with him a very important matter. Singh went on to say that inaction on the part of the government towards his gun-toting, motorcycle-riding 'army' should not be construed as its weakness. If the government so desired, they could put a stop to their activities in no time. Further, if he and the Akalis continued with their agitations, it would bring great harm to Punjab in general and Sikhs in particular. Singh told Bhindranwale that his advice was that before the government was compelled to take any drastic action against him and his armed men, he should withdraw his agitation and move back to his gurudwara at Chowk Mehta and concentrate on religious activities.

Singh ended by saying that with the approval of Indira Gandhi he was trying to work out a compromise that could help the Akalis withdraw their agitation. He told Bhindranwale that if he had any reasonable demand of his own, he should feel free to discuss it with him and, as far as possible, he would try to accommodate it once a compromise formula with the Akalis was worked out.

At first Bhidranwale expressed his usual grievances with the 'Hindu' government's discriminatory attitude towards Sikhs. Swaran Singh advised him that he had better not get involved in such demands as these were a part of Akali demands also. Singh was finally able to bring down Bhindranwale to one small demand, which was the unconditional release of Amrik Singh and Thara Singh. Bhindranwale also agreed to move back to his Mehta Chowk gurudwara once a final settlement was reached and his men were released.

Swaran Singh had been keeping Indira Gandhi informed about the outcome of his meetings at regular intervals, including the one with Bhindranwale. He also 'conveyed to her the details of the agreement on Anandpur Sahib Resolution and the distribution of waters, the two principal demands. She accepted the settlement and praised him for his painstaking efforts. She, however, told him that she would like the matter to be placed before a cabinet sub-committee, which she constituted immediately, with Pranab

Mukherjee, R.Venkataraman, P.V. Narsimha Rao, and P.C. Sethi as its members.'[14] Indira Gandhi also agreed that senior Akali leaders be called to Delhi for formal discussions with the sub-committee.

'Ghosts Behind Every Bush'

At this stage I would like to mention that I came to know about the negotiations with the Akalis sometime in early October 1982. Since I had already come to know, through my friend from Patiala, about the Congress conspiring to win the next general elections through a dramatic solution to a deliberately manufactured crisis in Punjab, I told my father-in-law that if my information was correct he would not be able to work out a compromise formula, and it would be sabotaged on one pretext or the other. He said, 'You intelligence people are in the habit of seeing ghosts behind every bush.' I wished him success. In my mind, I decided that the success or failure of my father-in-law's efforts to broker a compromise would be a litmus test for the veracity or otherwise of the information my friend had conveyed to me.

His discussions with Akali leaders and Bhindranwale over, and Indira Gandhi's approval of the formulae worked out by him obtained, Swaran Singh travelled back to Delhi on or around 30 October 1982 and stayed with us in our Satya Marg, Chanakyapuri, flat. From what I observed during Singh's stay with us, Longowal had detailed Parkash Singh Badal and Balwant Singh as his messengers for exchange of messages or information to and from Swaran Singh. On the government's side, Swaran Singh interacted by phone with Pranab Mukherjee, then finance minister, who had been his colleague in Indira Gandhi's cabinet till November 1975.

Swaran Singh met members of the cabinet sub-committee on Punjab affairs and briefed them about his meetings with the Akali leaders and Bhindranwale. Regarding Bhindranwale's demand for the release of Amrik Singh and Thara Singh, Swaran Singh told them that in his view, based on his knowledge of criminal law, the cases against the two were weak and they would be released by the court on their very first appearance. So why not oblige Bhindranwale in a case which was bound to fall in court in any case? (In fact, both were subsequently discharged in the summer of 1983 and died during Operation Blue Star.)

Four senior Akali leaders – Parkash Singh Badal, Gurcharan Singh Tohra, Jagdev Singh Talwandi and Balwant Singh – reached New Delhi to participate in discussions with the cabinet sub-committee. On 2 November 1982, the two sides had detailed discussions on various issues related to the Akali demands. Consequently, it was agreed that all the religious demands be accepted, including the broadcasting of gurbani from the Golden Temple, enactment of the All India Gurudwara Act, allowing the carrying of a small kirpan on domestic flights, and the closure of tobacco, meat and liquor shops within a certain radius of the Golden Temple. There was agreement on some of the political demands too. However, the modalities had to be worked out and the concerned states consulted before a final decision was taken. There was some understanding on the Chandigarh issue too.

On the morning of 3 November, the cabinet committee met in P.V. Narasimha Rao's room in the Parliament House. Principal secretary to the PM, P.C. Alexander, Cabinet Secretary C.R. Krishnaswamy Rao Sahib, Home Secretary T.N. Chaturvedi and Special Secretary, Home, P.P. Nayyar, were also present. Swaran Singh also attended the meeting. His plea was that the Akalis should be given a way out to withdraw their agitation before their planned meeting on 4 November. That could be done by making a conciliatory announcement on the basis of what had been agreed with the Akali leaders on 2 November. It was decided that Home

Minister P.C. Sethi would make a statement in parliament on the morning of 4 November on the government's stand on the Akali demands, and a copy of it would thereafter be passed on to the Akali Dal leadership at Amritsar. It appeared at that point that everybody involved was satisfied with the outcome of the meetings on 2 and 3 November.

Swaran Singh and the cabinet committee met once again in the afternoon on 3 November. A draft statement, which was to be made in parliament the next morning, was prepared. The gist of the statement, as I learnt from my father-in-law some time later, is given below:

1. All religious demands were to be fully met.
2. Regarding devolution of some Central powers to Punjab as envisaged in the Anandpur Sahib Resolution, a commission would be appointed to go into the entire gamut of Centre–state relations, and make recommendations about which powers could be transferred to the states.
3. Regarding sharing of river waters, efforts would be made to suitably compensate Punjab for the loss of water resulting from agreement signed 31 December 1981.
4. About Chandigarh, efforts would be made to compensate Haryana, financially and otherwise, in lieu of Haryana not insisting on the transfer of Fazilka and Abohar areas as a condition for the transfer of Chandigarh to Punjab.
5. Finally, a brief mention was made of the role of the Sikhs in the freedom movement and the contribution made by them after independence.

Although most of the concessions were of a futuristic nature, they were specific enough to give the Akali's reasonable grounds to withdraw the agitation without losing face.

The meeting was over by 5 p.m. and the statement was informally shown to a representative of the Akali Dal delegation, who approved it. Satisfied at the cabinet committee's favourable view of their demands, Badal, Talwandi, Tohra and Balwant Singh returned to Amritsar on the evening of 3 November.

Around 6 p.m., G.S. Chawla, senior correspondent of the *Indian Express*, visited Special Secretary (home) P.P. Nayyar in his room. Nayyar was dictating a letter from the home minister to the speaker, informing him that he would like to make the enclosed statement in parliament the next morning. Nayyar told his personal assistant to take that letter with the earlier approved statement as its enclosure to the home minister for his signature, and after that deliver it to the speaker. A copy of the letter with the enclosure was also sent to the prime minister. On Chawla's request, Nayyar allowed him to publish a story on this development, provided he sought approval from a member of the cabinet sub-committee. Instead, G.S Chawla spoke to Swaran Singh and sought his clearance for publishing the report. Nayyar told Chawla to go ahead with his report, which appeared as a front-page lead story in the *Indian Express* on 4 November 1982.[15]

On 4 November, senior Akali leaders were sitting at the SGPC office at Amritsar to announce their next programme. Those who had participated in the talks in Delhi were hopeful that the statement in parliament would enable them to announce the withdrawal of their morcha. Around 10 a.m., Swaran Singh received a call from Amritsar (from either Badal or Balwant Singh) telling him that they were awaiting receipt of the statement shown to them the previous day in New Delhi. Swaran Singh called Pranab Mukherjee, who told Singh that a copy of the statement would be delivered to the Akalis at Amritsar soon after the home minister had made the statement in parliament.

After a couple of hours, the same caller from Amritsar told Swaran Singh that the letter from Delhi had been received, but it had been significantly altered both in 'tone and content'. The caller also said it was a case of downright betrayal of the promise made to them at the sub-committee meeting on 3 November. He also said that Longowal had asked it to be conveyed to Swaran that in the light of this development it would not be possible for them to postpone or withdraw their Dharam Yudh Morcha.

Swaran Singh then called Pranab Mukherjee to check the veracity of the information he had received from the Akalis. Confirming it, Pranab Mukherjee wanted Singh to suggest ways and means of retrieving the situation. Swaran Singh told Mukherjee that he had tried his best to save Punjab from the deepening crisis, but in view of the overnight change in the earlier approved statement he would not like to be associated with the negotiations in future

I am reproducing here the text of the statement actually made by Home Minister P.C. Sethi in the Lok Sabha on 4 November.[16]

> Government has been deeply distressed over the situation in Punjab. The Prime Minister and senior members of the cabinet have met delegation of the Akalis several times. The Prime Minister has indicated to them that practically all religious demands could be accepted subject to details being worked out but this could not be finalized because of their other demands.
>
> During the recent agitation, Government made further efforts to resolve the crisis and has been considering the demands conveyed recently by the 5-members committee of Akali leaders through Sardar Swaran Singh. Certain areas of agreement have been identified in respect to some demands. The others concern various states also. Therefore, consultations

> have to be held with Punjab and other concerned Governments and also with representatives of other communities before a decision can be taken. This process of consultations has been initiated and I have been in touch with the respective Chief Ministers and others including, leaders of opposition parties and Members of Parliament. It is likely that this process will take some more time.
>
> In taking any decision, the Government cannot ignore the overall interest of national unity, integrity, and the welfare of all sections of people.
>
> Government hopes and trusts that the representatives of the Akali Dal will look at their problems in the larger context. We repeat our invitation to them to come for further discussions and to create the right atmosphere for this by calling off or suspending their agitation. I hope that in the present circumstances nothing will be done which may escalate tension or will give rise to violence and suffering. I appeal to all parties to extend their cooperation.

The above statement, though also futuristic, deviated from the original statement shown to the Akalis in that it lacked the specificity that made it acceptable to them in the first place. There was no mention of a commission to look into Centre–state relations, no mention of river waters, no mention of Chandigarh. On top of that, instead of recognizing the contributions made by the Sikhs to the freedom struggle and nation building, oblique aspersions were being cast on their commitment to national unity and integrity.

Anxious to find the reason for this overnight change of statement, Swaran Singh left home soon after these calls. He went to Parliament House, where he met G.S Chawla, who asked him,

'Sardar Sahib, why this change in the government's stance?' Swaran Singh replied, 'This is neither the same statement nor the same spirit. Now I am going to withdraw from the negotiations,' and told Chawla that he could be quoted on this.[17] After that Swaran Singh decided not to get involved in future negotiations with the Akalis. Though he was repeatedly requested by Indira Gandhi to play some part in solving the Punjab problem, he kept away.[18]

There were various versions regarding the government's volte face. A few days after the statement was made in parliament, P.P. Nayyar told Chawla in strict confidence that it was changed by Indira Gandhi herself at 11 p.m., and a new statement was sent to the speaker and the home minister.[19] Chawla is of the view that despite becoming the president of India in July 1982, Giani Zail Singh had played a dubious role in what had happened.

Zail Singh, who had carried tales regarding Swaran Singh in the immediate aftermath of the declaration of Emergency, citing Singh's open criticism of the move, did not want any Sikh leader to get the credit for solving the Punjab imbroglio. He reportedly told Indira Gandhi that credit for solving the Punjab problem should go to Rajiv Gandhi, as it would help the fledgling politician build his reputation as a national-level political leader.[20]

Referring to the failure of the talks, Mark Tully and Satish Jacob mention in their book that Swaran Singh 'was bitterly disappointed and never became involved in the negotiations again'.[21]

Asian Games shenanigans

The Akali leaders, who were waiting at the SGPC office in Amritsar for the home minister's statement on 4 November, were stunned by the betrayal and in response immediately issued a threat to disrupt the ninth Asian Games in order to focus world attention on the 'persecution of the Sikhs in India'.[22] The Games were to be held in New Delhi from 19 November to 4 December 1982.

Meanwhile, a short one-act play began in New Delhi, with its stated aim being to yet again find a peaceful solution to the Punjab problem. The main actors this time were Rajiv Gandhi, Amarinder Singh and a couple of Rajiv's close friends from the 1 Akbar Road group, and Badal, Balwant Singh, Ravi Inder Singh (former speaker of the Punjab assembly) and R.S. Bhatia representing the Akalis. The government was represented by Defence Minister R. Venkataraman, Home Minister P.C. Sethi, Law Minister P. Shiv Shankar, Home Secretary T.N. Chaturvedi and Principal Secretary to the PM P.C. Alexander.

According to Alexander, the meeting was called at Amarinder Singh's instance. Amarinder suggested that the government consider holding informal talks at a level lower than the PM's. However, according to Chawla, the idea for these talks actually came from Giani Zail Singh so that credit for their success might go to Rajiv Gandhi. Zail Singh also felt that involvement of his political protégé Amarinder Singh would further the latter's prospects of replacing his (Zail Singh's) arch political rival Darbara Singh as chief minister of Punjab.[23]

In line with the past pattern of negotiations, the two days of talks held on 16 and 17 November appeared to have produced some results, and it was decided that an announcement along agreed-upon lines could be made. It was also decided that after getting final clearance for this from the prime minister, the home secretary would fly to Amritsar on 18 November to obtain the approval of Longowal and other senior Akali leaders, and then make the announcement over television and radio the same evening.

What happened next is narrated by P.C. Alexander,

> ...some unforeseen development took place, which prevented the formal conclusion of the proposed agreement between the government and the Akalis. Just an hour or so before the Home Secretary was to board the special plane for Amritsar, carrying with him the draft of the minutes of the talks, we had to suddenly face very strong opposition to the whole proposal from an unexpected source' [24]

The 'unexpected source' was Indira Gandhi's loyal follower Bhajan Lal, ever willing to curry favour with her at the slightest pretext. According to P.C. Alexander, Bhajan Lal, who had been informed of the proposal, in this instance adopted a 'determined' stand against giving any concessions to the Akalis on Chandigarh and water-sharing issues without adequately protecting Haryana's interests.[25]

Only a year ago, Darbara Singh had been summoned to Delhi to jointly sign an agreement with the Congress party chief ministers of Haryana and Rajasthan to withdraw a case filed by his predecessor Akali chief minister Badal in the Supreme Court. If a person like Darbara Singh could be made to do this, making a pliant loyalist like Bhajan Lal agree to the latest draft agreement should have been much easier. There were various ways of communicating to Bhajan Lal what Indira Gandhi wanted him to do, or not do, at a particular juncture if that was the intention. Incidentally, Bhajan Lal was the leading exponent, if not the father, of the '*Aya Ram Gaya Ram*' practice in Indian politics (party hopping based on political opportunism; literally, someone who comes and goes) before he joined the Congress party.

The Asian Games were to begin on 19 November in Delhi. Haryana police, who controlled the main access points from Punjab to Delhi, were ordered not to let any Sikh enter the capital without proper verification. Consequently, not even persons like former Air Chief Marshal (later Marshal of the Air Force)

Arjan Singh and Lt Gen. Jagjit Singh Arora (Retd), who accepted the instrument of surrender of the Pakistan Army at Dhaka at the end of Bangladesh Liberation War (both residents of Delhi returning from Punjab), were spared by the Haryana police. They were allowed to proceed only after being subjected to search and questioning. A total of 1,500 Sikhs were detained as potential demonstrators. Though the Games passed off peacefully and Rajiv Gandhi got accolades for a job well done, it left a bitter taste in the mouth for Sikhs in Delhi and Punjab.

The failure of the November 1982 talks and the ruthless manner in which Haryana police treated the Sikhs in Haryana and those transiting through Haryana to reach Delhi led Harchand Singh Longowal to call a convention of ex-servicemen at the Golden Temple in December 1982. Over 5,000 former officers and soldiers turned up at this meeting.

Alarmed at the turnout and the mood of the participants at that meeting, the Central government resumed negotiations with Akali Dal leaders on 24 January 1983. To these talks, opposition leaders were also invited. Senior Communist Party of India (Marxist) leader and MP from Punjab Harkishan Singh Surjeet was one of them. He told Mark Tully that significant progress was made and that these talks would have succeeded had the government allowed the use of the same amount of river waters by Punjab as it was drawing at that time, pending the final decision of a tribunal on that issue.[26]

Though the talks with the Akalis had failed by February, Indira Gandhi subsequently visited Gurudwara Bangla Sahib in New Delhi and abruptly announced that the government had accepted all the religious demands of the Sikhs. As it turned out these were mere words, with no matching follow-up action. Then, in June 1983, she announced the constitution of a 'one-man commission' headed by a retired Supreme Court judge, Justice R.S. Sarkaria, to look into the structure of Centre-state relations as enshrined in the Constitution and suggest changes, if any, that were required to meet the growing aspirations of the states.

Had the prime minister made these concessions to the Akali Dal delegation during the latest round of negotiations that failed just a few months before in February, the Akalis could have projected them as their own achievement, giving them some reasonable grounds to withdraw their morcha. In the context of the failed February talks, Surjeet said it was the third time in six months that Indira Gandhi had backed out of agreements. It was during this time that Mark Tully met Bhindranwale in his room at Guru Nanak Niwas. When Tully asked him a direct question, 'Do you or do you not support the demand of Khalistan, Sikh independent state?', Bhindranwale replied, 'I am neither in favour of it nor against it. If the government gives us, we won't reject it.'[27]

Following this, a number of rounds of talks and negotiations continued to take place between the Akali Dal and Central government functionaries/nominees in the period leading up to Operation Blue Star. All met with the same fate as the earlier ones. However, in this intervening period one internal discussion held by Akali Dal in Amrtisar, and the last round of talks between the Akalis and the Central government in New Delhi merits special mention.

Following the failure of the talks in February 1984, Longowal called a meeting of Akali Dal leaders at Amritsar, to discuss the future course of their Dharam Yudh Morcha. It was generally felt that as the morcha had been hijacked by Bhindranwale, which was doing more harm than good to the Sikhs, it would be better to suspend or even withdraw it unconditionally. While a consensus was emerging in favour of that decision, Balwant Singh, former finance minister in the Badal government, stood up and made a provocative speech, saying that after having made so many sacrifices, suspension or withdrawal of the morcha would be a betrayal of the Sikh cause.

According to G.S. Chawla, Balwant Singh was beholden to Alexander for his help in furthering his personal business interests. Chawla mentions that soon after the meeting was over, senior Akali leader Atma Singh telephoned someone at Rashtrapati Bhavan and told that person that so far his own impression had been that the government truly wanted the agitation to end, but from the speech made at the meeting by Balwant Singh, it now appeared that the government was not interested in finding a peaceful solution.[28]

With no solution in sight to the Akali Dal's dilemma and disturbed by Bhindranwale's unimpeded hijacking of the morcha, Longowal gave a call on 23 May 1984 for intensification of the Dharam Yudh Morcha from June 3 onwards. The agenda included non-payment of land revenue, water and electricity charges, and stopping the movement of food grains out of Punjab. Expectedly, P.C. Alexander writes, 'Indira Gandhi did not want to miss even the faintest chance of settlement through negotiation and, therefore, she asked us to get in touch with Longowal once again and ascertain his willingness to depute a team of senior leaders for talks.'

On receipt of the message from the prime minister, Longowal sent Badal, Tohra and Barnala to New Delhi, and secret talks were held on 26 May at a guest house in Vasant Vihar, with cabinet ministers P.V. Narasimha Rao, Pranab Mukherjee and P. Shiv Shankar in attendance. The government's representatives insisted on the transfer of some Punjab villages to Haryana in lieu of Haryana surrendering its claim over Chandigarh. The Akalis were not in a position to give concessions on any such issue due to their weakened position vis-à-vis Bhindranwale.[29]

About this matter, Kuldip Nayar writes:

> Narasimha Rao, then Home Minister, called us, the Punjab Group, and suggested that we should hold discussions with the Akalis and persuade them to divide Chandigarh, one part becoming the capital of Punjab and other of Haryana, as if the Centre had agreed to concede the other Akali demands. We were able to persuade the Akalis to agree to split Chandigarh, but the strange thing was that we were unable either to get an appointment with Narasimha Rao or to convey the Akalis' consent to him over the phone. He was simply unavailable so we feared something fishy was in the air.

Nayar was shocked but not surprised when the army moved into the Golden Temple on 3 June. As a member of the Punjab Group he felt defeated because Rao had entrusted them with the task of talking to the Akalis only ten days before the army moved in. Nayar had learnt from Maj. Gen. K.S. Brar, who led Operation Blue Star, that the army had been told about the assignment about a fortnight earlier. This meant that the government had already made up its mind to storm the Golden Temple even before Rao had spoken to them. Naturally, Nayar was surprised as to why Rao had hidden that fact from them.[30]

Thus ended the prolonged charade of finding a peaceful solution to the Punjab problem through negotiations with the Akalis. These prolonged rounds of talks had served the purpose of the 1 Akbar Road group and were no longer required. Instead, as per the Op-2 plan, the time had come to implement the 'final solution' to solve the Punjab problem, for which they had waited four long years.

6

Indira Gandhi's 1982 US State Visit

PRIME MINISTER Indira Gandhi was to reach New York on 27 July 1982 for an eight-day state visit to the US. Director (R) Suntook called me about a fortnight before and said that according to the information he had, the chances of a threat to her life from US and Canada-based Sikh extremists had considerably increased. We had to do everything possible to see that the visit passed off without any untoward incident. His information was of a general nature and he did not tell me any specifics as to who, how and wherefrom that threat could emanate and how it was going to be executed. Providing physical security to the PM was the job of many other people and this would in any case be taken care of by the concerned agencies. But keeping in view Suntook's instructions, to look out for related intelligence it was clear that I also needed to do everything possible within my means to prevent any harm to the prime minister.

I told Suntook that rather than trying to find a needle in a haystack by meeting my friends and contacts spread over various parts of Canada and the US, I would reach New York a couple of days before Indira Gandhi's arrival. Thereafter, I would commence by getting in touch with certain knowledgeable friends and contacts by phone to gather the required intelligence. I would then concentrate on such functions or meetings as could be used by suspected Sikh extremists to cause physical harm to the PM, by keeping a watch out for any suspicious activity. With Suntook's approval, I reached New York around 25 July and booked my room in a hotel close to Carlyle Hotel on East 76th Street, where the prime minister and members of her delegation were to stay.

'An honour to us'

Soon after my arrival, I started calling my relatives, friends and contacts spread across Canada and the US one by one, and that process continued till the end of Indira Gandhi's visit. What I learnt was that although anti-Indira and anti-Congress feelings were running high among a segment of the Sikh diaspora due to the happenings in Punjab, there was nothing to support apprehensions of a threat to her life during that visit.

Some of the contacts, however, did ask me what had happened to their suggestions given to me during my December 1981 visit. According to them, rather than the situation improving, things were getting gradually worse as Hindu-Sikh relations had been vitiated further and some Sikhs were even suspected of nursing pro-Khalistan feelings. I didn't have any clear answer to that, other than to say that I had passed on their suggestions to the concerned authorities and it may take some time before the situation improved.

The prime minister's delegation reached New York on the afternoon of 27 July. After a formal reception at the airport, she drove straight to the Carlyle Hotel. The Indian delegation had a full complement of a VVIP security team from the Intelligence Bureau, led by Joint Director S.C. (Subhash) Tandon (IPS 1952 Rajasthan, later commissioner of Delhi Police, from April 1983 to 12 November 1984, including the period of the anti-Sikh pogrom in Delhi), his two deputy directors – S.D. Trivedi (IPS 1960 Uttar Pradesh) and my batchmate and friend Ratan Sahgal (IPS 1964 Madhya Pradesh) – and their supporting staff.

During her stay at New York, Indira Gandhi's itinerary included a visit to the Metropolitan Museum on 28 July to attend the inauguration of an exhibition on India, followed by lunch. On her way to the hotel, a brief meeting with UN Secretary General Javier Perez de Cuellar was scheduled. The same afternoon, she was to leave for Washington on a two-day visit, for meetings with Secretary of State George P. Shultz and President Ronald Reagan on 29 July, followed by a banquet that night at the White House.

On her return from Washington on 31 July, there were three meetings at Carlyle Hotel, one with office bearers of various associations of persons of Indian origin, another with scientists, and a third with US businessmen of Indian origin. In the evening she was to watch a show at Broadway. On the morning of 1 August, there was the crucial (from my point of view) visit to Richmond Hill Gurudwara. At forenoon on 2 August, she was to receive the U Thant Award for encouraging cultural understanding between the East and West, followed by a call on the mayor of New York, Ed Koch. After that would follow a big contributory luncheon organized in her honour at the Waldorf-Astoria by the Foreign Policy Association, the Asia Society, the Far Eastern American Council of Commerce and Industry and the Indian Chamber of Commerce of America, where about

1,500 guests were expected to turn up. In the afternoon she was scheduled to leave for Los Angeles.[1]

On returning to my hotel room, I studied her programme carefully to prepare my action plan. Of all the listed functions I decided to focus on two – the meeting with prominent members of associations of persons of Indian origin on 31 July at Hotel Carlyle, and the visit to Richmond Hill Gurudwara on 95-30, 118th St South Richmond, Queens, on 1 August. For the function on 31 July, I sat in the hotel lobby and observed the guests walking into the hotel to attend the meetings. As expected, the function passed off peacefully.

In an interview to the *New York Times* on 31 July, Tejinder Singh Kahlon, president of the Sikh Cultural Society, which had invited Indira Gandhi to Richmond Gurudwara, described her impending visit as 'an honour to us'.[2] She was expected to reach the gurudwara at 9.30 a.m. I reached about forty-five minutes before her arrival, which gave me enough time to have a close look at the premises and the kind of people who were coming to attend the function. For security reasons, only one entry with a small door was kept open, and was guarded heavily.

'Where are your gunmen?'

On her arrival, Indira Gandhi was received by Kahlon and some other members of the gurudwara management committee (of the Sikh Cultural Society Inc.). I entered the gurudwara following her entourage. The hall was almost full. There were about ten officers, five on each side of the entrance, from the New York Police Department, the FBI and some plainclothesmen. S.D. Trivedi and Ratan Sahgal were standing in the left-hand row. On the other side, Subhash Tandon was in close proximity to Indira Gandhi.

I stood just behind Trivedi and Sahgal, from where I could see everyone entering the gurudwara. There was a large fixed glass window on the wall to the right, through which I could observe what was happening in the area just outside the entrance. My attention was divided between what was happening in the area around the Guru Granth Sahib and the movement of people both inside and outside the gurudwara's main entrance. Indira Gandhi, wearing a lightly embroidered crimson salwar-kurta with a matching chunni to cover her head, was her usual elegant self.

After the customary welcome address by Tejinder Singh Kahlon, a siropa (scarf of honour) was presented to Prime Minister Gandhi by the granthi (head priest) of the gurudwara. She was then requested to address the gathering. She was speaking very softly, and I, standing at a distance, could hear her say, 'We should follow the path shown by Gurbani which would help us in overcoming difficulties in our way.' Meanwhile, my attention was diverted towards a group of four Sikhs standing outside but not very far from the entrance. I identified one of them as the Toronto-based self-styled 'consul general of Khalistan', Kuldip Singh Sodhi, from Jagjit Singh Chauhan's outfit (see Chapter 1).

Sodhi was agitated and appeared to be having an argument with one of the people with him. It also seemed that with the help of two of the men, he was trying to prevent the fourth from entering the gurudwara. This animated discussion continued for another five minutes. Upon observing them, I made a mental note that if they attempted to enter the gurudwara I would tell Ratan Sahgal to ask the local police to stop them, lest they should start shouting anti-India or anti-Indira slogans. But Sodhi appeared to have finally prevailed upon the others and they did not enter the gurudwara. The function was over in another ten minutes and Indira Gandhi left soon afterwards, through the side door.

While she was leaving, Trivedi turned to me and suddenly out of the blue asked, 'Sidhu, where are your gunmen?' Taken aback, I replied that I had not told him anything of the sort. He then said, 'But your department created a scare.' It was obvious that the IB had been forewarned by the R&AW about the possibility of an incident taking place during Indira Gandhi's visit, especially during her visit to the gurudwara. Naturally, the IB officers and the local security officers, who had been suitably briefed by Tandon, were extra cautious during the PM's visit to the gurudwara.

That was also perhaps the reason for the minor scare at Broadway, where Indira Gandhi had gone to watch a show the previous evening. While the play was on, someone from the rear seats had had a heart attack, resulting in a flutter in the area, which was viewed by the over-cautious security staff posted there as a possible assassination attempt. The patient was soon evacuated from the hall, and the show resumed after a few minutes.

As soon as Trivedi and Sahgal left, I sought out Sodhi, who was talking to some visitors outside the gurudwara. Sodhi had met me once before in March 1979 at a Toronto hotel (Chapter 1) after a Sikh conference. He recognized me and came over to meet me. I took him aside and asked him the reason for the altercation earlier. He said, 'What should I say? One of the persons [he didn't tell me his name] in our group was carrying a gun and wanted to shoot Indira Gandhi inside the gurudwara.'

This was the reason why he and the others with him were trying to stop that man from entering the gurudwara. Sodhi said they could not allow any such thing to happen in the US or Canada as their security agencies would have immediately clamped down on all their activities in North America. Sodhi said the person with the gun was from Toronto and had developed a strong animosity towards Indira Gandhi because of what was happening in Punjab.

Sodhi then said that he had come to know about this man's plan to kill Indira Gandhi during her visit to the gurudwara about a month back. From then onwards Sodhi had been keeping a close watch on the man's activities. Given the sensitivity of this information, I requested Sodhi to join me for lunch, where I wanted him to meet some important persons. As his flight back to Toronto was not until late afternoon, he agreed to accompany me. I booked a table for five for lunch at a Chinese restaurant on the ground floor of the building where the Permanent Mission of India to the United Nations was located.

Keeping in view Trivedi's uncalled-for snide remarks, I contacted Subhash Tandon by phone and informed him that I would like him to meet someone who had information relating to a threat to Indira Gandhi's life. Tandon was busy and so sent Trivedi and Sahgal to meet us at the restaurant. On our way there I told Sodhi that we would be meeting two senior officers from the IB who, as members of prime minister's security detail, had been on duty that morning.

Soon after we arrived at the restaurant, Trivedi and Sahgal joined us. I introduced them to Sodhi. Both were familiar with his name and the position he held in Jagjit Singh Chauhan's set-up at Toronto. Frail, five-foot eight inches tall, fair-complexioned and with a thin, greying beard, Sodhi did not fit the image of someone involved in pro-Khalistan activities. A little later, pointing towards Trivedi, I told Sodhi that he didn't believe there was any threat to Indira Gandhi's life during her visit to the gurudwara that morning. I requested him to share with them what he had told me earlier.

Everyone listened to him in rapt attention and in total silence. No questions were asked. Afterwards, I took Sodhi in a cab to drop him at LaGuardia airport so he could catch his flight to Toronto. I asked him how his 'business' was doing. He replied that thanks to Indira Gandhi's mishandling of the situation in Punjab, a fairly large number of Sikhs in Canada and the US had started believing in what his organization had been propagating so far. In a mischievous tone, he asked me to convey their special thanks to her for all that she was doing in Punjab.

After dropping Sodhi at the airport, I sent a message to Suntook about what had happened during the day. I left for Los Angeles on the afternoon of 2 August, to reach the Holiday Inn hotel an hour or so before the arrival of the prime minister's entourage. By the time she arrived at the hotel it was getting dark, but one could still see about fifty or sixty Sikh demonstrators standing at a distance of about 200m across the road, shouting anti-Indira slogans. The overall tone of the sloganeering was somewhat muted. Within twenty minutes of her arrival they had dispersed.

On 3 August, Indira Gandhi had two engagements at Los Angeles. In the morning, Mayor Tom Bradley presented her with a key to the city. During that time I quickly went to meet my sister Preet and her husband Harnek Grewal at their home in Diamond Bar, a suburb of Los Angeles. I returned in time for Indira Gandhi's address to prominent members of the local Indian community that evening. She called upon them to help improve India's image in the US. 'Spare a thought for India,' she said. She left for Honolulu the same evening for a fourteen-hour stopover. The delegation checked into Hotel Kahala Hilton late at night.

On the morning of 4 August, while Indira Gandhi was formally presenting a baby elephant to the Honolulu zoo, I did a quick round of the city accompanied by a friend from the delegation. We bumped into a Sikh driver of a Honolulu-based fishing magnate. I still remember his name. Operationally he was of no use to us, even though he was an interesting character. I parted company with the prime minister's entourage in the evening and left for New Delhi, with a night halt at Tokyo. I left Tokyo on 5 August by Air India 307 and reached New Delhi in the evening.

One-upmanship

The next morning, on 6 August, I met Suntook in his office and handed over a short note about my visit. He remarked, 'I didn't know that you can also indulge in one-upmanship'. I knew what he was referring to. I told him that it was Trivedi who had first taunted me and blamed the Department for creating an unwarranted scare. Further, as it was actionable intelligence, I felt that the IB's VVIP security team should be made aware of continuing danger to Indira Gandhi's life as soon as possible, as the PM's state visit was not yet over. Suntook didn't say anything more.

Having worked with him over a period of time, I knew him extremely well and also knew that he had full faith in me. I could walk into his room any time after checking with his PS as to whether someone else was with him. But from his demeanour I could make out that Suntook didn't like my having confronted Trivedi with Sodhi.

I tried to visualize the real reason for Suntook's remarks. Did I inadvertently expose a R&AW source to the IB? It might have been so. Sodhi was not my source when I was posted at Ottawa, since the Department was not interested in Khalistan-related activities at the time. It's possible my successor had cultivated him in view of the changed requirements.

It is also possible that information relating to a threat to the prime minister could have come directly from London-based Jagjit Singh Chauahan through high level operational R&AW contacts established with him, to keep a tab on his organization's links with Pakistan and the ISI. Incidentally, despite Chauhan's best efforts, he had not succeeded in creating any noticeable following in North America for his cause until then.

In that context, the following excerpts from a report in *India Today*'s 28 February 1983 issue corroborate my views on the subject (Chapter 1): 'Until the spring and summer of 1981, the voice of pro-Khalistan elements was like a cry in the wilderness. Then came the sudden influx of more than 2,000 Sikhs seeking political asylum in Canada, claiming oppression and brutality at the hands of Mrs Gandhi's government.'[3]

Did the Indian government deliberately overlook such an exodus? Were Chauhan's men allowed to ferry so many Sikhs to Canada? At that time it was widely believed, both in Canada and Punjab, that most of the so-called seekers of political asylum (including a full Boeing 747 load which landed in Toronto) were directly or indirectly sponsored by Jagjit Singh Chauhan's set-up. There could not have been a more effective way of increasing the number of pro-Khalistan residents in Canada. To justify their claim of persecution by the Indian government for their political views, those asylum seekers had to necessarily get involved in pro-Khalistan activities.

Getting back to Trivedi's snide remarks, they were a bit too much for me to digest. Also, if I had not done what I had, the IB would have thought that there was actually no danger to the prime minister's life at Richmond Hill Gurudwara or, for that matter, during the rest of her state visit to the US. Incidentally, Sodhi avoided meeting me the next year when I visited Toronto in September 1983. We only talked on the phone. Also, I didn't see him among the two busloads of Sikhs who had come from Toronto to demonstrate in front of the UN building in New York, where Indira Gandhi was to address the UN General Assembly session at the time (Chapter 8). As far as Suntook was concerned, things were back to normal from the next working day onwards.

7

A State of Controlled Chaos

THE SITUATION in Punjab in early 1983 can be summed up as follows: the moderate Akali Dal leadership was demoralized by their repeated failure to get any face-saving concessions from the Central government that would enable them to withdraw their morcha. In the face of Bhindranwale's criticism, they had to keep increasing the level of their demands. Bhindranwale's profile was on the ascendant, and he continued to carry on with his unbridled acts of extremism to instil fear in the minds of the Hindus of Punjab, which had an impact on Haryana too. The Punjab government was frustrated, as they were left with very little initiative to take on-the-spot independent decisions. A dispirited Punjab Police and the Central Reserve Police Force (CRPF) were accusing each other of being communal in the discharge of their duties. It was a recipe for disaster.

The national elections were still two years away. Therefore, the main challenge for the 1 Akbar Road group at that time was to ensure that the pressure caused by the continued insecurity and chaos did not cross the threshold that would force them to make a premature intervention before the end of 1984. This was not an easy task. To ensure this, a three-member informal think-tank comprising senior officers Cabinet Secretary C.R. Krishnaswami Rao Sahib, Principal Secretary to the PM P.C. Alexander and Home Secretary T.N. Chaturvedi (succeeded later by M.M.K. Wali) was created to micro-manage the affairs of Punjab.

Unfortunately, they had little experience of Punjab. Perhaps their ignorance was considered a plus point by Indira Gandhi, as they had only to sustain a certain level of chaos in the state and not find a solution to it. Rajiv Gandhi had also started associating with this think-tank's activities and influencing its decisions when a higher-level consultation was required. On occasion, when the situation in Punjab appeared to be worsening, the think-tank, on behalf of the Central government, took some administrative measures. These included suspension of the Punjab government, change of governor and DGP, posting of some advisors, and a show of (and not use of) force, to reassure the Hindus that the government was not insensitive to their growing concerns.

As desired, the impact of such measures was transient, and the situation would eventually return to its previous – if not higher – level of turmoil. In short, Punjab was like a pressure cooker whose temperature control, to maintain the right amount of pressure, was in the hands of the above-mentioned three-man think-tank working under the close supervision and guidance of Indira Gandhi, assisted by Rajiv Gandhi who was himself under the influence of others, including Makhan Lal Fotedar and Arun Nehru.

The 'killer Squad' and unabated violence

While Harchand Singh Longowal and other Akali leaders were fast losing credibility, Bhindranwale did not miss any opportunity to criticize them for their weak-kneed attitude towards the Central government. By then he had built a team of trusted lieutenants to help manage his various activities. The team included Harminder Singh Sandhu, general secretary of the All India Sikh Students Federation (AISSF), Dalbir Singh, his political advisor, and Rachpal Singh, his secretary. His right-hand man, Amrik Singh, president of AISSF, and his second-in-command, Thara Singh, who had been arrested on 19 July 1982, resumed their activities after their release in the summer of 1983.

Lest anyone should refuse to accept his authority, Bhindranwale constituted a 'killer squad'. That comprised, among others, four deserters from Punjab police (Amarjit Singh, Sewa Singh, Kabul Singh and Gurnam Singh), an escaped convict, Talwinder Singh, and Surinder Singh Sodhi.[1] Bhindranwale also started holding 'court' to settle personal disputes and began dispensing quick justice through the killer squad in cases he saw as serious violations of the Sikh religious code of conduct or where he saw a challenge to his authority.

The violence in Punjab continued unabated. In addition to the Nirankaris, senior leaders and functionaries of the ruling Congress party were not spared either. Chief Minister Darbara Singh survived an attack. A bomb was thrown into the house of a cabinet minister of Punjab as well as into the house of a Congress member of the Punjab legislative assembly. Bombs were also thrown to disturb India's Republic Day celebrations at Amritsar on 26 January 1983. On 27 January, a branch of the Syndicate Bank was robbed. There was another attempt to rob a bank in April 1983. But specific and targeted killings, which destroyed the morale of the police, were yet to come.[2]

To reassert his leadership, in April 1983 Longowal launched a 'rasta roko' (block the roads) agitation, which attracted significant response from the Sikhs of Punjab. The transport system was completely paralysed, and bloody clashes with the police followed. The response to his call for agitation encouraged Longowal to order Bhindranwale to take an oath of loyalty to him, which the latter reluctantly did. But the bonhomie didn't last long. During the course of the agitation, a Home Guard armoury in Ferozepur district was looted by extremists. In the last week of April 1983, Longowal announced in Amritsar the creation of a voluntary force of one lakh Sikhs, to be known as 'marjiwares' – the do-or-die squad.[3]

'By this time Bhindranwale and his men were above the law. It needed sanction of the prime minister's think-tank before they could be arrested and that sanction was not coming.'[4] Bhindranwale's unbridled activities were terrorizing the Hindus of Punjab, who wanted an end to his reign of terror as soon as possible. However, the time had not yet come. The 1 Akbar Road group was busy trying to ensure two things. First, hopes of a negotiated settlement with the Akalis were to be kept alive for some more time. For that the Akalis had to continue their agitation programme to build pressure on the Central government to invite them for another round of negotiations. For this, it was necessary that the Akalis didn't lose faith in the process. Second, care had to be taken that Bhindranwale did not go too fast and too far in his extremist activities, which could force the government to intervene much before the predetermined time.

The 1 Akbar Road group had enough time to place their own trusted men in the Bhindranwale circle to win the confidence of Bhindranwale and influence his decisions. This they did either through party workers or through intelligence agencies. Harminder Singh Sandhu, general secretary of the AISSF, was suspected to be one such person.[5] As Harminder knew English well, Bhindranwale used him as an interpreter whenever an English-speaking visitor came to meet him. Sandhu was also suspected to be an agent run by the R&AW for intelligence on Bhindranwale and on Pakistan's involvement in Punjab-related violence (though not to my knowledge). Incidentally, Sandhu was the only one among Bhindranwale's inner circle who surrendered to the army during Operation Blue Star. There might have been many more such moles, especially among those who escaped from the Akal Takht/ Golden Temple complex on the eve of Operation Blue Star.

During that period I had heard of one such person (name withheld, as desired by the source of information) who won Bhindranwale's trust by presenting him with a brand-new revolver, which he liked and asked for a second, which was promptly procured and presented, courtesy of one of the two intelligence agencies concerned. This man also escaped from the Golden Temple complex a few days before the army moved in.

Both these tasks had to be manged by the 1 Akbar Road group through their contacts or through reliable second-level Congress leaders and the three-man think-tank. The Akali Dal leaders could be manipulated through people like Balwant Singh (who was close to P.C. Alexander) and a couple of others who might have risen through the ranks of the Akali Dal or gained importance because of the support of persons or agencies of the Central government. For an informed reader it should not be difficult to shortlist the names of some such Akali Dal leaders.

Similarly, it was not difficult for these persons and agencies to manage the activities of a person like Bhindranwale, who was originally the creation of the 1 Akbar Road group itself, but who over a period of time started drifting – or more appropriately, was intentionally allowed to drift – from his original mentors, to help him shake off the impression that he was actually the creation of the 1 Akbar Road group. Naturally, the group had no objection to that, provided Bhindranwale's activities did not cross their 'comfort zone', which could force them to act prematurely or run the risk of Indira Gandhi further losing credibility.

A police officer is murdered

As mentioned in Chapter 4, Avtar Singh Atwal, DIG of police, Jalandhar Range, and former senior superintendent of police of Amritsar district, was shot dead on 25 April 1983 on the steps of the Golden Temple. The emasculated state machinery let his body lie where he fell, in full public view, for over two hours before it was 'allowed' to be retrieved. The message that it conveyed was, if the government could not act against Atwal's killers hiding in the Golden Temple complex or in Guru Nanak Niwas, how could it save the lives of ordinary citizens from the same killers, now emboldened by the government's inaction? This instilled yet even more fear in the minds of the general population. Little did anyone realize that taking action against the killers at that stage did not fit in with the 1 Akbar Road group's plan.

While posted as SSP, Amritsar, Atwal had been able to plant one of his sources in close proximity to Bhindranwale in order to secure information on his and his men's activities. It was through this source that Atwal came to know that on 15 March 1983, two members of Bhindranwale's killer squad were planning to carry out an assigned task. Based on that information, Atwal deployed SP Hqr, Amritsar, G.D. Pandey, to lay a trap at Manawala bridge on the Grand Trunk Road going towards Jalandhar.

As expected, at around 4.30 a.m., a jeep stopped in front the temporary naka (barrier) installed by Pandey's men. Finding their way blocked, the occupants of the jeep threw a hand grenade towards the police party blocking the road, who returned fire. Pandey was injured. One of the occupants of the jeep, Hardev Singh Chhina, was killed, and three others were injured. The driver of the jeep, Gursant Singh, reversed the vehicle and took the dead body to Guru Nanak Niwas. Gursant narrated the incident to Bhindranwale, who issued a statement accusing the police of murdering one of his associates in cold blood. Atwal's source was soon identified and the nature of his connection with Atwal extracted from him. His mutilated body was found later outside Guru Nanak Niwas. As a result, Atwal became a marked man on Bhindranwale's hit list.[6]

On 25 April 1983, Atwal entered the Golden Temple complex through the Clock Tower entrance at around 10 a.m. Like any other Sikh, he undertook the parikrama of the sacred sarovar (tank) before paying homage to the Guru Granth Sahib in Darbar Sahib. He then came out, received prasad and walked towards the Clock Tower side exit. Holding the prasad, he climbed the thirteen marble steps and was about to leave the complex when he was shot from behind. Riddled with seven bullets, Atwal died on the spot and his body lay there in broad daylight in full view of a large number of people. Policemen at a nearby post remained mute witness to their senior officer's murder, despite knowing that the person responsible for it was hiding a short distance away at Guru Nanak Niwas.

Reportedly, Brigadier Tejinder Singh Grewal, a close relation of Atwal's, and his friend Jarnail Singh Chahal, an IPS officer of the Punjab cadre, had asked Atwal to come to Amritsar on 25 April for discussions on an important matter. Grewal was at that time posted at the army headquarters in New Delhi. Chahal was the person who had negotiated Bhindranwale's surrender at Chowk Mehta in 1981. According to the slain DIG's family, Atwal initially resisted going to Amritsar but was persuaded by the two officials over the telephone. The three had a long discussion before Atwal went into the Golden Temple.

Both Grewal and Chahal had been hobnobbing with Longowal and Bhindranwale for some time.[7] In fact, at the precise moment that Atwal was gunned down, Chahal was alone with Longowal and Grewal was also in the vicinity. Rather than go to the scene of crime, where Atwal's body lay unclaimed, both Grewal and Chahal left for Chandigarh in haste, where they met Governor A.P. Sharma (former Union minister of state for industries and later governor of West Bengal) and then at night, Chief Minister Darbara Singh. They did not attend Atwal's bhog – last rites – lest they should be accused by Atwal's family of responsibility for his murder. Incidentally, the investigation of the case was handed over to the CBI, bypassing the Punjab Police who had the original jurisdiction. Also, CBI Director J.S. Bawa was asked to personally handle the case and report directly to Indira Gandhi.

The visit to the Golden Temple from Delhi of a senior serving army officer along with a serving Punjab police officer of SP rank, and their request to a Punjab police DIG to join them would not have been done without instructions from above. It appears there was some plan afoot, which went awry with Atwal's unexpected murder.

Why did neither Punjab Police nor the CRPF not enter the Guru Nanak Niwas to capture Bhindranwale or his killer squad responsible for Atwal's murder remains an unanswered question. Darbara Singh told Mark Tully and Satish Jacob, 'I consistently told Central government that the Guru Nanak Niwas (Rest House) was not a part of the Temple complex, that the police should be sent in there. But they told me they were afraid of inflaming Sikh sentiments.' The authors conclude, 'In the national outcry that followed [Atwal's murder], very few Sikhs, except those already committed to Bhindranwale, would have raised any objection.

In fact, many Sikhs, especially those living outside Punjab, would have welcomed it.'[8]

With that I fully agree.

Bhindranwale's 'hit list'

Within a couple of months of Atwal's murder two close associates of Bhindranwale's – Thara Singh and Amrik Singh (whose release was the only condition Bhindranwale asked for in November 1982 when Swaran Singh had gone to meet him) – were released from jail. Soon after his release, Amrik Singh, as president of the AISSF, called a meeting of the organization at the Golden Temple, where Hindus were specifically targeted in slogans, songs and speeches. Bhindranwale was the main attraction at the meeting, and Longowal appeared to play second fiddle to him.[9]

It would be interesting to note here that many in Amritsar were aware that R.L. Bhatia, president of the Punjab State Congress party and the local Member of Parliament for whom Bhindranwale had canvassed during the 1980 elections, continued to maintain contact with Bhindranwale through Amrik Singh till as late as May 1984.[10] It is obvious that Bhatia was maintaining that connection on behalf of the 1 Akbar Road group. Though Amrik Singh's release at this point was described as a mistake, it could also have been the result of a move by the 1 Akbar Road Group to introduce a more sinister dimension to the already chaotic situation. The proceedings of the AISSF conference Amrik Singh organized would bear this out.

Soon after this, friction between Longowal and Bhindranwale surfaced. The two started spending most of their time in their respective rooms in Guru Nanak Niwas. The activities of Bhindranwale's 'killer squad' also gained momentum. At least five bodies were found in the sewers close to Guru Nanak Niwas in

August and September 1983. During this period, unverified stories of Bhindranwale's 'hit list' began circulating. The list reportedly included names of police officers and government officials, Hindus as well as Sikhs, with whom Bhindranwale had scores to settle.

A police officer, Bichhu Ram, who had forcibly trimmed the beard of a Sikh, was killed within six months of the incident. Bhindranwale and his men also started sending threatening letters to newspaper editors and journalists, including Khushwant Singh and Prem Bhatia, the editor of the Chandigarh-based daily, the *Tribune*. Bhindranwale's interpreter at the time is reported to have said, 'No one can refuse Santji's orders.'[11]

Communal discord

Following inflammatory anti-Hindu speeches at the AISSF meeting at the Golden Temple on 28 September 1983, some Sikhs fired upon a group of Hindu morning walkers at Jagraon, a small town near Ludhiana. On 5 October, a group of Sikhs hijacked a bus near Dhilwan village in Kapurthala district, separated Hindu passengers from the rest and shot dead six of them at point-blank range. Consequently, on 6 October, Chief Minister Darbara Singh was made the scapegoat. The Congress government in Punjab, led by a powerless but secular chief minister, was dismissed for its failure in maintaining law and order in the state.

Soon after this development, Mark Tully met Darbara Singh at Chandigarh, and the latter 'blamed the faction in the Central government loyal to Zail Singh for his downfall'.

> A senior colleague of Darbara Singh went so far as to claim that President Zail Singh was still in daily contact with Bhindranwale.

> ... there is no doubt that Darbara Singh had worked to take action against Bhindranwale, and that it was the Central government which had refused to allow him to send the police into the Temple Rest House, which the Sant had made his headquarters. Darbara Singh was one of the very few Congress leaders who had the courage to attack Bhindranwale by name ... Darbara Singh matched his words with deeds as far as the Central government allowed him ... The other problem was, of course, that Darbara Singh's police were not allowed to tackle the problem at its root [meaning Bhindranwale].[12]

Following the Dhilwan village incident, as a measure to reassure the local Hindu population, a CRPF contingent conducted a route march through the streets of Amritsar. Within a week, the state administrative machinery at the top was overhauled. Governor A.P. Sharma was sent to West Bengal, and in his place former cabinet secretary, the well-regarded civil servant B.D. Pande, was posted as governor on 10 October. Four senior civil servants were sent from the Centre to help him run the administration of Punjab: P.S. Bhinder, husband of Sukhbans Kaur Bhinder, Congress MP from Gurdaspur and a close confidante of the Gandhi family, was posted as DGP, Punjab.

Even as Indira Gandhi was trying to reassure the people of Punjab that she was doing her best to restore peace in the state, terrorist activities continued unabated. On 12 October 1983, an assistant superintendent of jails was beaten up by Bhindranwale's men in the Golden Temple; one of Bhindranwale's Sikh critics was shot dead in Jalandhar; a shop owned by a Hindu was looted. Within two weeks of governor's rule, the Kashmir Mail going to Kolkata was derailed while passing through Punjab. As a result, nineteen passengers were killed and 129 injured. On 18 November, another bus was hijacked and four Hindu passengers were shot dead.

Simultaneously, friction was building between the highly demoralized Punjab Police and the CRPF. The latter felt that the Punjab Police were partisan and did not want to act against Sikh extremists. Within a couple of months of the imposition of president's rule in the state, even Congress MPs started expressing doubts about the efficacy of the government's 'weak-kneed' policy towards Punjab. During a debate in parliament, members from both sides demanded the arrest of Bhindranwale.

Bhindranwale, still living in Guru Nanak Niwas, now faced threats from two avenues. There was the fear of arrest by the police, and a challenge from members of the Akhand Kirtani Jatha and the Babbar Khalsa, who had come to protect Longowal and other moderate Akali Dal leaders living in Guru Nanak Niwas from Bhindranwale's killer squad. The Akhand Kirtani Jatha was led by Bibi Amarjit Kaur, widow of Fauja Singh, who had died in the attack on the Nirankari convention on 13 April 1981. She would openly criticize Bhindranwale as a coward.

The Babbar Khalsa, also a product of the Sikh anti-Nirankari movement, was fiercely anti-Bhindranwale too, and well-armed. Its leader, Sukhdev Singh, claimed that his group had killed forty-five Nirankaris. Both Bibi Amarjit Kaur and Sukhdev Singh were strongly opposed to the murder of Hindus and to the violence unleashed by the 'coward', Bhindranwale, in Punjab. Babbar Khalsa men entered Guru Nanak Niwas and ordered Bhindranwale's men to get out. While the latter claimed they did so on their own, the Babbar Khalsa claimed they had fled when threatened. Bhindranwale shifted to the safety of the Akal Takht on 15

December 1983 with the help of the SGPC chairman G.S. Tohra, who was still nursing ambitions of becoming chief minister of Punjab for which he was soliciting Bhindranwale's support.

Sermons on the roof

Soon after shifting to the Akal Takht, Bhindranwale started holding his darbar (congregation) on the langar roof, delivering sermons which were mostly anti-Hindu in content. Sometimes he would criticize Indira Gandhi by using derogatory names. His tape-recorded speeches, spewing venom, were freely available at shops and were actively distributed in villages, unrestricted by the police. He and his posse of armed men would walk across from the Akal Takht building to the langar roof very casually, as if there was no fear of any action by security forces.

Conscious of the fact that he was being criticized by many as an agent of the Congress party, Bhindranwale described his critics as 'power hungry' individuals out to destroy the unity of the 'panth' (synonymous with Sikhs as a religious group). He soon started demanding implementation of the Anandpur Sahib Resolution in its entirety, favouring greater devolution of power to states. He also exhorted every Sikh village to raise a group of three baptized, motorcycle-riding Sikhs armed with revolvers.

This last bit caused Longowal to issue a statement criticizing it and to Bhindranwale's call in general to Sikhs to support terrorism. Soon afterwards, on India's Republic Day (26 January 1984), the Khalistan flag was flown on a building close to the Golden Temple. To match Bhindranwale's utterances, Akali Dal leaders also demanded an amendment to Article 25 of the Indian Constitution, which mentioned that reference to Hindus included persons professing the Sikh, Jain and Buddhist religions. This was neither a part of the Akali Dal's original demands nor a part of the Anandpur Sahib Resolution. To up the ante, Akali Dal leaders announced that if their demand was not met they would burn copies of the Indian Constitution. They also decided to launch an agitation reviving their original demands. As a result, other than Longowal, senior Akali leaders, including Badal and Tohra, were arrested and sent to jail. The Akali Dal called for a general strike on 8 February 1984. Hindu shopkeepers in Punjab were forced to close their shops. To prevent loss of life and property, the government cancelled all train and air services to Punjab.

To deal with the situation arising out of the general strike, Akali leaders were once again called for negotiations on 14 February 1984, to which opposition leaders were also invited. On the same day, six policemen at a post near the Golden Temple were abducted by Bhindranwale's men. One of them was killed and the rest released after some time. Also on the same day, a general strike was called in Punjab by the Hindu Suraksha Samiti (Hindu Defence Committee) by its Patiala-based leader Pawan Kumar Sharma.

Authors Mark Tully and Satish Jacob described Pawan Kumar as '... a young man with a criminal record brought into politics by a Sikh Congress (Indira) member of Parliament. Pawan Kumar also had close links with the Haryana Chief Minister'.[13] But according to G.S Chawla, 'Seema Mustafa, then working for the *Telegraph*, Calcutta, had visited Patiala and interviewed the mother of Pawan Kumar Sharma, who said that she did not understand why the Maharaja Patiala, Amarinder Singh, was spoiling her son. Amarinder Singh's car used to pick up Pawan Kumar Sharma.'[14]

In the violence during that strike, fourteen persons were killed, mostly Sikhs. As a result, Akali leaders walked out of the negotiations saying they would return to the talks only when peace returned to Punjab.

Riots, and more killings

Following the Hindu Suraksha Samiti-led strike in Punjab, serious anti-Sikh riots broke out in the neighbouring state of Haryana, provoked by a speech by Chief Minister Bhajan Lal at Faridabad, in which he warned that the patience of Hindus was running out and they could retaliate any time. A gurudwara in Panipat was burnt down in the presence of the police. Sikhs were pulled out of buses and forcibly shaved, and Sikh-owned shops were looted. Eight Sikhs were clubbed to death. Considering the gravity of the situation, traffic on the main Grand Trunk Road had to be halted. The violence stopped as suddenly as it arose, 'which suggests that it was not quite as spontaneous as it appeared at first sight. Bhajan Lal had shown his strength and Haryana's position was not ignored again'.[15]

On 28 March 1984, the president of the DSGMC, H.S. Manchanda, pro-Congress and a bitter critic of the Akali Dal morcha, was shot dead in broad daylight at the busy ITO traffic crossing in Delhi. To deal with the worsening law and order situation, on 3 April the whole of Punjab was declared a disturbed area and the National Security Act was promulgated, giving powers to the police to detain people without producing them in court. The day this was done, a prominent member of the Bharatiya Janata Party, Harbans Lal Khanna, was killed at Amritsar.

The next day, 4 April, Vishva Nath Tiwari, a professor at Punjab University and a member of the Rajya Sabha, was shot dead in Chandigarh while on a morning walk. On 22 April, an air force officer was hacked to death in his home. On 26 April, a young Sikh motorcycle rider shot a Hindu commission agent in Bhikiwind village in Amritsar district, and in another similar incident, a Hindu shopkeeper was shot in Samadh Bhai village in Faridkot district.

On 30 April, former deputy superintendent of police Bachan Singh, who had reportedly tortured Amrik Singh while he was in police custody, was shot dead along with his wife and daughter. On 12 May, Romesh Chander, son of the late Lala Jagat Narain, was shot dead in Jalandhar. In the two months of April and May 1984, at least eighty persons were killed and 107 injured in Bhindranwale-led extremist activities. Some Hindus started growing beards and wearing turbans to save their lives. The Hindu industrialists of Punjab started thinking of moving their businesses to the neighbouring state of Haryana.

By early March 1984, Bhindranwale's armed men were freely moving in the Golden Temple complex, and some of them had taken positions at vantage points in nearby buildings and houses overlooking the complex. Gun positions around the Akal Takht were being prepared, and arms and ammunition were moving into the Akal Takht complex with the knowledge, if not connivance, of officials of the Punjab government. Maj. Gen. Shahbeg Singh, who had played a significant role in the training of the Mukti Bahini for their role in the liberation struggle of Bangladesh but was subsequently dismissed on charges of corruption during his posting as a divisional commander, also moved into the Akal Takht. He started preparing the defences around the Akal Takht in case of an attack on it. Bhindranwale's control over government machinery through fear can be gauged from the fact that the telephone exchange would handle on priority calls made by him and his men.

The final break between Bhindranwale and the Longowal-led Akali Dal was reached when Surinder Singh Sodhi, a member of Bhindranwale's killer squad, was killed on 14 April just outside the Golden Temple complex. Bhindranwale suspected the hand of the moderate Akali Dal leaders behind the killing. Soon, a couple,

Surinder Singh 'Chhinda' and his girlfriend Baljit Kaur, were killed for their suspected involvement in Sandhu's murder. In an attempt to reassert his authority, Longowal called a meeting of senior Sikh leaders but found that sixty of the 140 persons who came to attend the meeting had walked over to Bhindranwale's side.

One day before that meeting, Longowal had a long telephone talk with Indira Gandhi. He told her he had lost control of the situation and requested her to make some concessions to enable him to withdraw his morcha. The contents of that conversation were conveniently leaked to the press, further eroding his credibility. In desperation, Longowal contacted five head priests to issue a hukamnama (edict) to Bhindranwale to vacate the Akal Takht. Within days, Bhindranwale got three of his critics, including the former head granthi of the Akal Takht, Giani Pratap Singh, killed to instil terror among the five serving head priests.

Meanwhile, Gurcharan Singh Tohra and Parkash Singh Badal, who had been jailed for burning copies of the Indian Constitution, conveyed their agreement to the withdrawal of their morcha if only Chandigarh were to be transferred to Punjab. As opposed to the earlier stance of the Centre, of requiring the transfer of both Abohar and Fazilka in exchange to Haryana, the prime minister now agreed to the transfer of Abohar only, through an award by a commission, the results of which would be guaranteed in advance. With that understanding, the charges of sedition against Tohra and Badal were withdrawn and they were released from jail on 11 May.

The last round of talks was held on 26 May and was conducted by External Affairs Minister P.V. Narasimha Rao and two other cabinet ministers, with the help of the three-member think-tank, where T.N. Chaturvedi had now been replaced by M.M.K. Wali, the new home secretary. Tohra, still hopeful of becoming chief minister, met Bhindranwale to get his approval of the agreement, but Bhindranwale insisted on acceptance of the Anandpur Sahib Resolution in its full form.

How these talks failed is described at the end of Chapter 4. Amarinder Singh, who did not participate in the February talks nor this latest round, explained his reasons for non-participation to Mark Tully as follows, 'Mrs Gandhi's think-tank was too bureaucratic in its attitude to the demands for river water and Chandigarh, and did not understand the political pressure on the Akali leaders.'[16] With the last round of talks having failed, on 26 May 1984 Longowal announced a new programme to intensify the Akali agitation, starting from 3 June. This involved blocking transport of food grains from Punjab to other states, non-payment of taxes due to the government, and regular courting of arrest by Sikhs.

It was now time for the 1 Akbar Road group to reap the bitter harvest, the seeds of which had been sown in 1980. But before dealing with the next stage, Operation Blue Star, there are a few issues which need to be explained, to allow the reader to understand the developments in their correct perspective.

8

My Third Visit to the US and Canada

MY THIRD and last Punjab-related visit to Canada and the US took place in September–October 1983, when Prime Minister Indira Gandhi was to address a session of the United Nations General Assembly at New York. As was the case during my previous two visits, I actually held the charge of deputy director overseeing two of the most sensitive divisions at the R&AW headquarters (the second one after it fell vacant in the middle of 1982). The work handled by these divisions had nothing to do with the coverage of Sikh extremist or Khalistan-related activities abroad. However, I was called upon as a sort of firefighter, to perform a special task in the US and Canada, report compliance of the orders to the director (R), and get back to my officially assigned duties.

At this time, Punjab was on the boil. DIG A.S. Atwal had been murdered a few months before, on 25 April 1983. Amrik Singh had criticized Hindus openly in the presence of Bhindranwale and Longowal at an AISSF conclave (described in the preceding chapter). Within days of Indira Gandhi's return from New York, six Hindus were dragged out of a bus on the night of 5 October and shot dead. That incident led to the dismissal of Darbara Singh's Congress government and imposition of president's rule in Punjab. Naturally, the developments in Punjab also had a serious impact on the Indian diaspora in the US and Canada.

Girish Chandra (Gary) Saxena (IPS 1950 Uttar Pradesh, later governor of Jammu and Kashmir), had taken over as director (R) in April 1983 on Suntook's retirement. Though very senior to me, we both belonged to the Uttar Pradesh cadre and I knew him well from before we joined the R&AW. Gary called me in the second week of September 1983 and told me that the prime minster was due to visit New York for about six days, from 26 September to 2 October, to address the thirty-eighth UNGA session on 28 September, and would also attend some other functions.

According to him, the situation in Canada and the west coast of the US had worsened as far as the Sikh diaspora was concerned, and the threat to the PM's life from extremists had escalated as well. We needed to be extra cautious to ensure her safety during that visit. Also, to avoid adverse publicity in front of foreign heads of state attending the UNGA session, we needed to ensure that no demonstration by pro-Khalistan Sikhs took place in front of the UN building while she was addressing the UNGA. If that was not possible, we should at least see that the demonstrations remained a low-key affair.

I had no control over such developments or over the people who might be behind them as it was not a part of my current charge at the headquarters. Gary was, in fact, aware that what I had been doing so far on this front was based on my personal goodwill and friendship with persons who were in the know of things. Therefore I told Gary that I could not guarantee anything but I would try my best to comply with his instructions. I then discussed the details of my programme with Gary, to which he agreed.

I reached Ottawa on 21 September. By that time, High Commissioner Gurdial Singh Dhillon, whom I had met in December 1981, had been replaced by Sivarama Krishnan. On the completion of his tenure, my successor too had been replaced by another R&AW officer. I had a detailed discussion with our man on the prevailing situation in Canada, after which I called on the high commissioner alone. Both our man and the high commissioner were worried about the significant increase in pro-Khalistan activities in Canada, especially in the Toronto and Vancouver areas, but did not know what could be done to deal with the situation without any clear instructions from their respective headquarters. Neither of them had any information on any likely attempt on Indira Gandhi's life during her visit to New York, but were expecting demonstrations in front of the UN building on 28 September.

I also met some of my Sikh friends that day and the next day too. I talked to some friends from the west coast of the US, and from the Vancouver and Toronto areas on the phone in the evenings, and later too throughout my stay in Canada and the US. This time I did not go to Vancouver. Nor did I visit the US west coast, as I felt visiting Toronto and meeting Kuldip Singh Sodhi, the so-called consul general of Khalistan, would be more fruitful in completing the two assigned tasks. I contacted Sodhi by phone and some other friends from the Toronto area too, fixing meetings with them on 24 September. However, before leaving Ottawa I requested our man there to shift to Vancouver during the period of the PM's stay at New York and keep me and the Department posted about information of interest that came to his notice.

On the morning of 24 September I left Ottawa for Toronto. On my arrival I called Sodhi again to fix a meeting at a local restaurant. I was surprised to find that he was a bit hesitant and excused himself from meeting me on the pretext of being unwell. It appeared to me that he had not got clearance from his bosses in London for the meeting, presumably due to his meeting with me outside Richmond Hill Gurudwara in New York the previous year, during Indira Gandhi's visit (Chapter 5). Maybe he was in touch with my successor, the current station head at Ottawa, who did not give Sodhi *his* clearance to meet me, which is normal in such cases.

The good thing was that Sodhi was still willing to talk. To my direct and brief questions, he mentioned that as far as he knew there was no threat to Indira Gandhi's life during her visit to New York. He also told me that two or three busloads of Sikhs would leave Toronto for New York early on the morning of 28 September, to demonstrate in front of the UN building. He was not sure whether he would be accompanying them. When I requested him to somehow convince the demonstrators not to use foul language or derogatory slogans against Indira Gandhi, he said he had no control over their behaviour. He did agree to give it a try, though.

A disappointed diaspora

Here I would like to sum up what I had gathered from my personal meetings and phone conversations with my friends, contacts and relatives during my ten days in Canada and the US. All of them enquired as to what happened to their suggestions (which they had made during my first visit in December 1981, and which are mentioned in Chapter 3). They emphasized again their anguish at the continued irresponsible and biased coverage of Punjab by the Indian media, especially the vernacular press, which was fanning communalism in Punjab and widening the schism between Hindus and Sikhs in their respective countries too.

They drew my attention towards the killing of innocent Hindus in Punjab and the Haryana police's repression of Sikhs. They informed me that gurudwaras in the US and Canada were increasingly coming under the control of hard-line Sikhs; there was a lack or total absence of institutional support from Indian missions in their respective areas or countries to help maintain cordial relations between Hindus and Sikhs. They were quite frank in saying that it seemed that Bhindranwale was being encouraged by some senior Congress leaders for political gains, which in turn was helping the pro-Khalistan elements in Canada and the US to attract Sikh youth towards their ideology.

I had no convincing answer to their questions as to what had happened to their suggestions made to me in December 1981. Actually, by then I had realized that what they were saying was largely true, especially about the root cause of the worsening situation in Punjab, but could not openly express my views because of my official position. By the time I finished my visit I had got the impression that if the situation in Punjab did not improve, which I felt it would not till the next parliamentary elections, very few of my contacts and friends from those two countries would meet me or talk to me again on that subject. None of them was a paid source. What they were sharing with me was out of friendship and their concern for the deteriorating situation in Punjab and its impact on their lives in the countries they had settled in.

A job done

After spending a night in Toronto, I reached New York on the morning of 25 September and checked into a hotel close to the upscale and well-equipped Hotel Helmsley Place on Madison Avenue where the prime minister and her delegation would be staying. After spending four days (20–24 September) on her state visits to Cyprus and Greece and making a brief stopover at Paris on 25 September, Indira Gandhi and her delegation reached JFK airport late in the evening on 26 September.

Compared with her state visit of the previous year, the reception at the airport was a low-key affair. Only two Indian press reporters, including G.S. Chawla of the *Indian Express*, had accompanied her on the flight. Against a full complement of three senior IB officers in charge of her security the previous year, only one officer was in attendance this time – Ratan Sahgal, with his supporting staff. There was hardly any press coverage of her arrival or her activities during her entire stay in New York. Even her speech at the UNGA was not covered by the local press.

Sometime after her arrival at the hotel, I got a copy of her New York itinerary. In addition to her speech at the UNGA on 28 September, she was to meet US President Ronald Reagan and chair two informal get-togethers of twenty-four leaders from Non-Aligned Movement (NAM) countries on 27 and 29 September. There were some press interviews as well. This time she made it a point to address US-based members of the Indian press, whom she could not meet as a group during her previous visit. Also, there were the usual rounds of discussions with editors, dinners with a few groups and friends, addresses to prominent persons from the local Indian community, inauguration of a photo exhibition on Jawaharlal Nehru, visits to some shows, and shopping.[1]

On the morning of 27 September I visited the consul general of India's (CGI) office in New York to see if I could meet someone known to me there. On arrival, I saw that they had set up a control room there in connection with the prime minister's visit. In addition to meeting Indian high commissioner to Canada Sivarama Krishnan who had also reached New York, I also ran into K.C. Singh (IFS 1974) who was posted in the CGI as head of chancery (HOC) and consul in charge of economic relations. We are both from Patiala and our families were known to each other.

I had by that time seen through the game the 1 Akbar Road group was playing. I cryptically told K.C., 'These people are using Sikh officers to further their own interests.' I told him he should be careful and not do anything which he would regret later on. When he asked me to explain what I had just said, I replied that I would do that at an appropriate time in the future. K.C. Singh later served as India's ambassador to the UAE and Iran and retired as secretary in the Ministry of External Affairs. We would meet at the Delhi Golf Club often. But I only got around to speaking to him at length on the phone on 26 May 2020, specifically to know more about his experience of working as deputy secretary with President Zail Singh during the November 1984 anti-Sikh pogrom in Delhi. He still remembered what I had told him at New York in September 1983.[2]

During Indira Gandhi's visit I decided to hang around the hotel lobby and other venues while she met with the Indian press and persons of Indian origin, and also focus on the expected protest outside the UN building on 28 September. That day I reached the UN building about half an hour before the session was to start. I walked around the UNGA hall and other adjoining areas, including the Security Council wing, to ensure that there was no suspicious person or activity. That was out of sheer habit, as the R&AW officers were not supposed to look after the PM's physical security, which was the responsibility of Ratan Sahgal and his team from the Intelligence Bureau and, of course, the local security agencies, including the New York Police Department and the FBI, in close cooperation with each other.

After spending about ten minutes inside the UN building, I came out and saw two buses full of Sikhs and bearing Canadian number plates, parked some distance away, to the left of the entrance to the UN building. There were some policemen keeping a watch over them. They had cordoned off the area where the buses were parked with a tape running across the road. As there was still some time for Indira Gandhi's arrival, I went to meet the occupants of the two buses. Kuldip Singh Sodhi was not among them.

I introduced myself as a former first secretary of the High Commission of India at Ottawa and told them I was part of Indira Gandhi's delegation and had come out specially to meet them for old times' sake. A couple of them remembered my name, as I had left Canada only four years ago. I told them that they were not in India where they could say anything or shout any kind of slogans against Indira Gandhi. They were in New York, in front of the UN building, where a number of foreign heads of state or government could observe their conduct. As they could be easily identified by their turbans, I requested them that as true Sikhs, they should observe the maryada (ethics) of their religion and not insult a woman, and that too in public, even though she happened to be the prime minister of India.

After initial protests, they finally agreed that that they would refrain from using foul language in their slogans, posters and placards. Keeping my fingers crossed and hoping that they would keep their promise, I entered the UN building to be close to the

UNGA hall where Indira Gandhi was to speak in a short while. I later came to know that they indeed kept that promise. After her speech was over, the prime minister, accompanied by Sonia Gandhi and others, started moving out of the building, but she was stopped in the foyer by a couple of reporters who had questions to ask.

A painful decision

It was time to return to India. As the prime minister's special aircraft was to leave in the forenoon of 2 October, I had booked my seat on an Air India flight from JFK the same afternoon. Fortunately, from our point of view, nothing of the sort that Gary had apprehended had happened. In fact, a few simple and friendly words spoken in an earthy language were all that it took to convince the so-called hard-line Khalistanis in front of the UN building to exercise restraint. Normally, I should have been happy about a task completed satisfactorily. But throughout my return flight I was tormented with the recollection of my interactions with my Sikh friends and contacts during the trip.

Was I actually doing something that was against the national interest? If so, should I continue serving the vested interests of some persons, even at the cost of the larger interests of the nation? If not, how should I tell Gary to take me off such assignments in future? Would he mind, and what would be the consequences of that? By the time my plane landed in New Delhi I had made up my mind – irrespective of the consequences, I would tell Gary that I would no longer like to be associated with any work or operation related to the ongoing developments in Punjab and request him to relieve me of the charge of the two top secret and sensitive divisions to avoid meeting him almost daily, sometimes more than once.

I called on Gary the first thing next morning to apprise him of my activities during the visit. As soon as I entered his room, he stood up, shook hands with me and congratulated me for a job well done. 'Now get ready to move to Bangkok, as head of the R&AW station there,' he told me. I thanked Gary for his appreciation but politely said, 'Sir, I am not going anywhere. I think something terrible is going to happen before the end of next year and I would like to be in India at that time.'

'Sir,' I continued, 'I don't want to be associated with anything which serves the interest of one person, one party or one family, which has the potential of shaking the foundations of the country. In view of that, please relieve me from my present posts and commitment to special assignments and post me to an analysis division.'

Gary was surprised, if not shocked, at this completely unexpected response to his words of appreciation. In the normal course, no one sought to be transferred from high-profile and sought-after divisions to a nondescript analysis division, and neither to decline an attractive posting to head the most important station of the R&AW in south east-Asia. Also, no one in his normal frame of mind was supposed to blame the policies followed by the prime minister, and that too one of Indira Gandhi's stature, as reasons thereof.

Gary sensed that what I had just told him was not simply an emotional outburst but was based on my knowledge of certain facts, which he wanted to avoid discussing further. I was, however, confident that Gary had enough faith in me to also believe that I would not divulge what I had just told him to anyone else outside his room. But from his expression I could sense that what he wanted to tell me was that while I could say anything of the sort I had said to him and get away with it, if he had to say something similar to the prime minster, he should be carrying his resignation letter in his pocket and be prepared for harsh consequences. Instead, absolutely calm and composed, he told me that it would take him some time to find my replacements for the two divisions, and until then I should continue with my work as usual. He did not say anything about Punjab-related assignments, but it was implied that I would not be associated with anything like that in future.

There was no doubt that while subsequently briefing Kao about my visit to the US and Canada, Gary would have informed him of what I had said that morning. Kao, who had closely supervised my Sikkim operation (1973–1975) as secretary, knew that I would not say what I had without any basis. Besides, as senior advisor to the PM since August 1981, he was fully aware of what was happening at the decision-making level and knew who were influencing Indira Gandhi's decisions. His advice to Gary might have been to allow me a respite from such activities.

When I met Gary the next day in connection with some official work, things were normal, and he gave me the impression that nothing had happened the previous day. I was finally relieved of my two charges sometime in November 1983 and posted as deputy director in charge of an analysis division covering a fairly large area, of which Sri Lanka was an important part. That was the time when Sri Lanka was recovering from anti-Tamil riots that had caused the death of approximately 4,000 Tamils across that country in retaliation for the killing of thirteen Sri Lankan soldiers by the Liberation Tigers of Tamil Eelam (LTTE) in an ambush at Jaffna on 23 July 1983.

That, in fact, marked the beginning of prolonged and fierce hostilities between the LTTE, other Sri Lankan Tamil militant groups such as the Peoples Liberation Organization of Tamil Elam (PLOTE), Eelam People's Revolutionary Liberation Front

(EPRLF), Eelam Revolutionary Organization of Students (EROS) on the one side, and the Sri Lankan security forces on the other.

There was an interesting incident that needs to be recounted here. At an official dinner a few months after my taking over the new charge, Gary walked over to where my wife and I were standing. Addressing my wife, Gary said, 'Bali, do you know that your dear husband is the Bhindranwale of R&AW?' To which Bali replied, 'Mr Saxena, I cannot imagine GB (my nickname) doing anything anti-national.' To which he significantly remarked, 'That is the problem.' The tone of Gary's conversation with Bali was akin to that of a man who might be telling his younger brother's wife about her husband's behaviour, either in appreciation of his courage or in exasperation at his sheer stupidity. Which of the two was applicable in this case, Gary left it to Bali to guess.

My relations with Gary continued to be excellent, even after our retirement. But we could not stay in regular contact with each other. Vikram Sood, former secretary, R&AW, has settled in Gurugram after his retirement. We are in regular touch on the phone and at occasional dinners and luncheons hosted by members of a group of senior retired officers living in Gurugram. Having served with Gary at an important R&AW station in the West, Vikram had continued to remain in regular touch with Gary even after his retirement.

Vikram is one of the very few persons with whom I have shared some of my experiences of the 1980s relating to Punjab. I had been thinking of seeking out Gary for some time in order to discuss why I had said what I did on my return from New York in September 1983. In that context, I suggested to Vikram that we should both call on Gary one day, and that I should share with

Gary my knowledge of Op-2. Unfortunately, that didn't happen due to my wife's indisposition. When she passed away in January 2017, Gary was in Goa. Though he was unwell himself, he called me to convey his condolences on Bali's demise. He mentioned that it was the turn of persons like him to go, not Bali. Unfortunately, Gary did not live for very long after that and passed away within three months of my wife's death.

9

The Aborted Heliborne Commando Operation

R.N. KAO, during his nine years (1968–77) as head of the R&AW and director general, security (DGS), was well aware of the capabilities of the elite SFF (Special Frontier Force, an adjunct of a bigger group known as Establishment 22) commando unit to handle hostage taking and other terrorism-related activities. As the R&AW and DGS were both part of the cabinet secretariat, functioning directly under the charge of the prime minster, Indira Gandhi of course knew the purpose for which SFF was originally raised. When the situation was hotting up in Punjab in the latter half of 1982, Kao began contemplating an SFF-led heliborne operations to remove Bhindranwale from Chowk Mehta gurudwara, and later, from the Golden Temple complex with as little loss of life and property as possible.

As mentioned earlier, I was at that time handling the additional charge of the liaison division, dealing with representatives of some of the foreign intelligence agencies posted at the various missions in New Delhi. In those days, all requests for meetings with liaison contacts, including those from the IB, were handled by the head of the liaison division of the R&AW. In addition to arranging such meetings, the head had to be personally present. Only the director (R), and later, its successor post secretary (R), could meet these liaison contacts alone without the presence of the liaison division head. This arrangement changed in the 1990s, when a decision was taken, for whatever reason, to allow the IB too to have direct access to some of those liaison contacts.

The foreign hand

It was the middle of November 1983 and I had not yet handed over charge of my two sensitive divisions. Gary Saxena told me that Kao wanted to meet the MI6 (UK's foreign intelligence agency) representative from the British High Commission. I picked up my MI6 contact and took him to Kao's office on the ground floor of the office block of the cabinet secretary, in the southern wing of Rashtrapati Bhavan.

Kao, after I introduced the contact to him, asked me to wait in the room of the officer on special duty Ratnakar Rao. The meeting lasted for about half an hour. I wondered what could have been the reason for Kao to ask me to keep away from the meeting. Due to some Op-2 related work that Kao was doing at that time, it seemed as if he was discussing something about Punjab. Just a month previously, on my return from New York, I had expressed to Gary Saxena my reservations on the way the situation in Punjab was being handled, or rather, mishandled. Perhaps Kao, who must have been in the know of that, did not want me at the meeting with the MI6 representative. Incidentally, on my return to office I informed Gary Saxena of Kao meeting my liaison contact alone, to which he did not react. Soon afterwards, I handed over charge of the liaison division to my successor.

B. Raman, in his book *Kaoboys of R&AW,* published in 2007 writes that two MI5 (typo for MI6; the MI5, UK's domestic intelligence agency, did not have any declared representative in New Delhi at that time) intelligence liaison officials at the British High Commission had scouted the Golden Temple complex in December 1983.[1] Most likely, their visit had resulted from Kao's meeting in November 1983 with my MI6 liaison contact, and he might have been one of the two officers who visited the Golden Temple complex.

The real purpose of that visit became clear when Phil Miller, an independent researcher and journalist, went to the British National Archives at Kew in Surrey, UK, looking for information on the involvement of the Special Air Services (SAS, the elite commando force of the UK) in Sri Lanka. Instead, he found some letters which showed a British connection to a planned Indian commando operation. According to these letters, declassified under the thirty years rule, Prime Minister Margaret Thatcher had agreed to a request (routed through the chief of MI6) from the Indian intelligence coordinator (R.N. Kao) to send an officer of the UK's elite commando force, SAS, to Delhi to advise the Indian government on 'expulsion' of Sikh militants from the Golden Temple.

Miller posted this information on a blog, highlighting the post-colonial role played by the UK in ongoing conflicts around the world. He referred to 'the apparent hypocrisy of Indira Gandhi who, the letters show, was highly critical of the involvement of British intelligence personnel in Sri Lanka, only to request their assistance herself at a later date.' This revelation, posted by Miller on his blog on 13 January 2014, was immediately picked up by the British press.[2]

Following this revelation, leaders of UK's Sikh community and some members of the House of Commons (especially those representing constituencies with large Sikh populations) objected to such a collaboration and to the alleged role of the SAS advisor in the planning of Operation Blue Star. Fearing a backlash, Prime Minister David Cameron ordered an inquiry by Cabinet Secretary Jeremy Heywood. Heywood consulted around 200 files, which included more than 23,000 documents covering the period from December 1983 to June 1984. But some documents had been destroyed in 2009 as part of a process that allowed the ministry of defence to review files after twenty-five years. The cabinet secretary also published details from five additional documents and interviewed former foreign secretary, Lord Howe, former home secretary, Lord Brittan and Margaret Thatcher's former private secretary, Lord Butler of Brockwell.[3]

The Heywood Report was presented in the British parliament by Foreign Secretary William Hague on 4 February 2014. Hague admitted that one SAS officer had visited India from 8 February to 17 February 1984 and had conducted a 'ground recce' of the Golden Temple with some members of the Indian special forces (SFF). The officer's advice was that 'a military operation should only be put into effect as a last resort, when all attempts at negotiation had failed. It recommended including in any operation an element of surprise and the use of helicopter-borne forces, in the interests of reducing casualties and bringing about a swift resolution.'[4]

Quoting the Heywood Report, Hague mentioned that 'with a view to reducing casualties, the UK military advisor recommended assaulting all objectives simultaneously, thereby assuring surprise and momentum. The advice given to the Indian authorities identified (the use of) sufficient helicopters, and the capability to insert troops by helicopter as critical requirement(s) for this approach.'

Further, 'The UK advice also focused on command and control arrangements, and night time coordination of paramilitary with Indian special group forces.' The report mentioned that there were 'significant differences' between the plan proposed by the SAS and the eventual operation that was mounted (Blue Star). The UK's assistance was purely 'advisory' and given months beforehand. It noted, 'Operation Bluestar was a ground assault, without an element of surprise, and without a helicopter-borne element.'

The British cabinet secretary's report concluded that the SAS officer's advice had limited impact on Operation Blue Star. It also tried to underline the absence of British involvement in the eventual Operation Blue Star by publishing correspondence between Indira Gandhi and Margaret Thatcher dated 14 June and 29 June 2014, which did not make any such mention. An analysis conducted by the British military for Heywood also concluded that the eventual operation was carried out by the Indian army in June 1984 in a wholly different way from what was suggested by the SAS.

Furore in British parliament

When details of this inquiry were revealed in the House of Commons, there were shouts of 'shame' from the ruling Conservative Party benches too. John McDonnell, the Labour MP for Hayes and Harlington, said Britain should apologize because it had willingly provided military support to desecrate Sikhism's holiest site. William Hague accused McDonnell of wild distortion, pointing out that the SAS officer who was sent to India in 1984 had provided advice to the Indian intelligence service (R&AW) and its special group (SFF) with the aim of minimizing casualties. This was ignored when the Indian army took charge of Operation Blue Star and stormed into the Golden Temple in June that year.

Hague also said there was no evidence that the SAS officer was sent to India to help British defence sales to India. But Tom Watson, a former Labour minister, said the House of Commons had been told that a protest march (by UK Sikhs) to commemorate victims of Operation Blue Star was not permitted on public-order grounds. He also quoted from newly released cabinet minutes from that time, which said: 'In view of the importance of the British political and commercial interests at stake it would be necessary to explore every possibility of preventing the march taking place. Export contracts worth five billion pounds could be at stake.'[5]

To this, Hague told Watson that the cabinet secretary was 'making a different point about a different event' because there was no evidence in the files that Britain provided military advice to boost defence sales.

Douglas Alexander, Labour's shadow secretary of state for foreign and commonwealth affairs, said, 'Labour welcomes what light the Cabinet Secretary's report sheds on the allegations of British involvement in Operation Blue Star, but despite the publication of this report, serious questions will continue to be asked.' He went on to say, 'It remains unclear, for example, why the government has today chosen to publish Mrs Gandhi's letter to Mrs Thatcher, but not Mrs Thatcher's letter to Mrs Gandhi. The pain and suffering still felt by many about the tragic events of

1984 places a particular duty on the government to provide what answers it can to address very genuine concerns.'

Winding up the debate, Prime Minister David Cameron said, 'I hope the manner in which we have investigated these dreadful events will provide some reassurance to the Sikh community, here in Britain and elsewhere.' He said, '... a single UK military officer provided some advice. But critically this advice was not followed, and it was a one-off'.

It is beyond the scope of this book to ascertain how much defence equipment the UK was able to sell to India or for that matter the kind of economic or diplomatic advantage some similarly placed Western countries might have taken of India in view of this self-created problem of India's. However, Margaret Thatcher was able to persuade Rajiv Gandhi to buy twenty-one Westland-30 helicopters for 65 million pounds, under a UK grant-in-aid scheme.[6]

Thatcher's foreign secretary, Sir Geoffrey Howe, wanted the Scotland Yard to ban protests planned by British Sikh groups, including the 'Republic of Khalistan', because a 'Sikh march in present circumstances would carry very serious risk, both for Indo-British relations and law and order in this country'. British High Commissioner to India Robert Wade Grey informed the foreign office that the celebrations by British Sikhs in the UK following Indira Gandhi's assassination could have a direct impact on this deal. Geoffrey Howe's private secretary, Leonard Appleyard, was more specific when he sent a note to the home office, saying, 'Contracts which would be potentially at risk from a trade boycott amount to some 5 billion pounds.'

Finally, India bought twenty-one of the Westland helicopters, which were inducted into the Pawan Hans fleet in 1986, to fly from Mumbai to offshore oil rigs and to ferry pilgrims to the Vaishno

Devi shrine from Jammu. Two of these helicopters (nicknamed 'flying coffins') crashed, one in 1988 in Jammu and one in 1989 in Nagaland, killing ten. The troubled fleet was grounded soon after, following endless wrangling over their obvious design flaws.[7]

'Snatch and grab'

Taking a lead from these revelations in the British press, an investigative report by journalist Sandeep Unnithan appeared in *India Today* in its issue of 31 January 2014. It said a 'snatch and grab' heliborne top-secret operation codenamed 'Operation Sundown', to grab and whisk away Bhindranwale from his Guru Nanak Niwas hideout, was planned by the director general, security, and presented to Indira Gandhi for her approval at her residential office, 1 Akbar Road, in the presence of Senior Advisor R.N. Kao.

However, Gandhi shot it down citing unaffordable civilian casualties that could result from it. Though the article was an excellent piece of investigative journalism, it had a few discrepancies, a major one being that when that operation was planned, Bhindranwale had already shifted to the Akal Takht and was no longer at Guru Nanak Niwas. Second, the plan was to grab him while he was delivering his sermon from the langar roof, and not from his room in Guru Nanak Niwas.[8]

It may be mentioned here that this was not the first attempt or plan by the SFF or the Indian army or security forces to arrest or abduct Bhindranwale from his hideouts. One such attempt at getting the army involved in his arrest from Chowk Mehta gurudwara after Lala Jagat Narain's murder in September 1981 has been described in Chapter 3.

Kao was even planning an SFF-led heliborne operation to abduct Bhindranwale from Chowk Mehta before the latter shifted to Guru Nanak Niwas on 19 July 1982. Sometime in the second half of June 1982, Director (R) Suntook called me to ascertain if it would be feasible for me to do a 'casing' (reconnaissance and preparation of a detailed map of the targeted area) of the Chowk Mehta complex. After a detailed discussion of the pros and cons of my 'casing' visit, I told Suntook that there was every chance of my being recognized by somebody at the complex, which could in turn alert Bhindranwale about the likelihood of such an operation.

I later learnt that someone else from the R&AW was actually sent to 'case' the Chowk Mehta complex under the guise of a reporter, but he was chased out as a suspected intelligence agent. Most likely it was this visit of a R&AW officer, followed by the arrest of Amrik Singh and Thara Singh on 19 July 1982, that prompted Bhindranwale to seek refuge in the safety of Guru Nanak Niwas.

To this day I have not been able to figure out the real motive behind the 'casing' operation. Possibly, Kao wanted to collect all relevant information well in advance, which could be useful when a decision to abduct Bhindranwale from Chowk Mehta was taken by the PM. Or the 1 Akbar Road group thought Bhindranwale's stature needed a further boost through a dramatic abduction. Or they wanted Bhindranwale to be suitably alerted that Chowk Mehta was no longer safe. That was perhaps the reason why an easily identifiable person like me was the first choice for the 'casing' operation. The job could easily have been done by someone else without being noticed, as it was later done by DGS R.T. Nagrani, to plan an SSF-led commando operation at the Golden Temple in April 1984.

For the 1 Akbar Road group, Bhindranwale's move to Guru Nanak Niwas had several advantages. First, Bhindranwale could carry out his extremist activities without any real threat of being arrested by the police. The Niwas, though not a part of the Golden

Temple complex, provide a better cover, being an official guest house of the SGPC, where police would normally not enter without approval from the concerned Central government authorities, which was not that easy to get. Second, anything said or done by Bhindranwale or his followers on his behalf from the Niwas or the temple complex would attract greater attention in national and international media. Third, his presence at Guru Nanak Niwas was expected to build pressure on the moderate Akali leadership, led by Longowal, to keep the pot boiling in Punjab.

Planning 'Operation Sundown'

I met Ram Tekchand (R.T.) Nagrani, former DGS, at his Vasant Vihar residence on 16 April 2019, and a couple of times after that too, to seek his views on the SFF heliborne operation that had been planned by the directorate general of security. Born in 1928, Nagrani is over ninety years old now. He had a serious heart problem in November 2014 when he was hospitalized for six days. Though physically somewhat weak, he regularly went for morning walks and played bridge at Vasant Vihar Club in the afternoons. Fortunately for me, he still remembered crucial details of the planned SFF-led heliborne operation to abduct Bhindranwale from the Golden Temple complex in April 1984.

An IPS officer of the 1951 batch (Andhra cadre), Nagrani came on deputation to the Government of India at SP rank, first to the CRPF. Soon afterwards he joined the Intelligence Bureau as assistant director in charge of the SFF. On bifurcation of the Intelligence Bureau and creation of the Research and Analysis Wing in September 1968, he moved over to the R&AW, where he served in various capacities both in India and abroad. He finally took over as DGS in 1982. Normally, the director of the R&AW used to be the ex-officio DGS too. But, as Nagrani was a 1951

IPS (regular recruitment) officer, and as Director Gary Saxena, entering service through the special recruitment quota, was given 1950-1/2 seniority, it was decided to give independent charge of DGS to Nagrani to oversee the affairs of the SFF, the Special Service Bureau (SSB) and the Aviation Research Centre (ARC).

The SFF, in addition to having a large contingent of persons of Tibetan origin meant specifically for Tibet-related operations, had a highly trained professional commando unit to deal with hostage taking or other serious situations resulting from terrorist activities. This commando unit comprised 150 young men, 50 per cent of them on short-term deputation from the army, and the rest from the BSF and CRPF. The cell had two Mi4 helicopters for heliborne operations. Besides, it had the facility to use suitable aircraft from the Aviation Research Centre as and when required.

Incidentally, when the Sikkim guards were being disarmed by the Indian army on 9 April 1975 at Gangtok, Nagrani, as staff officer to the R&AW Secretary R.N. Kao, had called me to seek a 'blow by blow' account of the disarming operation for the benefit of his boss.

Soon after the assassination of Indira Gandhi, Nagrani was asked to raise a distinct new commando force, the National Security Guard (NSG) as its first director general. He raised it with the help of some SFF commandos and clerical and ministerial staff, who formed the core of the newly created outfit.

Nagrani told me that it was towards the end of December 1983 that Kao called him to his office and asked him to plan an SFF-led heliborne operation to abduct Bhindranwale from the roof of the Golden Temple's langar (dining complex), where he delivered daily sermons till late evening, and whisk him away with the help of the CRPF. Nagrani confirmed to me the planned operation included an SFF unit and two Mi4 helicopters and the use of bulletproof vehicles to take Bhindranwale out of the complex from an adjoining road after he was captured. For that, Nagrani had requested a three-layered CRPF cordon of the area to be put in place just before the heliborne commandos were to strike.

Before the operation was planned, Nagrani selected a civilian employee of the SFF and assigned him the task of spending a few days at the Golden Temple complex. The employee's task was to prepare a detailed sketch map with special emphasis on the langar area and mark the most suitable points of entry and exit. He was also to observe the activities and movements of Bhindranwale and his armed guards from his residence in the Akal Takht to the langar complex rooftop. The observer was asked to suggest the most suitable time and place for Bhindranwale's abduction by heliborne commandos. With all this information gathered in three or four days, a model of the Golden Temple complex highlighting the langar area and nearby escape routes was prepared in Sarsawa near Saharanpur in Uttar Pradesh.

The following were the salient features of that operation:

Just before the heliborne commandos were to approach the Golden Temple complex, a sufficient number of armed CRPF personnel would throw a cordon around the complex to prevent entry and exit of people and material till the operation was over. Two teams of SFF commandos, travelling in two low-flying Mi4 helicopters, would approach the spot where Bhindranwale addressed his sermon on the roof, as his talk was about to end. Taking advantage of the lax security around Bhindranwale at that moment, the two teams would rope down.

Some of the commandos would rush towards Bhindranwale and grab him, while the rest would neutralize his armed security guards, who would naturally react as soon as they saw the commandos, possibly even before they had landed on the rooftop.

Simultaneously, the remaining SFF commandos and CRPF personnel would divide themselves into two lots. One would enter the Golden Temple complex to block Bhindranwale's access to the sanctum, in case he escaped from the langar roof, and capture him. The second lot would reach the road between the langar complex and Guru Nanak Niwas in bulletproof vehicles, take charge of the captured Bhindranwale from the heliborne commandos and whisk him away to a predetermined place, where he would be handed over to the authorities concerned.

The heliborne and ground-based SFF commandos were specifically instructed that Bhindranwale should in no case be allowed to go towards the Harmandir Sahib sanctum to take refuge, as capturing him from there without causing damage to the building would not be possible and causing damage to the main Harmandir Sahib structure was unacceptable.

According to Nagrani, the Golden Temple complex model used to plan the operation, along with the SFF personnel being trained, was shifted to the National Capital Region of Delhi towards the end of March 1984 to facilitate closer cooperation with the CRPF. Nagrani distinctly recalled the visit of the advisor from SAS. He specifically mentioned that the advice given by the advisor was meant exclusively for the SFF heliborne operation and not for the army-led Operation Blue Star, which was not even at the planning stage at the time. He, however, mentioned that as it turned out, his SFF commandos were later requisitioned by Lt Gen. K. Sundarji for Operation Blue Star at short notice.

Briefing Indira Gandhi

In early April 1984, R.N. Kao told Nagrani that Indira Gandhi wanted a briefing on the heliborne operation at 1 Akbar Road, at her private office wing adjoining her residence, 1 Safdarjung Road.

Nagrani was initially hesitant and did not want to brief her. He therefore requested Kao to brief the PM personally, since Kao was also fully conversant with the details of the operation. Ultimately however, Nagrani relented and briefed her in Kao's presence. After the briefing, the PM pointedly asked Nagrani about the number of casualties that could be expected. Nagrani said he could lose both the helicopters and about 20 per cent of the commandos.

Indira Gandhi then specifically asked him about the possibility of civilian casualties. Nagrani had no answer to that. The operation would coincide with Baisakhi (April 13) celebrations at the Golden Temple. He could not guess how many civilians might be present at the time. Finally, he said that about 20 per cent of the civilians coming in the way of the operation could also be killed. The PM said she could not afford such a large number of civilian casualties. The operation was killed there and then.

When I asked Nagrani about the selection of Baisakhi day for the operation, he said nobody at that time thought of postponing or bringing forward the date of the operation. Significantly, towards the end of the briefing, Indira Gandhi, in a pensive mood, remarked that she knew that, sooner or later, she would be killed by Sikh extremists, but she was not worried about that. Her main concern was what would happen to her children after her death.[9]

Let us examine the number of casualties that would have resulted from this operation. An Mi4 helicopter can carry between eight to sixteen passengers. Let us assume that two SSF Mi4 helicopters were carrying twelve fully equipped commandos each for the operation. If the casualty rate were 20 per cent, then five of the twenty-four commandos would be lost. Let us also assume that around 300 persons including Bhindranwale's ten guards, constituted his audience on the langar complex rooftop at the time of the operation. The normal reaction of the civilians would be to run for cover or escape on seeing the helicopters approach. Even if we presume that all 300 people came in the way of the operation, the total civilian casualties would amount to sixty persons per the estimate.

As the exit route would already have been sanitized by the CRPF, nobody would have come in the way of the commandos leaving with Bhindranwale from the side road. Both Kao and Nagrani were very cautious in projecting such estimates and would not have made tall claims or promised what they could not deliver. Given their propensity to err on the side of caution, even the estimates of expected casualties shared by Nagrani with the prime minister at the special briefing would have been on the higher side. Contrast the estimated losses from this operation with the horrific loss of life and the scale of destruction eventually caused by Operation Blue Star.

M.P.S. Aulakh (IPS 1970 Gujarat) held charge of the crucial post of assistant director at the Subsidiary Intelligence Bureau (SIB), Amritsar, from 1982 to 1985. In that capacity, he was in the know of Bhindranwale's day-to-day activities and related developments. A nephew of a close friend, Aulakh was known to me since his school days at Patiala. He recently told me that if the government wanted to abduct Bhindranwale and take him away to a predetermined place, it was not very difficult.

This was because Bhindranwale had a fixed routine of going on foot from the Akal Takht to the roof of the langar complex and returning the same way. He was always accompanied by eight to ten armed men, who would hang around him casually, without any apprehension of being attacked or arrested. If the day and time for such an operation had been carefully chosen (when there were fewer pilgrims in the complex), the number of civilian casualties could have been minimal. In fact, moderate Akali leaders and most of the general public of Punjab would have welcomed such a move, as they were getting sick of the continued instability in the state resulting from Bhindranwale's activities.[10]

Was Indira Gandhi's rejection of the SFF operation motivated only by her concern for civilian casualties, or was there was another reason, of which Nagrani was not aware? If one were to take this question a step further, would the abduction of Bhindranwale at this juncture have helped the Congress win the upcoming Lok Sabha elections? Actually, as per information obtained from the Punjab government through the ministry of home affairs by RTI activist Navdeep Gupta in 2017, till the day Bhindranwale died there was neither any actionable First Information Report (FIR) lodged against him nor any criminal case pending against him. Gupta is of the view that Bhindranwale's 'was basically a political murder.' Gupta's search for the truth behind Operation Blue Star continues, with a view to bringing the guilty to the court of justice.[11]

From the point of view of the 1 Akbar Road group, Bhindranwale had done the job for which his help had been enlisted. Bhindranwale alive and in detention at that time would have been a liability for the government. His arrest, even under the most dramatic circumstances, would not have ended militancy in Punjab. On the contrary, he could have spilled the beans about his connections with some senior Congress leaders. His arrest could also have provided a reason for Sikh militants to fan out in Punjab and target innocent Hindus in retaliation. It would have been difficult, if not impossible, to control that situation before the elections, which were due within the next eight months. Obviously, the 1 Akbar Road group would not have done anything to jeopardize their chances at the hustings.

It was time for Bhindranwale to go. The precise time, and the manner in which the 'final solution' would be implemented, remained to be worked out. In view of his 'ferocious' image, so very carefully cultivated over the last three years, Bhindranwale could not be seen to have gone meekly. His last fight had to be befitting his image so people could realize what a tough enemy he was. It would, therefore, appear that the Akal Takht's fortification through the smuggling of arms was deliberately overlooked so that when the time came for the 'final solution', Bhindranwale should go fighting till the last man.

It would thus appear that Indira Gandhi's rejection of the SFF operation was based on these considerations rather than on her concern for the lives of innocent civilians. This would become evident from the way Operation Blue Star was conceived, approved and ruthlessly executed, without any concern for civilian casualties or for its impact on the stability of a strategic state like Punjab, and of the nation as a whole.

10

P.C. Alexander, R.N. Kao and B. Raman

IN THIS chapter, I will examine, very briefly, the roles played in Op-2 by P.C. Alexander, principal secretary to the PM, R.N. Kao, senior advisor, and B. Raman, a senior R&AW officer, during the period from early 1981 to November 1984. Their respective working styles were also, to a large extent, symptomatic of the three different ways of functioning of government servants in the country.

The first category comprised those who would do anything to please their bosses, in the hope that their services would be suitably rewarded at an appropriate time. While nursing such ambitions they acted as front persons, created deniability, did their best to cover their tracks, and justified controversial actions taken by or on behalf of their bosses, under all circumstances.

The second category rendered appropriate advice on all occasions, based on their experience, expertise and knowledge, without expecting anything in return. They also came up with alternative plans and solutions to problems as and when they thought things were not moving in the right direction. But once a decision was taken by their bosses, they abided by it till the end.

To the third category belonged those hardworking and conscientious officers who had no personal axe to grind and carried out the tasks assigned to them in right earnest as part of their normal duties. While performing their duties, they somehow convinced themselves about the righteousness of the cause for which their services had been enlisted.

The ambitious P.C. Alexander

P.C. Alexander belonged to the first category. A highly successful IAS officer of the 1948 batch (Madras, first batch of IAS, post-Independence), he held a number of important posts and assignments during his career. After working in his home cadre and in various ministries at New Delhi, he became Prime Minister Indira Gandhi's principal secretary in May 1981 and continued to serve in that capacity with Rajiv Gandhi till January 1985, when he had to resign after the infamous Coomar Narain spy scandal, in which his personal secretary and two assistants were involved.[1,2] They were caught passing on copies of top-secret documents received by Alexander to their handlers linked to some embassies located in New Delhi. Originating from highly sensitive departments such as the R&AW, Atomic Energy Commission and India's space agency, ISRO, their safe custody was Alexander's to ensure.

In terms of the scandal's impact on the R&AW, in addition to the leakage of sensitive information contained in those notes, the names of issuing officers (including my own), their designations and areas of responsibility were also compromised. Following that, it was decided that the R&AW officers authorized to issue such notes would use their designations only and not their names. From that day onwards, a number of officers working in the R&AW, a department directly under the charge of the prime minster, became truly nameless and faceless entities, even for the PM's office.

It was a serious lapse on Alexander's part. He got away only with his resignation from the post of principal secretary to the PM, with his PS and two assistants going to jail. He was soon rehabilitated and sent to London for two years (1985–87) as India's high commissioner. On his return, he was appointed governor of Tamil Nadu (1988–90) and then of Maharashtra (1993–2002). The NDA (National Democratic Alliance) government led by Prime Minister Atal Bihari Vajpayee wanted to nominate him to the post of president of India in 2002. But the proposal fell through because of lack of support from the Congress. Following that, he was made a Rajya Sabha member (2002–2008) by the NDA government. Not only had he managed to get out of a sticky situation unscathed, he had also endeared himself to two prime ministers from two opposing parties, Indira Gandhi and later Atal Bihari Vajpayee.

I have had no direct access to or interaction with Alexander. Therefore, my assessment of his role in Punjab affairs is essentially based on the contents of his book and references to his role by other authors. In his memoirs, *Through the Corridors of Power: An Inside Story*, Alexander devoted one full chapter of ninety-two pages to the 'Akali Agitation'. In it he has mentioned that there were twenty-six rounds of talks with the Akalis between October 1981 and May 1984, to seek a solution through peaceful negotiations.[3] Surprisingly, he has not mentioned a single word about the most important round of these negotiations, the one mediated by Swaran Singh, which Alexander attended.[4] On the other hand, Alexander gives very minute details in his book of the Rajiv Gandhi-led talks, which followed within a fortnight of the sabotage of the Swaran Singh-led talks on the night of 3-4 November, 1982. In that context, the following paragraph from Alexander's book is rather interesting:

> As one who knew Indira Gandhi's thought process well and as one who participated in all the talks, I can assert on the basis of direct knowledge, that she sincerely believed till the last minute that a solution could be found through talks and, therefore, wanted to avoid use of force. There have been some highly mischievous reports that Indira Gandhi had initiated these talks and kept their momentum only to create the impression of seeking a settlement through negotiations but that she had always planned to crack down on the Akalis. Nothing could be farther from the truth.[5]

Alexander says Indira Gandhi 'sincerely believed till the last moment that a solution could be found through talks'. In fact, there was no need to stretch the negotiations till 'the last moment' in the first place as she could have settled the matter back in 1982 by sticking with her initial acceptance of the Swaran Singh formula. How credible can one consider Alexander's terming of these reports as 'mischievous', when he has himself completely omitted the most crucial round of mediated talks from his book?

In fact, the deliberate omission of reference to the Swaran Singh-mediated solution is not just limited to Alexander's book. A cover-up to remove its traces began as early as July 1984 with the Central government's white paper on Punjab, which was tabled in parliament within one month of Operation Blue Star. Noting the total absence of reference to the Swaran Singh-mediated talks in the paper, senior BJP leader, and later prime minister, Atal Bihari Vajpayee stated in parliament on 25 July 1984, 'there is no reference (in the white paper) to the efforts made by Sardar Swaran Singh. Has the Congress disowned even Sardar Swaran Singh? Did he make any efforts or did he not?'[6].

Alexander was one of the members of the three-man think-tank and, in his capacity as principal secretary to the PM, was in a position to influence the views of the other two by dropping subtle hints as to what his boss would appreciate. Also, all three members of the think-tank (Alexander, Cabinet Secretary C.R. Krishnaswamy Rao Sahib and Home Secretary Chaturvedi) were highly experienced officers who, as the saying goes in Urdu, 'could count the feathers of a flying sparrow'.

They knew very well the Indian bureaucratic ways of holding and prolonging fruitless discussions, best described by the dictum '*naksha,* meeting *aur salaam*' – which means prepare maps or collect a lot of relevant data, hold protracted discussions without conceding anything substantial while keeping the hope of another session alive. Unfamiliar as the think-tank was with Punjab affairs to begin with, it would not have been difficult for them to work out an amicable solution to the Punjab imbroglio, provided only that there was a suitable signal from the top.

Spymaster R.N. Kao

Rameshwar Nath Kao (IP 1940 United Provinces), a role model for the second category of bureaucrat, was recalled by Indira Gandhi from his retirement and appointed senior advisor in the cabinet secretariat in August 1981. Soon after his appointment, he established a three-man Policy and Research Group comprising Ambassador A.K. Damodaran (IFS, Retd) and two former R&AW officers, G.S. Mishra and S.K. Chaturvedi, mainly to help him in foreign policy-related matters, especially for China. Before his retirement, Mishra was one of the Department's leading experts on China and had served in Beijing, while Chaturvedi had been head of the R&AW's economic division.

While Kao and his personal staff functioned from both the ground floor of the cabinet secretary's office block in Rashtrapati Bhavan and from Bikaner House Annexe, the activities of the Policy and Research Group were confined to Bikaner House Annexe alone. Kao used the Rashtrapati Bhavan office for official meetings, but operational work and related meetings were conducted from Bikaner House Annexe.

In Alexander's words, Kao was a member of a three-man core group dealing with national security matters. The other two members were Alexander himself and Cabinet Secretary C.R. Krishnaswamy Rao Sahib. In addition, Kao was also involved in carrying out special operations directly assigned by Indira Gandhi. One such instance was his visit to Washington DC to remove the Reagan administration's misunderstanding about her policy on Afghanistan. This visit took place sometime before the PM's state visit to the US in July 1982, and for that purpose Kao had used the good offices of his old friend George H.W. Bush (director, CIA, 1976-77, vice president of the US, 1980–84, and later the forty-first US president, from January 1989 to January 1993).[7]

The second assignment related to a visit to Beijing, facilitated by Yugoslav intelligence, to test the waters of a possible visit to China by Indira Gandhi as well as the possibility of establishing R&AW's liaison relationship with the ministry of state security (MSS), China's intelligence, security and secret police agency responsible for counter-intelligence, foreign intelligence and political security. In fact, Kao was in Beijing on 31 October 1984 when he came to know of Indira Gandhi's assassination. His hosts provided him with a special aircraft to take him to Hong Kong so he could catch the Air-India flight to New Delhi the same afternoon.

The liaison relationship was established soon thereafter, but the PM's visit had to wait till 1988, when Rajiv Gandhi paid a visit to China. Incidentally, I was at that time joint secretary, looking after China analysis, and was asked to prepare notes in connection with that visit. Kao was also involved in some other foreign policy-related visits and a couple of secret operations related to internal matters. Here, however, we need to examine Kao's role in Op-2 only.

B. Raman and two other officers from the R&AW accompanied Kao to London and Zurich to meet 'Khalistani elements' and seek their cooperation in getting Bhindranwale and other extremist elements to vacate the Golden Temple complex. Raman's job was to discreetly record their conversations, transcribe them and give Kao the transcripts in order to brief Indira Gandhi on his return. It appears the visit took place in January–February 1984, by which time Bhindranwale had shifted to the Akal Takht (15 December 1983).

According to Raman, 'A Khalistani leader from the US, who met Kao at Zurich, offered to try to help if he was allowed to go into the Golden Temple and meet Bhindranwale. As proof of his good will, he claimed that the Khalistani elements in the US had planned to kill the R&AW officer in Washington DC, but he prevented them from doing so. I was told that Indira Gandhi was against accepting his proposal to send him inside the temple. She felt that if this person also stayed behind and joined Bhindranwale it could add to the problem of the Government of India.'[8]

Though Raman has not named him, it is obvious that the 'Khalistani leader' he refers to was the Washington DC-based Ganga Singh Dhillon, head of the Nankana Sahib Foundation.

Dhillon was earlier allowed, if not encouraged, to visit Chandigarh in mid-March 1981 to preside over a Sikh education conference, where he had moved a resolution for the creation of Khalistan. His visit suited the Congress party at that time. Now it did not. The time was not opportune to allow a US national of his background to meet Bhindranwale in the Golden Temple complex. He could have stayed back or been held hostage by Bhindranwale.

Also, the presence of a US national in the Akal Takht at the time of Operation Blue Star would have created a number of problems. The US Embassy in India would have taken every possible measure to get him out alive before Blue Star began. But Dhillon, by that time, would have noticed or come to know quite a few things that the Indian government would not have wanted him to know. Also, though the chances of Dhillon convincing Bhindranwale to leave the Akal Takht were remote, Indira Gandhi possibly did not want to risk Bhindranwale walking out of the temple complex alive. It could not be the 'final solution' to the Punjab problem.

Given his charter, Kao could not have returned from London without meeting Jagjit Singh Chauhan, head of the 'National Council of Khalistan'. Besides, Kao must have met a number of prominent Sikh leaders from the UK and other countries. Regarding Kao's meetings with 'Khalistani elements', I don't think any one of them was in a position to convince Bhindranwale to vacate the Golden Temple complex, which Kao might have soon realized, if he did not know it before he left Delhi.

Obviously, those meetings did not produce any results. But Kao's secret and mysterious meetings with them in a quiet place like Zurich or even London might have created an impression on the Sikhs whom he met that the prime minister, who had specially sent Kao to talk to them, was actually serious about finding a peaceful solution to the Punjab problem. It was the same impression that the repeated negotiations with Akali leaders were creating in India.

On the basis of what has been written earlier in this book, the contents of Raman's and Alexander's books, and my own personal experience of dealing with Kao, the following things emerge about Kao's role during that period:

Kao knew about the overall requirements of Op-2 and did whatever was possible within his means to help it along. Regarding my own very limited role in furthering the cause of Op-2, I undertook my first visit to the US and Canada in December 1981 upon Kao's instructions conveyed through Suntook, and on return reported the outcome of my visit to him. It was again upon his instruction that I met the PIO to the PM, Sharda Prasad, and handed over the note I had prepared for Kao's perusal, which was unfortunately used for doing just the opposite of what I had suggested. My two subsequent visits to the US and Canada in July 1982 and September 1983 were undertaken as per Kao's suggestion to Suntook and then to Gary Saxena.

It is, however, not clear when Kao came to know about the real nature of the 'final solution' to the Punjab problem. From some of his actions, it appears that he might have come to know of it within a year or so of his appointment as senior advisor as he had started exploring softer solutions for the Punjab problem soon thereafter. His efforts to get Gurudwara Chowk Mehta 'cased' by me, and the aborted SFF-led heliborne operation, are indicative of that.

Kao, however, remained involved with the Punjab decision-making process till the very end and participated in the three meetings with General Vaidya on 25 May, 27 May and 29 May 1984, where the decision to launch Operation Blue Star was taken (next chapter). P.C. Alexander has not mentioned anything about

Kao posing questions about the operation at any of the meetings. However, it is my professional judgement, that an experienced person like Kao would not sit quietly during such meetings without asking General Vaidya how General Sundarji's revised plan would help clear a well-fortified Akal Takht without any significant loss of life. Moreover, if DIG BSF, G.S. Pandher (ref. next chapter), could raise such doubts at the meeting called by Maj. Gen. Brar on 3 June, Kao was much better equipped to have asked similar questions of General Vaidya.

It may be relevant here to compare Kao's performance in the pre-March 1977 period as secretary, R&AW, with his post-retirement comeback as senior advisor in August 1981. During his previous tenure, the R&AW achieved major successes within a few years of its creation in September 1968. These included two landmark operations – the liberation of Bangladesh and Sikkim's merger with India – which changed the maps of south Asia and India, respectively. Those achievements built his reputation in India and abroad as a master spy who commanded respect. During that period he had some good friends in P.N. Haksar, principal secretary to the PM, and P.N. Dhar, a close advisor to the PM. Before the implementation of the Emergency, Indira Gandhi had experienced cabinet colleagues capable of giving her independent advice. In her second tenure, the cabinet comprised only 'yes men' who dared not disagree with her, and this affected her capacity to take well-considered and sound decisions.

In the pre-Emergency period, Sanjay Gandhi's emergence as a new power centre did not have an impact on the functioning of the R&AW as he was not interested in its activities. But in the post-Emergency period, Indira Gandhi's decision-making, especially when it came to the Punjab situation, was influenced by the 1 Akbar Road group. In fact, the decision to win the next parliamentary elections due before January 1985 on the Khalistan issue had been taken by Sanjay and his close advisors before Kao had rejoined work. Sanjay Gandhi was tragically killed in a plane crash on 23 June 1980.

As senior advisor, Kao's role was largely shaped by the insecurity of a prime minister lacking the saner advice of her old senior cabinet ministers and independent-minded principal secretaries. That led her to depend heavily for advice on Rajiv Gandhi, who had entered politics following Sanjay's death, and his close advisors. Kao had to function within the parameters defined by the changed circumstances. Clearly, Kao, who had seen better days, in his own way did try his best to change the course of events, especially those related to Punjab, but did not succeed.

While he continued to receive unstinted support from the R&AW due to his past connection with it and the personal regard that Suntook, Gary Saxena and several of the officers had for him, getting support from the Intelligence Bureau was difficult. In 1968, Kao had walked out of the IB with some others to create a new department, which some senior officers of the IB did not like. Also, the IB was working directly under the charge of the home minster while Kao was a part of the cabinet secretariat. Therefore, all sensitive information was passed on by the IB to the PM, either directly by its director or though the home minister, keeping Kao out of the loop. Under the given circumstances, he might have faced coordination problems with the IB.

During his earlier tenure, (Congress) party work and government work, as far as possible, were kept separate. But during Kao's second phase at work, the actual decision-making process on Punjab and Sikh affairs had shifted from the PMO in South Block and the MHA in North Block to 1 Akbar Road.

As senior advisor, Kao was also responsible for Indira Gandhi's safety. Kao had set up a coordination committee for her security comprising senior representatives of security departments and intelligence agencies. It met daily under his chairmanship and discussed intelligence inputs related to her security and her daily programme. Rajiv Gandhi, who did not hold any position in the government at the time, took close interest in the actions taken to strengthen the PM's physical security. According to B. Raman,

> As per his desire, two of his closest personal advisors used to attend these meetings in order to give their suggestions and keep him informed of the discussions and the action taken. Since they too did not hold any position in the Government, they were not entitled to attend these top-secret meetings, in which classified information was discussed. Despite this, in order to satisfy him that everything that was required to be done for her physical security was being done, Kao let them attend even though they did not have the required security clearance, but the minutes of these meetings did not show their presence.[9]

Incidentally, Rajiv Gandhi and 'two of his close associates' also held a number of meetings with Akali Dal leaders in a New Delhi guesthouse of the R&AW. Raman 'was given the task of making arrangements for these meetings, recording the discussions, transcribing them and putting up the transcripts to Kao or briefing Indira Gandhi.'[10]

Regarding the removal and redeployment of Sikh security staff at Indira Gandhi's residence, B. Raman writes, 'The withdrawal of the Sikh officers from close-proximity duties came to the notice of Indira Gandhi. Some say she noticed it herself. Others say one of her close associates noticed it, ascertained from the Delhi Police that this was done on the orders of Kao and brought this to her attention. She expressed her misgivings over the wisdom of the decision. Following this, the withdrawn Sikh police officers were posted back to her residence. However, Kao instructed that no Sikh police officer should normally be posted alone in her close proximity and that, whenever a Sikh police officer was posted in her close proximity, he should be accompanied by a non-Sikh officer.'[11] It was the violation of these instructions of Kao's that created the conditions for her assassination.

It took Sweden thirty-four years, 10,000 interviews and 134 confessions to bring a closure to the case of the murder of their popular prime minister Olof Palme in February 1989. On 10 June 2020 it was finally determined that the real killer was the self-professed eye witness, Stig Engstrom. Though the killer could not be punished for his crime as he had died in 2000, the closure was needed to start the healing process of a nation troubled by its inability to find and punish the real culprit.[12] In that context though the real killers of Indira Gandhi got the punishment that they deserved, it is still not known as to who advised Indira Gandhi on the most crucial issue of recalling those armed Sikh guards who were removed from duty at PM's residence after Operation Blue Star on Kao's advice. Also why was Satwant Singh allowed to join Beant Singh against Kao's specific instructions of not letting the two-armed Sikh guards come together and that too within the inner circle?

One of the three notes written by Kao, which is at the Nehru Memorial Museum and Library (NMML) in New Delhi (and is closed for public view till 2027, i.e., till twenty-five years after his death), is on the assassination of Indira Gandhi. It would be interesting to see whether this note contains only details of what he did to protect her life or whether it has some other information too. To bring a closure to the whole issue and in the national interest, it would be advisable to open Kao's note.

In view of all these developments, I do wish that Kao had not come out of retirement. In that context I agree with B. Raman, who says, 'The almost three-year (1981 to 1984) post-retirement tenure of Kao as the Senior Advisor to Indira Gandhi in the Cabinet Secretariat did not have the brilliant dazzle of his tenure as the founder and head of the R&AW between 1968 and 1977.'[13]

The hard-working B. Raman

B. (Bahukutumbi) Raman (IPS 1961 Madhya Pradesh) represented the third category of officers mentioned at the beginning of this chapter. Raman was one of the most hard-working officers to have been employed at the R&AW. A bachelor, he was married to his work and had no other hobby. For him, his home was an extension of his office. He could rattle off facts and figures on the subjects he dealt with at will. He had all the qualities that a R&AW chief needed in his staff officer, and this endeared him to Kao also. But in his handling of Sikh affairs up to the period ending November 1984 and thereafter, he suffered the following handicaps:

First, as Sikh extremism was totally a new development for the R&AW till the end of 1980, there were no past records of such activities in the Department to consult or refer to. Some files on the activities (from within Pakistan and the UK and US) of the Pakistan-sponsored Jagjit Singh Chauhan's organization and the related activities of people like Ganga Singh Dhillon of Nankana Sahib Foundation in Washington DC might have been transferred from the R&AW's Pakistan division to the newly created division under Raman. It was natural that the R&AW officers already posted in areas (before the seven new stations started functioning one by one by early 1982) where there was a comparatively large presence of Sikhs, after being asked to watch out for pro-Khalistan or Sikh extremist activities, might have started sending their reports on the subject. But those would have been sketchy to begin with. So, Raman's information bank was initially mainly based on published information and the sketchy reports from existing stations based on the new charter of requirements.

Second, Raman did not go deep into the recent or early history of the Sikhs to really appreciate why the concept of Khalistan started attracting attention of some only after the Congress returned to power in January 1980. This lack of proper understanding of the subject soon started reflecting in the notes he produced on the basis of open information and inputs from the R&AW stations abroad, some of which might have actually resulted from 1 Akbar Road group-inspired moves. However, those reports were appreciated even at the foreign minister's level.[14] Though none of the senior-level consumers of the reports, including cabinet ministers, had any power to change the course of events predetermined by the 1 Akbar Road group, Raman's reports might have led them to think that events in Punjab required the strongest possible action to save India's unity, thereby providing some justification in their minds about the severity of action taken through Operation Blue Star.

Third, the principal information officer to the prime minster is usually not a recipient of the R&AW reports, for obvious reasons. But from the way Kao sent me to hand over my report to the PIO to the PM, H.Y. Sharda Prasad, in January 1982, it appeared that Kao and Sharada Prasad were working in tandem. It is also obvious that Sharada Prasad used my report as a barometer to measure the impact of his media management on furthering the cause of Op-2. That report might also have been used to assess what more needed to be done. It created a vicious circle, with Raman feeding information to Sharda Prasad, Sharda Prasad feeding that information to his high-level contacts in the Indian press, which information in turn appeared in some leading newspapers in the form of beefed-up lead articles on editorial pages written by influential journalists, and finally that information in the form of press clippings landing on Raman's table to confirm what he originally thought to be reliable and worth sharing with the consumers of information.

Fourth, while transcribing secretly recorded conversations of meetings of Akali leaders with senior Congress leaders, and of 'Khalistani elements' and influential Sikhs with Kao in London, Zurich and elsewhere, Raman was influenced by the views of Rajiv Gandhi and his friends in the first instance and by Kao's later, for reasons explained earlier. It is extremely difficult for most civil servants to not be influenced by the views of important people around them. Besides, in such an environment there is little scope for civil servants to hold or express independent views of their own. They usually become part of the system.

Last but not the least, perhaps the most significant shortcoming of Raman's reports and notes on Khalistan/Sikh extremist affairs was that he was both the operational and analysis head of the newly created division to cover Sikh extremism or Khalistan-related activities in India and abroad, specially the latter. On the one hand he was producing and collecting raw and unprocessed intelligence, and on the other, as recipient of that same information, he was analysing and assessing its value for dissemination to important consumers. This is against the very basic tenets of intelligence. An operational officer is highly protective of information or intelligence produced by him or his juniors and views it in a subjective manner. Being so, he or she cannot be absolutely dispassionate and strictly objective in assessing its real worth. Under normal circumstances, the information has to pass the analytical test of accessibility, reliability and, finally, acceptability, under the vigilant eyes of an independent, knowledgeable and experienced analysis desk officer before it is processed and disseminated in a suitable manner to consumers.

On instructions from both Suntook and Gary Saxena, whenever Raman was out of station his assistant director would show me the drafts of reports meant for consumers outside the Department. I used to make changes in some of those drafts as they had a perceptible bias and showed a lack of proper understanding of the subject in its historical perspective. This process continued till early 1984, even though I had moved over to an analysis division in November 1983.

To be fair to Raman, he was not a careerist who would ingratiate himself with the powers-that-be by suitably tweaking his reports. In fact, he was just the opposite. As additional secretary, because of his outstanding service record, in the proceedings of the departmental promotion committee (DPC), he had superseded some officers who were a couple of years senior to him for promotion to the next rank. He should have been promoted to the rank of special secretary, but he preferred not to represent his case and finally retired as additional secretary, as age was not in his favour for his next promotion in the normal course.

11

Operation Blue Star

OPERATION BHINDRANWALE-KHALISTAN-2 (Op-2) had a predetermined goal, a fixed time frame and an operational plan. These three aspects have been explained in previous chapters. By 1984, the time had come to roll out the 'final solution'. The essential ingredients for justifying strong action had converged – or, were made to converge – by the end of May that year. A majority of the Indian population, an efficiently managed Indian press, observant foreign media and governments (through their missions in India) – everyone appeared to have been sufficiently convinced about the 'sincerity' of Indira Gandhi's prolonged efforts to find a negotiated settlement to the Punjab problem.

The carefully controlled chaos in Punjab could not be allowed to drift any further without the prime minister losing the confidence, and votes, of the majority community. According to government figures, Bhindranwale-inspired extremists had already killed 165 Hindus and Nirankaris in the twenty-two months since the launch of the Dharam Yudh Morcha in August 1982. In addition, thirty-nine Sikhs had been killed for opposing Bhindranwale. The total number of deaths in violent incidents, including the so-called police 'encounters', riots, and the accident at the railway level crossing in which thirty-four supporters of the morcha were killed, stood at 410, while the injured numbered 1,180.[1] The Congress had already lost a state-level by-election in Uttar Pradesh, a stronghold of the party.

Senior Akali Dal leaders, troubled by the PM's dilatory tactics, were feeling helpless and suffocated within the Golden Temple complex because of Bhindranwale's presence and his extremist activities. Clandestine smuggling of arms and ammunition and fortification of the Akal Takht by Maj. Gen. Shahbeg Singh had started by March 1984, and were being conveniently overlooked by the security apparatus concerned.

The next general elections were due by January 1985, and the Congress needed adequate time to consolidate the gains arising out of the planned 'final solution'. Postponing it further would now be counterproductive. It was, therefore, time for Indira Gandhi to act decisively and live up to her by now somewhat dented image of a strong leader capable of taking the strongest possible action.

The planning stage

The justification for such an action was provided by Harchand Singh Longowal on 23 May 1984, when he announced that starting 3 June, no food grains would be allowed to move out of Punjab, and that Sikhs would not pay taxes and dues. With the Punjab police and paramilitary forces incapable of clearing the by-now heavily armed Akal Takht complex, army's involvement became inevitable. Consequently, the PM called Chief of the Army Staff General A.S. Vaidya on 25 May to discuss the situation. She told him to keep the army ready to help the civilian authorities in Punjab, to which General Vaidya replied that anticipating such an eventuality, he had already ordered troop movement in Punjab.

The initial plan, as explained by General Vaidya, was confined to siege-and-flushing-out operations in the identified gurudwaras, including the Golden Temple, by using adequate force to prevent movement of men, food stocks and weapons into these gurudwaras and force the extremists to surrender. Vaidya assured her that there would be 'maximum show of force and minimum use of that'. He also assured her that during the operation no damage would be caused to the targeted gurudwara buildings, especially to the Golden Temple complex.[2]

According to Alexander, Indira Gandhi clearly defined the main objectives of the army operation by saying that 'the top priorities of the army would be to effectively curb terrorism and violence, provide security to the people and restore normalcy in Punjab. The tasks involved flushing out the terrorists from their hideouts in certain gurudwaras, their arrest and the seizure of their weapons. Her expectation was that the very presence of the army and the demonstration of its strength through flag marches would, by themselves, act as deterrents. Consequently, she felt that there would not be any need for use of excess force by the army.'[3]

Simultaneously, she also called moderate Akali Dal leaders to Delhi for secret talks on 26 May with some of her cabinet colleagues. Expectedly, these talks also met with their predetermined fate (see Chapter 4). After the failed 26 May talks with Akali leaders, a meeting was held at the cabinet secretariat on the morning of 27 May, which was attended by Cabinet Secretary Krishnaswamy Rao Sahib, Senior Advisor R.N. Kao, Principal Secretary to the PM P.C. Alexander and General Vaidya. General Vaidya's 25 May plan was discussed in detail and he was given the go-ahead to implement it.

However, on General Vaidya's request, an urgent meeting was held at the prime minister's South Block office on 29 May, where both R.N. Kao and P.C. Alexander were present. Vaidya mentioned that he had discussed the 25 May plan with Lt Gen. K. Sundarji, GOC-in-C, western command, who was of the view that the plan could work only for smaller gurudwaras and not for the Golden Temple, as a prolonged siege of the Golden Temple could lead to a mass upsurge of Sikhs around the state, who could then march towards the Golden Temple.

Surprised at this sudden change in the plan, Indira Gandhi enquired about the implications of a stiff resistance by the terrorists holed up in the complex and their taking refuge in the inner sanctum of Harmandir Sahib. She also asked for a comparative analysis of the original plan with the alternative in terms of the number of casualties and the impact of the operations on serving Sikh jawans (soldiers) in the Indian army.

Fully supportive of Lt Gen. Sundarji's suggestion for revising the original plan, General Vaidya said no time should be lost and the army needed to make a quick entry into the Golden Temple and take the terrorists by surprise. According to him, the operation would be carried out with 'such swiftness and surprise that it would not result in any damage to the temple buildings.' The new plan 'would be executed so quickly that everything would be over by the time people came to realize what was happening.' He also mentioned that the extremists within the temple complex would be given enough time to surrender before army action was initiated. He ruled out any adverse reactions among Sikh jawans serving in the army. According to Alexander, Vaidya's explanation was so convincing that the PM felt the revised plan was the only option left to deal with the situation, and she gave her consent for its implementation as she respected the professional judgement of the generals.[4]

Keeping in mind the deliberations of the two meetings of 25 May and 29 May with General Vaidya, it is crucial to note that just a couple of months earlier, when the SFF-led heliborne operation targeted only at the langar hall rooftop, was being discussed with Nagrani in the presence of Kao, Indira Gandhi had asked pointed questions about the possible casualties involved and had rejected that operation outright, despite relatively modest estimates. Operation Blue Star was a much bigger operation and the main target, the Akal Takht, was heavily fortified with about a hundred fully trained and equipped Sikh extremists. Yet, she approved the operation on the basis of superficial and unchallenged assurances.

A few days before Operation Blue Star was launched, Sardar Swaran Singh was travelling in his personal car from Jalandhar to New Delhi. On the outskirts of Jalandhar he saw a large contingent of army troops on the Grand Trunk Road heading northwards. It was possibly the movement of troops from the Meerut-based 9th Division, which was to reach Amritsar by 30 May. The morning after he reached Delhi, he called Indira Gandhi's special assistant, R.K. Dhawan, and requested an urgent meeting with her, which was fixed for the same afternoon. Drawing her attention to the troop movement, he told the prime minister he was apprehensive that the army was possibly being deployed to clear the Golden Temple of extremists, including Bhindranwale. His advice to her was that she should not under any circumstances let the army enter the Golden Temple, as it could have serious repercussions for Punjab and the country as a whole.

Expressing surprise, she said, 'Sardar Sahib, how can you imagine that I would commit such a mistake?' She then became pensive, and said she knew that sooner or later she would be killed by Sikh militants. She was not worried about that but did not know what would happen to her children after her death. These were the same words she had spoken during her meeting at 1 Akbar Road in April 1984 with Kao and Nagrani, when she overruled the SFF commando operation. Perhaps it was her way of expressing her helplessness.

Incidentally, Swaran Singh met Indira Gandhi on or after 29 May, by when she had already given her approval to the revised plan as suggested by Lt Gen. Sundarji. However, Swaran Singh returned fully reassured, but remained so only till he witnessed the ferocity of the action taken, in the form of Operation Blue Star.

On 30 May, Prime Minister Indira Gandhi met President Zail Singh, who, by virtue of his position as Commander-in-Chief of the Indian Armed Forces, should have been taken into confidence, if not consulted, about the planned army operation at the Golden Temple. She spent over an hour discussing with him the new formula for reaching an agreement with the Akalis.[5] This option had already been closed on 29 May when the army was given the go-ahead to implement the revised plan for the operation. It meant that the person who had originally planned operation Bhindranwale-Khalistan (Op-1 and Op-2) for furthering the prospects of the Congress could no longer be trusted with a decision to use the army to flush out Bhindranwale and other extremists from the Golden Temple complex. Maybe she did not want to hear a 'no' from the Commander-in-Chief of the Indian Armed Forces for an army operation that she had already approved.

The Harmandir Sahib

The foundation stone of Harmandir Sahib, also known as Darbar Sahib, was laid in AD 1588, as per a personal request from the fifth Sikh Guru, Arjan Dev (AD 1563–1604), by a pious Muslim saint of his time, Mian Mir Mohammad of Lahore. The construction was completed in 1601. Meanwhile, the Adi Granth was compiled under Guru Arjan's supervision. On its compilation, the Granth Sahib was installed for the first time in Harmandir Sahib in 1604.

It was due to his insistence on retaining one particular hymn in the Granth Sahib and, subsequently, due to his refusal to embrace Islam that Guru Arjan was martyred at Lahore in 1604, under orders from the Mughal emperor Jehangir. Incidentally, Operation Blue Star was launched on the day Sikh pilgrims had gathered in the Golden Temple complex that year to mark the anniversary of Guru Arjan's martyrdom.

In the eighteenth century, Harmandir Sahib was desecrated a number of times. But the three better remembered cases of desecration are those of 1737, 1757 and 1762. In 1737, the Mughal governor of Lahore ordered the arrest and execution of Bhai Mani Singh, the custodian of Harmandir. Musa Khan (Massa) Ranghar, who was appointed administrator of Amritsar, started using Harmandir as a place of entertainment by getting dancing girls to perform there. In August 1740, two Sikhs entered Harmandir under the guise of tax collectors and beheaded 'Massa' Ranghar.

In April 1757, Ahmad Shah Abdali (Durrani) raided north India for the fourth time. While he was on his way back to Kabul from Delhi taking with him young Hindu men and women as captives, a group of Sikhs led by seventy-five-year-old Baba Deep Singh attacked Abdali's convoy near Kurukshetra and freed a large number of prisoners, also relieving Abdali's convoy of some of the valuables it was carrying. In retaliation, Harmandir's sacred sarovar (pool) was filled with filth and the entrails of slaughtered animals, including cows. After Abdali's return to Afghanistan, Baba Deep Singh marched towards Harmandir Sahib to liberate it and was joined by thousands of Sikhs along the way. On 13 November 1757, he died fighting in an attempt to liberate Harmandir Sahib.

In 1762, Ahmad Shah Abdali returned and blew up Harmandir Sahib with gunpowder and again filled its sacred sarovar with filth and the entrails of slaughtered cows before returning to Afghanistan. In 1764, Baba Jassa Singh Ahluwalia defeated the local Afghan contingent in the battle of Sirhind, collected donations and rebuilt Harmandir Sahib. It came to be known as swaran mandir (Golden Temple) after some of its portions were plated with gold in AD 1830, from donations made by Maharaja Ranjit Singh and his family members.

'Maybe tonight'

For several months, arms and ammunition had been reaching the Golden Temple complex, hidden in trucks carrying provisions for langar. The police seldom checked these trucks, reportedly under instructions from the authorities concerned. No follow-up action was taken when one such truck was intercepted and found carrying Sten guns and ammunition. Young Sikh militants were being imparted weapons training inside the temple complex by ex-service men under the overall supervision of Shahbeg Singh.

Leaving the main Harmandir Sahib untouched, Shahbeg had started fortifying the vantage points of all buildings and structures within the Golden Temple complex and the surrounding private houses. Special attention was paid to the Akal Takht because of the presence of Bhindranwale and his armed men there. Every strategically significant building in the temple complex was fortified in a similar manner. Seventeen private houses surrounding the temple complex were in constant touch with Shahbeg Singh by means of wireless communication.

For Operation Blue Star, troops from the Meerut-based 9th Division were ordered to reach Amritsar by 30 May. It was commanded by Maj. Gen. Kuldip Singh Brar, who was a clean-shaven Sikh from the same Jat Sikh gotra (sub-caste) of 'Brar' as Bhindranwale. Originally from Faridkot, the Brars are in turn a sub-clan of the Sidhus.

After attending an important meeting in the afternoon of 2 June 1984, Kao returned to his office slightly late and looking despondent. One of his close confidantes (name withheld on request) who was waiting for him in his office, asked him the reason behind this demeanour. Kao significantly remarked that for the last couple of years he had been trying his best to stop things coming to such a pass but could not succeed. When asked to elaborate his cryptic remarks, Kao told that confidante he would be well advised to listen to that night's AIR news broadcast, to understand what he had just told him.

The same night at 9.15 p.m., Indira Gandhi addressed the nation on the state-owned television and radio channels. She recounted details of the efforts made by her government to reach a peaceful settlement with the Akali leaders. Once again, she appealed to them not to go ahead with their agitation, which was supposed to begin on 3 June, and instead accept the peaceful settlement the government had offered. 'Let us join hands together and heal the wounds ... don't shed blood, shed hatred,' she appealed to all Punjabis.

Later that night the government announced on AIR that the army had been called to support the civilian authorities in Punjab and that Lt Gen. Ranjit Singh Dayal, chief of staff, Western

Command, would hold the key post of advisor (security) to the governor of Punjab. The police and paramilitary forces would work under the overall command of the army. Also, Lt Gen. Dayal, assisted by Maj. Gen. K.S. Brar, was put in overall charge of the Golden Temple operation, code-named 'Blue Star'.[6,7]

Simultaneously, by the evening of 2 June, the army sealed the international border with Pakistan from J&K to Sri Ganganagar in Rajasthan. At least seven divisions of the army were deployed in various villages of Punjab. By evening the media was gagged. Rail, road and air services in Punjab were suspended and a three-day curfew imposed in the whole of Punjab.

On 2 June, Mark Tully met Bhindranwale for the last time. Tully found him not his usual relaxed self, but somewhat tense. Always willing to give interviews to foreign correspondents, Bhindranwale said, 'You will have to hurry up. I have got more important things to do.'

The next day, when the *Times of India* reporter Subhash Kirpekar met Bhindranwale and drew his attention to the deployment of the army, Bhindranwale said the army would also behave the way the CRPF and BSF had been behaving in the past. When his attention was drawn towards the heavier deployment of the better equipped army, Bhindranwale said, 'Sheep always outnumber lions. But one lion can take care of a thousand sheep ... He is not a Sikh who fears death and he who fears death is not a Sikh.' When Kirpekar asked Gen. Shahbeg Singh when he expected the army action to start, he replied, 'Maybe tonight'.[8]

The ignored SOP

Lt Gen. S.K. Sinha was GOC-in-C, Western Command, before Lt Gen. Sundarji took over. Judging from the deteriorating situation in Punjab, Lt Gen. Sinha had sensed that one day in the not-so-distant future the army might be called to flush out Sikh militants from gurudwaras, especially the Golden Temple complex. To deal with such an eventuality, he had devised a Standard Operating Procedure (SOP), which included the following steps:

i. The whole operation has to be carried out in as transparent a manner as possible in the presence of some respectable local Sikh witnesses.
ii. There should be live TV coverage.
iii. The Golden Temple complex should be duly cordoned off to prevent entry or exit of unauthorized persons till the operation was over.
iv. If the siege persisted, water and power supply should be cut off, followed by a public announcement to encourage voluntary surrender.
v. Keeping in view the sensitivity of about 80,000 Sikh soldiers, both officers and men, they should be taken into confidence and sensitized about the reasons behind the operation and the precautions being taken in carrying it out.
vi. A temporary gurudwara must be established outside the Golden Temple complex with continuous recitation of the holy scriptures.
vii. Officers and jawans involved in the operation should remove their shoes, cover their heads and offer prayers at the temporary gurudwara before entering the Golden Temple complex.
viii. The operation should be carried out under the overall command of a senior Sikh army officer with a mix of Hindu and Sikh troops.[9]

Lt Gen. Sundarji did not follow this SOP, for reasons given at the end of this chapter.

Lt Gen. Sinha was transferred to army headquarters as vice chief of the army staff (VCOAS) towards the end of 1982. Being the senior-most lieutenant general in the Indian Army, he was expected to take over as chief of the army staff from General K.V. Krishna Rao upon the latter's retirement in July 1983. However, he was superseded by General A.S. Vaidya (six months junior to him) when the latter was appointed COAS on 31 July 1983. Lt Gen. Sinha sought voluntary retirement, and during the NDA government served as India's ambassador to Nepal, and as governor of Assam and Jammu and Kashmir.

During my meeting with the DGS, R.T. Nagrani (Chapter 8), he had told me that the services of SFF commandos were requisitioned at short notice for Operation Blue Star. To help prepare the commandos for their assignment, he had asked the help of the same civilian employee of SFF who had performed the 'casing' of the Golden Temple complex for the aborted SFF-led heliborne operation. This time, this employee stayed in the temple complex for a couple of days and prepared a detailed sketch of it with special reference to the Akal Takht, noting the most suitable points from where SFF commandos could enter with the least possible casualties. For the Akal Takht, he was asked to show the exact number and placement of gun positions, and the floor plan, including the approach route to Bhindranwale's living quarters. These were handed over to Maj. Gen. Brar by the commanding officer of SFF before Operation Blue Star was launched.

Nagrani also told me that the commanding officer of the SFF unit had specifically advised Maj. Gen. Brar that in view of the heavily armed and guarded approach to the Akal Takht, an attack from the front would not be wise. Therefore, it would be better to blast some portion of the rear of the Akal Takht touching the narrow lane behind the temple complex and create a small hole to let the commandos enter the living quarters of Bhindranwale and other areas of the Akal Takht. It was even possible to grab Bhindranwale and his men alive with the careful use of some stun/flash grenades, which disorient the targeted persons for some time. In addition to a high degree of training in the use of sophisticated techniques and weapons, stealth and surprise are the essential components of any commando operation.

This plan was, however, ruled out by the army top brass, on the grounds that no damage to the Akal Takht was acceptable. This can be contrasted with the actual damage that was done to the Akal Takht. Rather than let the SFF and para-commandos enter the Akal Takht building by creating a man-sized opening, a type of operation for which they are actually trained, Brar eventually made them sitting ducks in the open courtyard, in full view of Shahbeg Singh, who had planned machine gun positions to defend the Akal Takht.

On 3 June, morning curfew was relaxed in Amritsar for a couple of hours to allow pilgrims to enter the Golden Temple to celebrate the martyrdom day of Guru Arjan Dev. Taking advantage of this relaxation, about 200 Sikh extremists escaped from the Golden Temple. They were seen carrying wads of currency notes, reportedly given to them by Bhindranwale.

Dissent in the war room

Maj. Gen. K.S. Brar called a meeting of civil and military officers on 3 June at 7 p.m. to brief them about Operation Blue Star. Also present at the meeting were some senior Punjab police officers, including SP CID Punjab Pandit Harjit Singh, Deputy Commissioner of Amritsar Rameshinder Singh, DIG BSF (Amritsar) G.S. Pandher, DIG CRPF N.K. Tiwari, and Assistant Director IB (Amritsar) G.S. Aulakh. Brar told them that the Akal

Takht complex had been taken over by criminals and the Indian army would retrieve the shrine from them through a surgical operation in no time.

Reacting to this, Pandher said that the persons holed up in the Akal Takht complex were no ordinary criminals but about one hundred fully armed and trained Jat Sikhs, for whom there could be no bigger honour than to die protecting the Akal Takht complex. None of them, including Bhindranwale, would surrender. A better alternative would be to cut off water and electricity supply to the complex and starve the inmates for eight to ten days to weaken their will to fight, and then attack, if necessary. In the meanwhile, it could be ensured that innocent pilgrims trapped in the Golden Temple complex were induced to come out. In that case, the army could neutralize the militants with not more than twenty to thirty casualties from its ranks.

Maj. Gen. Brar, who didn't like Pandher's suggestion, said that he was also a Jat Sikh and knew the Jat Sikh psychology well. In response, Pandher said, 'Sir, don't mind me saying, but you don't look like a Jat Sikh. A Jat Sikh must have a beard on his face and turban over his head. Also, he should be born and brought up in a village, like me. In view of that I know their psychology much better. You can at best be considered a modified Jat Sikh.' A furious Brar insisted on carrying out the surgical operation as planned. Pandher told Brar that in that case he would like to get his orders in writing as to what was expected of him and his force, as he apprehended a judicial enquiry headed by a serving or retired Supreme Court judge later.

In that context, Pandher referred to the Hunter Commission appointed in October 1919 to inquire into the various aspects of the infamous Jallianwala Bagh (located next door to the Golden Temple) massacre of 13 April 1919. At that point, Maj. Gen. Brar lost his temper and thumped the table a few times, accusing Pandher of open mutiny, and adding that for a soldier, 'theirs not to reason why, theirs but to do and die'. Pandher responded with, 'Sir, this must be true for the army but police officers are trained to consider all available softer options before taking such a drastic action.'

After the meeting, Pandher sent a report to the BSF headquarters in New Delhi, giving his views on Maj. Gen. Brar's planned surgical operation as well as his own suggestions. Brar received a copy of that report from Delhi early in the morning of 4 June, and he held a second meeting of the same officers at 10 a.m. that day. He asked Pandher why he had sent a report to his headquarters, to which Pandher replied that it was his duty to keep his bosses fully informed of the ground situation and he would continue to do so in future too.

Not liking that answer, Brar had Pandher removed from the charge of DIG BSF, Amritsar, made him proceed on thirty days' leave and had him dropped to his village in Ludhiana district under police escort. Brar also recommended Pandher's summary dismissal from service under Article 311 of the Indian Constitution. The case reached the PMO. Someone pointed out that such an action could lead Pandher to join the Akali Dal, and he wouldn't be a pliant member either.

The state CID and CBI were asked to collect evidence in order to lodge a corruption case against him. His house at his village and his government flat in New Delhi were searched and his entire service record from the day he joined the Indian Police Service was screened. As nothing incriminating was found against him, he was repatriated to his cadre, Manipur, in early 1985. In due course he became director general of police, Manipur, and finally retired honourably as DG, Bureau of Police Research and

Development (BPRD) on 30 April 1998 with the additional charge of NSG.

Pandher laments that despite promises made in the Akali Dal's election manifesto during the 1997 state elections, of appointing a commission to go into the truth behind Operation Blue Star, no such action was taken by them even though the Akali Dal was in power in Punjab from 1997 to 2002 and then again from 2007 to 2017.[10]

The operation begins

On the night of 3 June, the army surrounded thirty-seven gurudwaras in Punjab to flush out suspected Sikh militants hiding there. Other than at Gurudwara Dukh Niwaran in Patiala, the army was met with hardly any resistance. As was the case with the Golden Temple, the Patiala operation too was commanded by a clean-shaven Sikh, Maj. Gen. Gurdial Singh. According to the army's official version, twenty persons were killed in that operation, but doctors at the Government Rajendra Hospital, Patiala, were reportedly of the view that at least fifty-six had died.

By the night of 4 June, practically all gurudwaras outside Amritsar were cleared of militants, and the army had arrested most of them and confiscated their weapons. However, the army was disappointed by the small number of militants they had captured or killed in those gurudwaras. Either there was not a large number of militants in the first place or they had already escaped.[11]

On 4 June, announcements were made over loudspeakers asking pilgrims inside the Golden Temple to leave the premises and the extremists to surrender with their weapons. But in the din and confusion that prevailed in the hostel complex of the temple, these announcements were not clearly audible. Only 129 persons came out of the temple area in the first lot. 'With no militant willing to surrender, army found itself suddenly faced with a situation that it had not anticipated and for which, therefore, it had not been prepared.'[12]

Thereafter, the army began bombarding the Ramgarhia Bunga, the overhead water tank and other positions. After destroying the outer defences, the army moved tanks and APCs (armoured personnel carriers) on to the road separating the main temple complex and the Guru Ram Das Sarai, Teja Singh Samundri Hall and Guru Nanak Niwas. Longowal and SGPC chairman G.S. Tohra were still in the SGPC office area of Teja Singh Samundri Hall, but Badal had left for his village. In view of his known proximity to Bhindranwale, Tohra felt he might be able to convince him to surrender. Therefore, soon after the firing stopped on the morning of 4 June, Tohra went to the Akal Takht (obviously, with the knowledge and approval of the authorities concerned) to meet Bhindranwale.

His advice was spurned by Bhindranwale, who accused Tohra of being Indira Gandhi's agent. Tohra and the authorities concerned should have known that by then Bhindranwale had talked himself into a position from where abject surrender before the army was unthinkable. He could not have lived with that humiliation for the rest of his life. He would rather die fighting and become a part of Sikh folklore, as a martyr who gave his life to defend the Harmandir Sahib complex.

The same night (June 4), foreign and Indian journalists working for foreign media were made to leave Punjab. However, Brahma Chellaney, a young Indian reporter working for Associated Press (AP), managed to stay on as he had arrived in Amritsar that very day and his name did not figure in the police list of journalists present in Amritsar.[13]

The main army action at the Golden Temple commenced on 5 June 1984. In his address to his troops before they were ordered to enter the Golden Temple, Maj. Gen. Brar identified Bhindranwale as 'the enemy' who had taken control of the Golden Temple complex, which now had to be wrested out of his control. They were also told that while doing so they must not fire either at the Harmandir Sahib or the Akal Takht without direct orders. The operation was launched at around 10 p.m. simultaneously from two sides, and the fighting that ensued continued till 7.30 a.m. the next day.

In a separate operation the same evening, the BSF and CRPF attacked militants hiding in Hotel Temple View and Brahm Boota Akhara, respectively, on the south-west fringes of the temple complex. By 10 p.m. both these buildings were under the forces' control.

One of the tasks assigned to Lt Gen. Sundarji by the government was to 'prevent internecine fighting' between the two major groups – Bhindranwale's group living in the Akal Takht and the moderate group of Akali Dal leaders, headed by Harchand Singh Longowal, living in Teja Singh Samundri Hall and the adjacent hostel complexes.[14] It was decided to segregate the two areas and clear the hostel-cum-SGPC office complex, comprising Guru Ram Das Sarai, Teja Singh Samundri Hall and Guru Nanak Niwas, of their inmates simultaneously with the clearance of buildings in the temple complex, including the Akal Takht. Most of the pilgrims and supporters of the Akali morcha and Akali Dal leaders had taken refuge in the hostel complex, where water and electricity connections had been cut. To allow the troops to enter the hostel complex, its strong southern gate had to be broken with the help of tanks.

The army entered Teja Singh Samundri Hall at about 1 a.m. on 6 June. Both Longowal and Gurcharan Singh Tohra, along with some other functionaries of the SGPC, were asked to stay put in the office room. One of the persons who surrendered was Harminder Singh Sandhu, general secretary of the All India Sikh Students Federation and a suspected Indian intelligence agent. He was reportedly sent by Bhindranwale to tell Longowal not to surrender, but could not or did not want to return.

According to SGPC secretary Bhan Singh, one of the survivors of the operation who was present in the complex, there were 250 other persons in Teja Singh Samundri Hall who were asked to come out and sit in the courtyard of Guru Ramdas hostel.[15] Some extremists threw grenades on them to stop them from surrendering. In the morning, about seventy dead bodies were found in the compound, including those of children and women. Though the Central government white paper issued in July 1984 admitted that seventy people including thirty women and five children died in that incident, the blame for it was put entirely on the militants.

According to Bhan Singh, the survivors were made to sit in the courtyard of Guru Ram Das Sarai without food, drink or medical aid till the curfew was lifted the next evening. Bhan Singh also told Khushwant Singh that he saw about thirty-five Sikhs brought out from the Teja Singh Samundri Hall, made to line up with their hands raised above their heads and shot dead by the army.

The Kumaon regiment also entered Guru Ram Das Sarai at the same time and ordered everyone to come out. According to one eyewitness, as quoted by Mark Tully and Satish Jacob in *Amritsar: Mrs Gandhi's Last Battle,* early in the morning of 6 June, all the pilgrims were taken into the courtyard and the men were separated from the women. The men were asked to take off their turbans, using which their hands were tied behind their backs. In addition, about 150 persons were taken out of the basement and asked to hold their hands up and shot after fifteen minutes.[16]

The persons from the basement were Bangladeshi Muslims whom the Pakistan government had refused to accept. According to a letter written to President Zail Singh by an elder of a village, a few of whose residents were locked in room 61 of Guru Ramdas Sarai, about sixty pilgrims were locked up in that room during the hot and sultry night between 5 June and 6 June. The only door and all windows of this room were shut. When the door of the room was opened at 8 a.m. on 6 June, fifty-five of the sixty pilgrims had died. The five survivors were arrested by the army and taken away to interrogation camps.[17]

Among the pilgrims who surrendered was a nineteen-year-old school teacher, Ranbir Kaur, who was staying in room 141 of Guru Ram Das Sarai with her husband and twelve children from a religious school she helped to run. She later told Mark Tully that she did not hear any appeals by the army to surrender or come out of the hostel. She thought they were safer inside and that the Indian army would not attack the temple.[18] Based on a petition moved in the Supreme Court in September 1984 by a Delhi-based social worker, twenty-two children who were picked up from the temple that day and lodged in Ludhiana jail were released. But most of them were subsequently re-arrested, on the plea that they had to be interrogated further for obtaining information about their relatives, who had probably been killed during the army operation. Ranbir Kaur was released at the end of August. She rejoined three of the children who had been released, but no one could tell her what had happened to the nine other children.

The hostel complex was eventually evacuated in the middle of the attack on the temple complex. Many innocent people were killed, many were injured and many were wrongly arrested. 'It was the least creditable part of Operation Blue Star.'[19]

The tanks roll in

As a part of the clearing-out process of the main temple complex, SFF commandos, 1 Para commandos and troops of 10 Guards were deployed to attack the Akal Takht from the main entrance side of the complex. Despite their repeated attempts, they failed to make a dent in the Akal Takht defences. In the process, the SFF and 1st Para commandos suffered heavy casualties. Additional troops from 26 Madras and 9 Garhwal Rifles, under the command of Brigadier A.K. Dewan, made another attempt to enter the Akal Takht. They too did not succeed, and suffered heavy casualties. At that point, Brigadier Dewan requested tank support.

While permission from Delhi was awaited, Maj. Gen. Brar made one more attempt to get his men into the Akal Takht with the help of the Skot OT64 armoured personnel carrier. The plan was to drive the APC right up to the Akal Takht so that men from the mechanized infantry could get in under the cover of a wall. But the APC soon came under attack from RPG (rocket propelled grenade) launchers. One of the grenades found its mark and the APC was knocked off.

Final clearance from New Delhi for the use of tanks came at about 7 a.m. on 6 June. Eight Vijayanta tanks from the 16th Cavalry Regiment with their main 105 mm high-explosive squash head shells were deployed. By the time the operation was over the tanks had fired about eighty shells, and the effect of the high-explosive squash-head shells on the building and its inmates was devastating.[20] In the process, much of the Akal Takht, the shrine which according to the original orders was to suffer as little damage as possible, was in a shambles.

There are conflicting views about the burning of the library, which had invaluable manuscripts of historical value, including copies of the Granth Sahib handwritten by some of the gurus. Some Sikhs believe the army deliberately set it on fire to destroy an important part of the Sikh cultural heritage. But, according to the government white paper, the library caught fire accidentally in the exchange of fire.[21]

By late afternoon on 6 June, the army was in control of the situation in both the complexes and curfew was lifted for two hours. During that period, nearly 250 people who were trapped in the main temple complex rooms overlooking the parikrama had surrendered.

After dealing with all the officials of the temple who surrendered that day, the army once again turned its attention to the Akal Takht. The sniping from there had died down, but Maj. Gen. Brar was not willing to risk losing any more lives by sending his men into the Akal Takht by daylight. He waited for dusk to fall before giving orders to his troops to storm the Akal Takht and shoot anyone who came in the way. There was no resistance from inside the building. Brar set a guard on it and decided to wait for daylight before starting a search of the premises. According to the army, it was during that search on the morning of 7 June that the bodies of Bhindranwale, Shahbeg Singh, Amrik Singh and Thara Singh were found in the basement.[22]

At about 4.30 a.m. on 7 June, Prem Kumar, special secretary (home), who was continuously monitoring the action by telephone and wireless from Amritsar, telephoned P.C. Alexander to confirm the report that Bhindranwale was dead and his body, which was lying in the basement of the Akal Takht, had been identified. The prime minister was immediately informed.[23]

The question of casualties

According to an army officer who was on duty at the makeshift cremation area just outside the temple complex, Bhindranwale was cremated at 7.39 p.m. on 7 June. A crowd of about 10,000 had gathered near the temple, but the army held them back. The bodies of Bhindranwale, Amrik Singh and Thara Singh were brought to the pyre. Captain Bhardwaj, who was on duty there, insisted on lifting the sheet covering Bhindranwale's body to identify it. When he asked the policemen why the body was so badly battered, they told him that the extremists had broken his bones.[24]

There is, however, some confusion over the timing of Bhindranwale's cremation, because as per the postmortem report the body was not brought into the mortuary until 7.30 p.m. on 7 June and was not examined until 8 p.m. According to the postmortem report, Bhindranwale was 'alleged to have died as a result of firearms' injuries'.[25] There are doubts about the accuracy of the postmortem reports. According to Shahbeg Singh's postmortem, his body was not brought to the mortuary until 9 June, and by then it was not possible to do a full postmortem of it because of the decomposition and putrefaction. There is no record of his last rites. He might have been cremated with the other bodies found in the hostel and temple complexes. Dead bodies from the complex had been piled into garbage trucks and taken to the cremation ground.[26]

The government white paper published in July 1984 said the army lost eighty-three men, including four officers. Twelve officers, and 273 men were injured. The main casualties were suffered by the SFF and 1 Para commandos. The Guards also suffered heavy casualties, with twenty dead and sixty injured.

The white paper said a total of 516 civilians/terrorists were killed and 592 apprehended. Brahma Chellaney, in his story based on information obtained from postmortem reports and other sources, said that 'several' inside the temple had been shot at close range with their hands tied behind their backs and that around 1,200 had died, around double the official figure. The story was picked up by the *London Times* on 14 June 1984.

As a result, Chellaney was charged with fanning sectarian hatred, and later with sedition. Though interrogated by the police for thirty-five hours, he escaped arrest because of the Supreme Court's intervention. His passport was impounded and his press credentials not renewed. It was due to international pressure including a scathing editorial in the *New York Times* in October 1984 that the charges against him were dropped in September 1985 and his passport restored and credentials renewed.

As per estimates gleaned from intelligence and Sikh religious sources by the BBC's Satish Jacob, '... no less than 2,000 people were killed including 300 army personnel. Another 800–900 army personnel were injured, many of them crippled for life. If the government had come out with the real figures then, it would have shown that the operation was a disaster.'[27] Due to widely conflicting claims, the exact number of civilian casualties resulting from Operation Blue Star can only be determined by a competent commission of inquiry appointed by the government.

Contrary to the assurance given by General Vaidya to the prime minister, many cases of mutiny by Sikh soldiers were reported from different places. On 6 June, 600 soldiers of the 9th Battalion of the Sikh Regiment mutinied in Sri Ganganagar in Rajasthan. While some managed to cross over to Pakistan, most were rounded up by men of the Rajputana Rifles. A large-scale mutiny took place in the Sikh Regimental Centre at Ramgarh, Bihar, where 1,461 soldiers including 1,050 new recruits, stormed the armoury, killing the commandant of the centre, Brigadier H.C. Puri, and injuring two others before they set out for Amritsar.

One half of them were engaged by army artillery at Sakteshgarh railway station in Uttar Pradesh. Those who managed to escape were rounded up by the 21st Mechanized Infantry Regiment. The others engaged with the artillery and troops of the 20th Infantry Brigade, during which thirty-five soldiers from both sides were killed. There were five more smaller mutinies in different parts of India. A total of fifty-five mutineers were killed and 2,606 rounded up.

Some senior retired army officers were of the view that the mutinies could have been prevented had the men been fully informed about the developments in Punjab. Lt Gen. Harbaksh Singh felt that to counter the soldiers' belief that that their villages were under attack, the Regimental Centre should have sent small parties of Sikh soldiers under the command of officers to Punjab to see for themselves what was actually happening on the ground and report it back to their colleagues. Lt Gen. S.K. Sinha said he would squarely blame the officer corps for the mutinies because they were apparently ignorant of what their men were thinking.[28]

Unfounded apprehension

One major justification for the progressively harsher and increasingly destructive measures adopted by the army as Operation Blue Star became prolonged was the apprehension that a mass upsurge of Sikhs from the rural areas might head towards the Golden Temple. Contrast this with the actual on-the-ground experience of *Indian Express* reporter Sanjay Suri on 7 June, the day the death of Bhindranwale and destruction of the Akal Takht became public knowledge. That day, Sanjay Suri did not visit any ordinary place but went straight to Bhindranwale's ancestral home in Rode village in Faridkot district.

Soon after AIR announced the news of Bhindranwale's death, Suri wanted to personally check on rumours about a massive uprising in Rode village. While asking for directions on his way to Rode, a young Sikh man offered to ferry him on the carrier of his bicycle and dropped him close to Bhindranwale's home. Suri saw a large number of Sikhs standing quietly outside. There wasn't a single non-Sikh among them. Everyone stood still and silent. Suri introduced himself to two family members as a reporter from the *Indian Express*. Within a couple of minutes, he was ushered into the house and offered a seat on the only piece of furniture (a charpoy) in the room.

He told the two family members the reason for his coming to Rode. Suri describes what followed:

> (one of the men) ... came carrying a thali with food – roti, daal, pickle and vegetables ... The kind host, because that was what this man had become, asked me if I had eaten anything through the day. I said I hadn't. He probably figured I was more in need of food than information, and in any case, he had no information to give ... Nothing remotely like an armed rebellion had erupted ...
>
> I was an alien Hindu when suspicions around alien Hindus in Punjab could have been at the peak. But I was offered rest, care and a meal ... Bhindranwale's family did not forget the age-old traditions of Punjab of welcoming a stranger, looking after him, making him feel at home ... I found a better Punjab than the headlines in the newspapers I worked for had led me

> to expect ... My gut told me, even if not all of my brain, that if this is how I could be welcomed at Bhindranwale's house that day, Punjab would be all right.[29]

Incidentally, within a week of Operation Blue Star, I had visited my own village and a couple of other adjoining villages located at the other end of Punjab, bordering Sirsa in Haryana. I met a number of Sikhs and Hindus during that visit. In my view, Suri's description most accurately describes the prevailing mood of the Sikhs in the rural areas of Punjab, at a time when the national and local press were busy maligning many of them as extremists who nursed anti-national feelings.

Costs and Responsibility

What went wrong with Operation Blue Star? Basically, the army is not meant to conduct such an operation. Under normal circumstances, it was a job meant for the police and paramilitary forces. But these were not used when they could have completed the task with far less loss of life and property. By June 1984, the situation was much beyond their capacity to handle.

As far as the actual operation was concerned, it was the case of a highly ambitious and proud General K. Sundarji nursing dreams of becoming a field marshal, trying to finish his job in a jiffy to please Indira Gandhi. In the process, he underestimated the capabilities, commitment and religious fervour of an equally proud group of Jat Sikhs, well equipped and trained by a professional and battle-hardened general, willing to sacrifice their lives to defend the Harmandir Sahib complex.

Being too proud to admit that the faulty planning and execution resulted from their over-confidence, Sundarji and his juniors later tried to pin the blame on intelligence failure. However, their allegation of intelligence failure rings hollow for a couple of reasons. First, they had had enough time and resources at their disposal to collect the requisite tactical intelligence and plan their operation based on it. If a single civilian employee of the SFF could do that job successfully on two previous occasions, the army, with its Intelligence Corps headed by a lieutenant general, had far superior resources at its command. Second, the commanding officer of the SFF had already advised Maj. Gen. Brar against a full frontal assault on the Akal Takht in view of the positioning of the defences. However, it appears that General Sundarji was in an inordinate hurry to prove his mettle in keeping with the promise made by General Vaidya to the prime minister.

Sundarji could have also chosen to follow the Standard Operating Procedure (SOP) laid down by his predecessor Lt Gen. S.K. Sinha. But Sundarji might have wanted the operation to have his personal stamp if he was going to take full credit for it. Also, the casualties would have been far less had the period of operation been carefully chosen. As was the case with the aborted SSF operation, which coincided with Baisakhi celebrations at the Golden Temple, Operation Blue Star was launched on the martyrdom day of Guru Arjan Dev, when a comparatively larger number of pilgrims visit the temple.

Did the 'final solution', which came in the form of Operation Blue Star, generate the desired momentum with which the 1 Akbar Road group could build a successful campaign for the upcoming elections? It appeared so. The vengeance with which Bhindranwale and his men were eliminated had brought a sense of great relief and satisfaction among a majority of voters. Indira Gandhi's image as a strong leader was restored. But many innocent civilians, including women and children, had to lose their lives in the process.

Lt Gen. K. Sundarji did win the battle for Indira Gandhi, and in March 1986 he became the army chief on General Vaidya's retirement. But at what cost? It was a pyrrhic victory. The developments set in motion as a result of Operation Blue Star led to the loss of a popular prime minister, at a time when the country needed her most. Though Op-2 achieved its objective and the Congress led by Rajiv Gandhi won the November 1984 general elections with an overwhelming majority, Indira Gandhi was assassinated and an anti-Sikh pogrom followed, ensuring that the country, especially the Sikhs, paid a heavy price for no fault of theirs.

Here it would be relevant to examine the pressures on Indira Gandhi which compelled her to approve Operation Blue Star despite being cautioned by a trusted and senior former member of her cabinet like Swaran Singh not to take such a drastic step, and despite Kao's comparatively soft solutions including a heliborne commando operation. Available evidence points the finger at the hawkish Arun Nehru, the politically shrewd M.L. Fotedar, Rajiv Gandhi, who was under their influence, and Arun Singh, who had become a member of the 1 Akbar Road group by that time. Of course, even if we believe that Indira Gandhi was forced to take that decision by this lot, she cannot be absolved of responsibility for what happened. It was she who had allowed extra-constitutional entities to usurp her powers as the prime minster of the country, forcing her to take decisions which she reportedly did not like. The buck stopped with her, and she must be held responsible for all those decisions even if taken under pressure from the 1 Akbar Road group.

This was not the first or the last time that religious and sectarian divides in Indian society was or would be exploited by the ruling or opposition parties for political gains. Such exploitation will continue as long as the country does not have a well-informed and politically evolved electorate, capable of seeing through such games and electing their representatives based purely on their past performance and/or future potential to look after their interests. However, this was the only time that senior leaders of the ruling party, soon after winning an election, started planning their party's victory at the next elections five years away, by first creating and then resolving a religious divide of gigantic proportions. That too, one between Hindus and Sikhs, where there is a very thin, in some cases even blurred, line dividing the two communities.

One can only wish and pray that such a thing never happens again in a secular and democratic India, which prides itself in the values enshrined in the Vedic Sanskrit phrase V*asudhaiva Kutumbakam*, which views the entire earth as family. This phrase is also engraved in the entrance hall of the Indian parliament. It appears that the architects of Op-2 were either totally oblivious of their Vedic heritage or could not care less about such values.

12

Indira Gandhi's Assassination and the Anti-Sikh Pogrom

BBC AND AIR news broadcasts announced Bhindranwale's death in the morning on 7 June 1984. When I reached office that morning, there was unusual excitement and the young officers were huddled in small groups in some of the rooms. Obviously, they were discussing Operation Blue Star and the developments of the past two days. I realized that the Sikh employees of the Department would have been appalled by the ferocity of army action and the damage to the Akal Takht and the Golden Temple complex. I took it upon myself to call all four Sikh section officers (SOs) at the headquarters to my room. In the functioning of government offices in India, including at the R&AW, SOs as heads of various sections occupy a crucial position. Having worked in different capacities in different sections, they come to know most of the staff members personally.

All four section officers were old Intelligence Bureau (IB) hands who had come over to the R&AW when the department was created in 1968. All four had worked with me in the past, three of them very recently in two sensitive divisions, where they were still working, and one in the personnel branch when I joined the R&AW in 1972.

I told them that what had happened was unfortunate and should have been avoided at all costs. It was neither indicative of any Hindu-Sikh divide nor was it motivated out of any genuine threat perception about the demand for Khalistan. In fact, these issues were deliberately created by some senior Congress leaders for electoral gains. I then told them that the main purpose of my calling them to my room was to tell them, and through them the rest of the Sikh staff members, that what had happened should have no impact on the performance of their duties in the Department.

Our primary responsibility was towards the nation and the protection of its security interests. Religious affiliation was secondary. Reminding them briefly of the sacrifices made by a large number of Sikhs during India's Independence struggle, I finally told them that within the next half hour they should contact all Sikh staff members working in the Department and inform them of my message, which they did. The rest of the day was spent in routine office work, which naturally proceeded at a comparatively slower pace.

'Duty to kill'

In the evening, accompanied by my wife Iqbal, young son Gagan and daughter Harmeeta, I visited Gurudwara Bangla Sahib to see if there was any impact of Operation Blue Star on the Sikhs there. While the Shabad Kirtan (recitation of sacred hymns) was going on inside the main hall, small groups of Sikhs were standing outside here and there, animatedly discussing the outcome of Operation Blue Star. A number of placards in Punjabi with inscriptions in red ink were also displayed prominently.

Both the contents of the placards and the animated discussions were highly critical of the government and especially the Congress, which was being held directly responsible for what had happened at the Golden Temple complex. I still remember the contents of one of the placards displayed near the langar entrance of the gurudwara. It read, '*Singh sahib, Bhai Amrik Singh ate Thara Singh nu tasehe de ke marya gaya hai. Hun is k ... Brahmani nu maran da har Sikh da farz banada hai.*' (Sikh brethren, be informed that brothers Amrik Singh and Thara Singh were tortured to death. Now it becomes the duty of every Sikh to kill this Brahmani).

The word 'Brahmani' was used for Indira Gandhi with a derogatory prefix. Incidentally, there was no placard that mentioned the death of Bhindranwale, as some Sikhs still believed that Bhindranwale had escaped just before or during Operation Blue Star. Going by the contents of the placard mentioned above, several Sikhs also believed that Amrik Singh and Thara Singh (and by implication, Bhindranwale) were captured alive and thereafter tortured to death.

The next morning, I called on Director (R) Gary Saxena in his office and informed him of what I had seen and observed in Gurudwara Bangla Sahib complex, especially the contents of the placard. I told him that going even by elementary knowledge of Sikh history, there would be a large number of Sikhs, specially from the rural areas, willing to risk their lives to avenge the damage caused to the Harmandir Sahib complex. Their target would be Indira Gandhi.

Coming straight to the point, I said that in my assessment there was a high probability of her being assassinated in the next six months, and it was the duty of the concerned security agencies to save her life at all costs. Gary asked me how, when and where such an attempt would be made. Based on my experience of working in Uttar Pradesh Police, where I had supervised some election rallies addressed by Indira Gandhi, I said that soon after her speech at an election rally, she would normally go towards the ladies' enclosure located on the left side of the rostrum, where she would meet and speak with women and receive garlands from them. In the haste and confusion that followed, she would be exposed to elements that were beyond the limits prescribed by her security set-up, thereby becoming an easy target. Tragically, it would be at an election rally that her son Rajiv Gandhi would be assassinated in a somewhat similar manner by a seventeen-year-old LTTE suicide bomber on 21 May 1991 at Sriperumbudur in Tamil Nadu.

Having heard my assessment, Gary remarked that if such a thing happened there would be large-scale killing of Sikhs in Delhi. It appeared the subject had been discussed the previous day at a high-level meeting, either at the cabinet secretariat or the PMO, where the likelihood of Indira Gandhi's assassination and its repercussions were also discussed. 'That is what they want,' I said. When Gary asked who 'they' were, I said, 'Obviously, Pakistan, and some Western countries, where there is a comparatively larger presence of Sikhs.'

As the implications of my remarks were rather obvious, no further discussion took place on the subject. It is, however, not known whether Gary's information about the large-scale killing of Sikhs in Delhi following Indira Gandhi's likely assassination was based on an intelligence input by the IB or was an observation by a perceptive officer who had attended the previous day's meeting of senior officers.

'Tomorrow may be too late'

October 21 was a Sunday. I had accompanied my wife and two children to the Lady Hardinge Medical College campus, adjacent to Connaught Place, to meet my wife's eldest sister Dr Paramjeet Panag. On our return journey, as we approached the crossing of Akbar Road and Safdarjung Road, while turning towards Gymkhana Club, I saw two young policemen posted at the corner of 1 Akbar Road, part of the prime minister's official residential complex. Both were armed with Sten guns.

One of them was a 5-foot-8-inch stocky Sikh who appeared to be in his mid-twenties with a closely trimmed beard. Seeing him posted there, I expressed my surprise to my wife as to why armed Sikh police security guards, who were removed from duty at the PM's residence after Operation Blue Star, had been redeployed. 'This is the surest and the easiest way of getting Mrs Gandhi assassinated!' I exclaimed in dismay. From the photographs that appeared in the newspapers later, I identified the young Sikh police constable I had seen as one of the two assassins, Satwant Singh.

On reaching office the next morning, I wrote a small note by hand and addressed it to Gary Saxena. In it I described precisely what I had observed the previous afternoon. In addition to writing that it was the surest and the easiest way of getting the PM killed, I specifically mentioned that all members of the Sikh VVIP security detail posted at the PM's residence must be removed at the earliest, for tomorrow may be too late. Also, a detailed enquiry should be conducted to find out who had recommended or decided their recall, and under what circumstances. Separately, I had asked my personal assistant Sita Lakshmi to prepare an envelope addressed to the director, marked, 'to be opened by addressee only'.

I then paused to consider the pros and cons of sending that note to Gary Saxena. Keeping in view the rural background of the police constabulary, still nursing a tribal mentality, and for whom avenging the attack on the Golden Temple complex was a priority over any other consideration, I had no doubt that an armed person like Satwant Singh, singly or in collaboration with one or more Sikh policemen, would make an attempt to assassinate Indira Gandhi sooner rather than later. But, I thought, if such an attempt was made the same afternoon or within a day or two, there was every chance that whoever was instrumental in bringing back the Sikh policemen on duty would try to deflect attention towards me by falsely accusing me of being part of the conspiracy.

In the prevailing environment of the time, a Sikh could become an easy target of any such insinuation. I reminded myself of the well-known proverb, 'Discretion is the better part of valour', and finally decided not to send the note to Gary. Therefore, when Sita Lakshmi returned with the envelope, I told her to leave it with me, and as soon as she left the room I shredded both the note and the envelope.

Afterwards, of course, I felt remorse for not sending that note to the director. I did come to know through the departmental grapevine that Kao had also expressed his reservations about the recall of Sikh guards at the PM's residence. He had suggested that in case it was not possible to remove them, no two Sikh armed guards should be posted together on duty at the same time and at the same place. That was precisely what happened on the day Indira Gandhi was assassinated. On the plea that he had an upset stomach, which may require him to visit the toilet often, Satwant Singh got his duty changed to the inner circle where Beant Singh was already deployed.

Intimation of danger

As mentioned in the Preface, at the time I had a car pool arrangement with four other officers living in the Satya Marg Chanakyapuri complex to commute to office. We would take turns in our cars and follow a shorter route, which ran alongside Safdarjung airport, crossing over to Tughlak Road via a loop connecting the INA bridge to that road. On 31 October, it was S.C. Mishra's turn to drive us in his car. We had heard the news of Indira Gandhi's assassination earlier that day while at office. She had been shot by Satwant Singh and Beant Singh at about 9.30 that morning.

Around 5.15 p.m., on our way back from office, passing the upscale residential area of Jor Bagh on our left, we were about to take the left turn from Lodhi Road to Tughlak Road towards the INA bridge when we noticed a smart-looking young man in his early twenties walking quickly from the side of the INA bridge. He was thin with sharp features, of wheatish complexion and about 5 foot 10 inches in height. On seeing me in the front seat from a distance, he started running towards us and almost stood in front of our car to stop it. We asked the young man what the problem was. He warned us not to go towards the INA bridge as he was concerned about my safety.

In his typical style, Amar Bhushan, who was sitting in the rear seat, said that in that case we must go via INA bridge only and that he 'would see who was going to touch Mr Sidhu'. When the young man persisted, I told Amar that we should heed his advice. Thanking him for his concern about my personal safety, we took another route via Ashoka Hotel and reached home safely.

At this time, Indira Gandhi's body was still at AIIMS and Rajiv Gandhi, who had returned from his election tour of West Bengal at around 3 p.m., had not yet been administered the oath as prime minister. Some days later I came to know about the reason for the young man's concern about my safety. At the very moment that he had stopped our car, Arjun Das, who had a scooter and car repair workshop on the corner of Lakshmi Bai Nagar market (adjacent to the INA Bridge) and was an associate of Sanjay Gandhi, and later of Rajiv Gandhi, was, with the help of some goons, dragging Sikhs out of their cars and scooters, manhandling them on the INA bridge and throwing some of them over the bridge onto the railway tracks below.[1]

The fact that the police did not stop Arjun Das and his men from what they were doing, at a place about 2 km from the PM's residence and only 1 km from Tughlak Road police station, and that too in broad daylight, indicated that Arjun Das and his goons enjoyed political protection.

The concern on the face of that young man for my safety amply demonstrates that there was no anger in the minds of the Hindus against Sikhs in general in the immediate aftermath of Indira Gandhi's assassination by her two Sikh police guards. It would, therefore, be obvious that the persons involved in the anti-Sikh pogrom were groups of organized goons abetted and, in some cases led, by Congress leaders in active connivance with the police.

'Golf 1, 2, 3'

I learnt about Sikhs and their properties being targeted in Delhi during the night of 31 October from some friends, and then from the BBC radio broadcast the next morning. In fact, the house of a friend in Defence Colony was attacked at around 9.30 p.m. that night and some of his belongings set on fire. Government offices were closed on 1 November. On 2 November, I preferred to stay at home as I didn't want to put my car pool friends in harm's way. On 1 November, at around 11 a.m., I got a call from Director

(R) Gary Saxena, who told me that sitting in his office (in the corner on the eleventh floor), he could see smoke pouring out of a number of buildings, obviously belonging to Sikhs. Due to the deteriorating law and order situation, he said he was sending a three-man SSB guard to my residence to ensure my safety.

A bit surprised at his gesture, I told him that as I was in a government residential complex there was no need for a guard. He said if I required any help I should call him immediately. Those days I had a powerful transistor radio which had all the frequencies and on which I could listen to major news broadcasts from around the world. It also had frequencies which could catch Air Traffic Control communication and the Delhi police wireless network. Obviously, these had been of no interest to me, but had been accidentally discovered while I tried to locate and lock in the frequencies of important radio news broadcasting stations in which I was interested.

After receiving Gary's call, I remembered that I could access the Delhi police wireless network on my radio. I started monitoring it intermittently for the next three days and even nights. I found that it had three call signs on a single frequency, which sounded like 'Gaff 1, 2, & 3'. Later, my batchmate P.S. Bawa, who had been additional commissioner of police, New Delhi range, before Gautam Kaul, and was at that time posted as IGP Goa, told me that these call signs were actually 'Golf 1, 2 and 3', and were used for messages meant for the police commissioner, joint commissioner and the two additional commissioners in charge of two police ranges, which were Delhi and New Delhi.

In October and November 1984, these posts were manned by Subhash Chander Tandon, Nikhil Kumar (under orders of transfer), Hukam Chand Jatav and Gautam Kaul, respectively. I was horrified by what I heard on this network. I wished I had recorded it. In fact, a whole 'book of shame' could have been written based on the contents of those conversations alone. For me, a person with a police background, listening to the communication on that network was a matter of shame and disgust. Only heartless, ruthless and gutless police officers who could sell their souls for career progression could have spoken in that manner.

What I heard on the police network was also a painful reminder of the Sikh persecution during the regime of Zakaria Khan, governor of Lahore (1726–45). Tormented by the exploits of the Sikhs against his rule, Zakaria Khan had laid down a graded scale of rewards for action against them – a blanket for cutting off a Sikh's hair; ten rupees for information about the whereabouts of a Sikh; fifty rupees for a Sikh scalp. Plunder of Sikh homes was made lawful; giving shelter to Sikhs or withholding information about their movements was made a capital offence.

The first thing which startled me was the information passed on by Chanakyapuri police station staff on duty at the nearby Yashwant Place market, which used to be part of the Chanakya Cinema complex. Some goons were looting Sikh-owned shops in that market and manhandling the owners. The same group was planning to loot the house of a Sikh officer in the first quadrangle of the Satya Marg D-I flats (the residential complex where I lived), who had recently returned from abroad and had a number of imported gadgets in his house. I immediately realized that this officer was Ranjit Singh Kalha, a 1965 batch IFS officer who had recently returned from London where he was posted as a counsellor in the high commission of India and was at that time posted as joint secretary (Americas) in the MEA. Incidentally, his flat was just below mine.

I did two things. I immediately called Kalha on the phone and, without disclosing the source of my information, told him that there was a plan to target his house. I asked him whether he had any weapons, and he told me that he had a 12 bore double barrel gun and a .32 bore revolver. Both were licensed but without ammunition. I then called Gary Saxena and requested him to send the SSB guard. Realizing the gravity of the situation and the likelihood of my flat also being targeted, I decided to shift out of my flat with my family and go across to my batchmate and close friend Sudhir Devare's flat in the second quadrangle and remain there till the arrival of the guard. We had come to know Sudhir, an IFS officer, and his wife Hema rather well when Sudhir and I were both posted at Gangtok.

Walking the 200m to Sudhir's flat felt like the longest distance I had ever walked. Lots of things came to my mind. I could visualize what might have been going through the minds of millions of Hindus and Sikhs who were forced to leave their homes in West Punjab, now part of Pakistan, and move to India in the wake of the Partition in 1947. And here was a government officer compelled to flee his home in a government colony in his own beloved country because he happened to be an easily identifiable turban-wearing Sikh, who had to be made to pay the price for the assassination of a popular prime minster. The new, less-than-a-day-old prime minister seemed to have abdicated his duty to protect the life, honour and property of thousands of Sikhs in the capital city and elsewhere, as he was mourning the death of his mother.

'We pay you taxes and you protect our lives and property' was the cornerstone on which the concept of a nation-state had evolved. Here was a prime minister of a twentieth-century 'democratic, socialist and secular' Republic of India, who had all the resources at his disposal to fulfil this basic constitutional obligation towards thousands of law abiding, innocent Sikh citizens of the country, but he chose not to. If the newly installed prime minster wanted to avert that tragedy, he just had to call Home Minister P.V.

Narasimha Rao (later prime minister) on the phone directly or tell his experienced principal secretary to convey his message to him. But he didn't, or chose not to, for the reasons mentioned below.

A new prime minister

Things were going as planned till Indira Gandhi's assassination. If allowed to go unavenged, this tragic loss had the potential of derailing the Congress party's election campaign and jeopardizing Rajiv Gandhi's succession as prime minister of the country. Director (R) Gary Saxena had already warned me on 8 June 1984 (mentioned earlier in this chapter) of the possibility of large-scale killings of Sikhs in Delhi in case Indira Gandhi was assassinated by a Sikh for her perceived role in the developments in Punjab leading to Operation Blue Star. It would thus appear that the 1 Akbar Road group had visualized such a possibility in the aftermath of Operation Blue Star and had planned for it, when and if the time came for its implementation.

Let us examine what members of the 1 Akbar Road group were doing on the day Indira Gandhi was shot, and how by that evening the riots had turned into an anti-Sikh pogrom. Rajiv Gandhi learnt about his mother being shot from Finance Minister Pranab Mukherjee while addressing an election rally at Contai (Kolaghat) in West Bengal. Cutting his speech short, both Rajiv and Mukherjee reached Kolaghat by road around noon, left for Calcutta by helicopter and took a special Indian Airlines flight to New Delhi at around 1 p.m., reaching New Delhi at 3 p.m. Incidentally, anti-Sikh riots started in some pockets of Kolkata soon after Rajiv's plane left Kolkata airport. In a West Bengal ruled by the CPI(M) with Jyoti Basu as chief minister, these riots were controlled by Kolkata police immediately.

Rajiv was received at New Delhi airport by Arun Nehru. Both left for AIIMS in the same car. What transpired between them is not fully known. One of the subjects discussed was obviously Rajiv's appointment as PM. As relations between Indira Gandhi and President Zail Singh had soured, especially after Operation Blue Star, Arun Nehru wanted Vice President R. Venkataraman to administer the oath of office to Rajiv Gandhi before the arrival of President Zail Singh, who was away on a state visit.

Zail Singh, who learnt the shocking news while on his way from Mauritius to Yemen, diverted his plane to New Delhi. At AIIMS, P.C. Alexander was able to convince Rajiv Gandhi to wait for President Zail Singh's arrival. Pranab Mukherjee left for 1 Akbar Road at around 4.10 p.m. in Arun Nehru's car, Kamal Nath being another passenger in the car. Meanwhile, President Zail Singh's plane landed at around 5 p.m., and he went straight to AIIMS, where his car was stoned and one of his staff members manhandled.

Around 6.30 p.m., Zail Singh administered the oath of office as prime minster to Rajiv Gandhi and four members of his cabinet – Pranab Mukherjee, P.V. Narasimha Rao, P. Shiv Shankar and Buta Singh.

M.L. Fotedar continued to hold the fort at 1 Akbar Road. It was only after his position as political secretary to the PM was confirmed with the appointment of Rajiv Gandhi as PM and Narsimha Rao as home minister that Fotedar called Rao on the phone and told him that for better coordination, 1 Akbar Road was taking over control of Delhi Police. While some scattered anti-Sikh riots had broken out even earlier – for instance, around AIIMS and the INA bridge – a large-scale coordinated pogrom now followed. It started from Kidwai Nagar, not very far from AIIMS and the INA bridge.

That such an eventuality had been foreseen could be borne out by the fact that on 31 October goons were carrying voters' lists to identify Sikh homes,[2] and some Congress leaders were supplying them with old car tyres, kerosene, oil and other incendiary material that would be used to burn Sikhs alive.

The information relating to Home Minister Narasimha Rao being asked to transfer control of Delhi Police to 1 Akbar Road was confirmed by Ambassador K.C. Singh (Retd) as well as journalist and academic Vinay Sitapati, author of *Half Lion: How PV Narsimha Rao Transformed India* (Viking 2016). In his interview by *In Focus* magazine of the *Economic Times*, in its issue of 26 June–2 July 2016, Sitapati made an interesting revelation in response to a question as to why he had described 1984 as the 'vilest hour' of Narasimha Rao in his book. This is quoted below:

> In the 1984 Sikh riots, the Delhi Police was reporting to Rao, the home minister. As I point out, he got a phone call in the evening of October 31 from someone very close to Rajiv Gandhi in the PMO that violence against Sikhs was likely and that there was a need for coordinated response and the PMO was going to take all the policing functioning into its hands. Rao could have disobeyed the orders and protected the Sikhs – he would have lost his job, but that would have been the honorable thing to do. When it came to choosing between protecting the lives of 2,733 Sikhs and listening to the Congress, he chose to listen the Congress. Every other Congressman did that but he was the only Congressman who was also the home minister of India. Morally that was his lowest point.[3]

That Rao's police powers had been fully usurped by 1 Akbar Road was further corroborated during a recent conversation I had with Ambassador K.C. Singh (Retd). He was posted as deputy secretary at the president's office at Rashtrapati Bhavan during those fateful days. K.C. narrated how, on the morning of 1 November, upon seeing smoke emanating from some buildings in the nearby markets and residential areas, Zail Singh had called Home Minister Narasimha Rao to check what was happening in the city. There was no response from Rao.

Later in the evening, Rao called Zail Singh back. However, instead of updating the president on developments in the city, Narasimha Rao surprised Zail Singh by seeking the latter's assistance to save one of his Sikh acquaintances, Manmohan Singh, who was living in a farmhouse in the Brijwasan area of South Delhi. Manmohan Singh (not to be confused with Dr Manmohan Singh, who later became PM) had a shipping business in Kolkata and interests in some Hyderabad-based industries. After that Zail Singh ordered his President's Guards to pick up Manmohan Singh and drop him at a safe place in New Delhi.

With the home minister's control over Delhi Police having been taken over by 1 Akbar Road, most senior Delhi police officers were aware of the kind of intervention that the powers-that-be wanted. Only a few brave and conscientious officers from various ranks chose not to pay attention to those signals and carried out their duties as per the law and in right earnest till the very end.

If there was any doubt about the complicity of 1 Akbar Road in what was happening in Delhi and elsewhere, Rajiv Gandhi removed it in his speech at an election rally on 19 November at the Boat Club in New Delhi. 'Some riots took place in the country following the murder of Indira ji,' he said. 'We know the people were very angry and for a few days it seemed that India had been shaken but, when a mighty tree falls it is only natural that the earth around it does shake a little.'[4] In that speech, Rajiv Gandhi trivialized the enormity of the pogrom by describing it as riots, hence sanctifying the use of this word to refer to the horrific events of those days. He also justified the pogrom as a natural outcome of the anger resulting from Indira Gandhi's assassination, overlooked, if not justified, acts of omission and commission by the concerned Delhi police officers, and sent a signal to the many commissions and committees that would inquire into various aspects of the anti-Sikh pogrom in future as to how to weigh the evidence presented before them.

Mob action, police inaction

A three-man SSB guard reached my flat in less than an hour of my conversation with Gary Saxena. Our household help informed us of their arrival. Thanking Sudhir and Hema for providing us refuge in our hour of need, we returned to our flat. The same evening, residents of D-I and D-II flats on Satya Marg and Vinay Marg held a meeting in the quadrangle in front of my flat, where the implications of the ongoing 'riots' for the residents of our complex were discussed. One of the residents openly said what was happening in Delhi was organized by some members of the Congress party. It was finally decided that two groups of college-going boys, each accompanied by a senior, would make the rounds of the colony at night in their cars and raise an alarm if anything suspicious came to their notice.

Fortunately, nothing of the sort happened in our area. Maybe the organizers of the pogrom had consciously decided against targeting Sikhs living in government officers' residential colonies, especially those located in Lutyens's Delhi. Incidentally, the DI and DII flats on Satya Marg and Vinay Marg were not very far from Arjun Das's workshop. He and others might have come to know about the unity of the residents there and the security arrangements they had made. There might have also been prior knowledge about the deployment of a guard at my residence and perhaps of my R&AW connection. That became obvious in the first week of January 1985, when out of the blue I received an India Post card with handwritten new year's greetings from Arjun Das. I wish I had kept that as a memento, but I was so furious on seeing his name that I tore it up immediately. Incidentally, Arjun Das was killed in his workshop by three motorcycle-borne Sikh terrorists on 4 September 1985.

In addition to the information regarding Ranjit Kalha, I picked up more from listening in on conversations on the police wireless network. Some of these conversations which I still clearly remember are briefly mentioned below.

Late afternoon on 1 November, policemen on duty at a market informed the Delhi police control room that some hooligans had set fire to a shop owned by a Sikh and they needed some help to control the hooligans. The response of the control room was that it was possible the fire had been caused by an electric short circuit and that they did not need to bother about it. In the end the policemen on duty were advised to move away from the place.

Later that evening, on receiving similar information through the police wireless network, I telephoned my batchmate Gunjit Singh from the Indian Revenue Service (IRS), who was posted in New Delhi as assistant commissioner, income tax, to inform him about vandalism taking place not very far from his house in J Block, Saket. Confirming the presence of about fifty hooligans not very far from his house, Gunjit was surprised how I had come to know about it. Appreciating my concern for his safety, he said the station house officer (SHO) at the Saket police station was known to them and he had assured them that no harm would come to them.

Later, on the intervening night of 1 and 2 November, policemen on duty at Dhaula Kuan crossing informed the control room that some hooligans were forcibly taking eight young Sikh girls towards a forested area of the nearby Ridge. They sought orders as to how to handle the situation. The caller used the word 'bhaisein' (buffalos) for the Sikh girls. The response from their control room was that the police force deployed there need not worry about them as the 'saands' (bulls) chasing them would take care of them.

Around the same time, policemen from Defence Colony started making frantic calls to the control room, informing them about the movement of an army vehicle carrying Sikh soldiers in that area. It appeared that a senior retired Sikh officer living in Defence Colony had sought help from the army unit stationed in the cantonment for his safety. Soon after, frantic messages started flowing in and out of the control room to ascertain who had sent the troops and under whose orders. That was the only time I witnessed the control room exhibit concern and urgency in dealing with a call received from the local police. The control room saw to it that the troops returned to their base as soon as possible.

Repeated calls the same night, over a period of a couple of hours, were received by the control room from policemen on duty at Tughlakabad railway station. According to them, a large crowd had gathered there and had planned to stop, even by tampering with the signals, trains arriving or passing through that station and going towards Delhi. It seemed they planned to kill Sikhs travelling on the trains. As the local police force was heavily outnumbered, they asked for reinforcements. They fetched no response from the control room. Very soon, they began informing the control room about the stopping of trains and killing of Sikh passengers by hooligans. Still there was no response.

Some of the above incidents were witnessed by Professor Madhu Dandavate, former Union minister for railways and finance and at that time Member of the Lok Sabha. He submitted his eyewitness account to the Justice Ranganath Misra Commission in the form of affidavits. On the night of 1 November, he was travelling by Rajdhani Express from Bombay to New Delhi. The train reached Mathura station in the early hours of 2 November. Nothing happened there as there was a large number of alert armed policemen.

> When the train reached Tughlakabad station on November 2 morning a large number of persons carrying iron rods, axes, crow-bars, etc., entered our train. They were searching for Sikh passengers in the train ... I found two Sikhs killed and thrown on the platform and then their bodies were set on fire ... The police standing on the platform made no effort to prevent either the killing or the burning of the Sikhs.

A Sikh railway employee who came out of the station master's office was also killed on the spot. The train halted there for four hours because of a rumour that a large crowd of Sikhs had gathered near Ashram Marg and they would stop the train and kill Hindu passengers. The train left only when the rumour was found to be false. Dandavate also stated in his affidavit that he discovered three more dead bodies of Sikhs in various compartments of the train. He was of the view that the murder of the Sikhs could have definitely been prevented if the police at Tughlakabad station had not remained passive spectators. Further, the police party standing at the foot of the overbridge turned out to be a group of tacit spectators and made no attempt to extinguish the fire when the two bodies were being burnt. According to one FIR, a request was also made to the police by the railway staff of Nangloi station to remove twelve dead bodies (of Sikhs) from there.

A total of seven FIRs were lodged in this connection. Forty-six trains were forced to make unauthorized halts, either at railway stations where they were not scheduled to stop, or outside stations. Justice Ranganath Misra observed that it was clear from these FIRs, as also from other FIRs where similar allegations had been made, that no arrangements were made to protect passengers, either of trains that were running or stood halted at railway stations.

If proper care had been taken and the police had remained active and played even the normal role of policemen, as Prof. Dandavate told the Commission, nothing untoward would have happened. The Commission took note of the difference in the arrangements at Mathura Junction in Uttar Pradesh and at stations within the Union Territory of Delhi. 'Whether it be RPF, Govt. Railway Police or Delhi Police, all appear to have become indifferent within the Union Territory.'[5] Unfortunately, other than a number of commissions and committees that followed, nothing happened to the known goons and murderers, who continued to roam freely without any fear of law or justice.

How the eyewitnesses who had submitted affidavits were treated by Justice Ranganath Misra when they were called to record their evidence would be clear from the following account. Journalist Sanjay Suri had covered the anti-Sikh pogrom in Delhi extensively for the *Indian Express.* He has written about it in his book, *1984: The Anti-Sikh Violence and After.* That book covers the mass killings, arson and rapes in colonies like Sultanpuri and Trilokpuri. Suri recounts an incident that occurred in the afternoon of 1 November outside Gurudwara Rakab Ganj, not very far from Teen Murti Bhavan where the mortal remains of Indira Gandhi were lying in state and mourners were walking past, some of them shouting '*khoon ka badla khoon*' (blood for blood).

When Suri reached Gurudwara Rakab Ganj on his scooter, he saw a crowd advancing menacingly towards the gurudwara in full view of a CRPF platoon and the additional commissioner police, New Delhi range, Gautam Kaul. Congress MP Kamal Nath (a member of the 1 Akbar Road group) was also standing nearby. Two Sikhs had just been burnt alive outside the gurudwara. According to Suri, 'Kaul stood static' alongside some CRPF men. The gurudwara was being targeted in the presence of a large police force. 'The designer [sic] police made no move to stop the men advancing on, Kaul made no move to order them to do so.'

According to Suri, 'Kaul later denied this; of course, he would.'

About Kamal Nath, Suri says, 'When the crowd surged forward at one point, Kamal Nath had only to gesture lightly, and they held back … What was the relation between Kamal Nath and that crowd that he had only to raise his hand towards it and it held back? … All that time he was there, the crowd had stayed there, violently and aggressively.' Further, Suri wrote, 'Kamal Nath had come down from Teen Murti Bhavan, the crowd too had come from there, as (the) Kusum Lata Mittal report into policing failure categorically declares.' Kamal Nath later said he was not leading the mob in any attack, that he had, on the contrary, only tried to control the situation.[6]

When the inquiry commission headed by serving Supreme Court judge, Justice Ranganath Misra, was set up in 1985, Sanjay Suri decided to submit his evidence through affidavits as to what he had seen during that period, including what he saw on

1 November at Gurudwara Rakab Ganj. After his evidence was recorded, he was cross-examined by two lawyers. The first asked him if he could produce an eyewitness who could testify that he had been at those places he had reported from.

When Suri mentioned that his evidence was based on his personal observation, the lawyer told him, 'Don't get excited. You must never get excited'; upon which Justice Misra nodded in agreement and said the witness should not get excited when presenting evidence. Suri says the second lawyer, who spoke kindly, asked him if he could produce a log book from the *Indian Express* that would 'list exactly where I was in the city and at what time and could such a book confirm that I was indeed at those places I had my eyewitness account from'.[7]

I don't have to comment on this and would like to leave to the readers' best judgement as to how the eyewitness evidence of reliable witnesses was treated by a commission headed by a serving Supreme Court judge.

Justice Misra later retired as Chief Justice of India. After retirement he was made chairman of the National Human Rights Commission and was finally elected as a member of the Rajya Sabha (1998–2004) on a Congress ticket.

Justice delayed, denied

On 11 January 2018, the Supreme Court constituted a three-member special investigation team (SIT) under former Delhi High Court judge, Justice S.N. Dhingra. The other two members were Abhishek Dular, a serving IPS officer of the 2006 batch from the Himachal Pradesh cadre, and Rajdeep Singh, a former IGP rank officer of the BSF. The purpose of the SIT was to examine the 199 cases that another SIT (appointed in February 2015 by the government and headed by IPS officer Pramod Asthana) had recommended for closure, along with forty-two other cases that a Supreme Court-appointed supervisory committee of two former judges had examined.

As Rajdeep Singh expressed his inability to join the SIT, the Supreme Court, in November 2018, allowed the remaining two to carry out the investigation. In January 2019, the court gave the SIT three months to file its report. The report was finalized and submitted to the Union law ministry by the end of April 2019. Though Justice Dhingra had been asking the law ministry officials for the past eight months to seek a date from the court so that the SIT's work could be brought to a closure, for reasons best known to the law ministry, it submitted his report to the Supreme Court in a sealed cover only in November 2019.[8]

The SIT report was finally taken up by the Supreme Court on 15 January 2020. The Solicitor General informed the Supreme Court that the Central government had accepted the recommendations of this Committee and would take action as per its recommendations.

In its report, the Dhingra Committee took special note of the Tughlakabad railway station incident. It observed that the Tughlakabad railway station massacre saw police recover seventy-one bodies, twenty-nine of which remained unidentified. The police said the rioters were very many in number, hence they could not prevent the massacre. The police did not identify a single rioter later.

Some of the other observations made by Justice Dhingra Committee are as follows:

1. Hundreds of affidavits about the riots were received by the Justice Ranganath Misra Commission in 1985, but those were converted into FIRs only in 1991 and 1992.

2. In almost all the cases, the trial judges to whom the cases were sent after investigation rejected the testimonies of witnesses on the grounds of delay in filing of the FIRs, delay in recording the statements of witnesses, and so on.
3. The police did not register FIRs crime-wise, and clubbed all complaints from one area into one FIR. It is humanly impossible for one investigating officer (IO) to investigate about 200 cases. Had the administration and police been serious about punishing the culprits, a special task force for investigating crimes committed within the jurisdiction of each police station should have been created by providing the necessary infrastructure. The police also did not preserve any forensic evidence with regard to unidentified bodies so that at a later stage, identification through forensic evidence could be done.
4. The Committee held the SHO of Sultanpuri police station, Suryavir Singh Tayagi, who was later promoted to assistant commissioner, to have been hand in glove with the rioters and recommended that his case be sent to the Delhi Police Riot Cell for action.
5. 'The whole effort of the police and administration seem to have been to hush up the criminal cases concerning riots.'[9]

Though the SIT report attracted a lot of attention in the media and generated hope for justice among the affected Sikh families, in his interview with Puneet Nicholas Yadav of *Outlook* (18 January 2020), Justice Dhingra mentioned that out of the 199 cases he could not recommend the reopening of investigation into even one case.

> At best, there are grounds for appeal in a handful of cases but none for investigation ... because of the manner in which

> they have been compromised by not just the police but also the judicial system. In most of cases, original records have been weeded out from the trial courts because of the long period of time that has elapsed. In several cases, we issued summons to witnesses only to learn that the individuals concerned had died many years ago.

In the end Justice Dhingra made some very pertinent remarks.

> I do not believe that a conviction in a ghastly crime or massacre, after 30 or 40 years having lapsed, amounts to justice. After such a long time, most of those who had lost their loved ones had died too. To those who are alive, how do you justify a sentence after 35 years? How do you call it justice? Justice after 35 years may make for good headlines for you people in the media, but for a human being who has lost everything because of that riot, it will mean nothing.'[10]

On 3 November 1984, with the SBB guard in place at my residence, I accompanied my car pool friends to office. On our way we saw some burnt taxis on Lodhi Road, presumably owned by Sikhs. But there were no dead bodies, which might have been removed from the scene. I told my car pool friends what I had heard on the police wireless network the previous two days and nights. Amar Bhushan still remembers this and also the incident of the young Hindu gentleman stopping us from going towards the INA bridge on the evening of 31 October.[11]

The anti-Sikh pogrom of November 1984 resulted in the death of about 2,800 Sikhs in Delhi and 3,350 nationwide (according to government estimates), while independent sources estimate the number of deaths to be not less than 8,000, with some placing it closer to 15,000. The Congress party won the general elections held in November 1984 with a thumping majority, because the Sikhs of Delhi and some other cities had been taught a lesson of their lifetime.

13

The Aftermath

RAJIV GANDHI, in his election speech of 19 November 1984 at the Boat Club in New Delhi had justified the anti-Sikh pogrom as a natural outcome of public anger generated by an earth-shaking event. What he did not realize was that sometimes minor tremors can also lead to a major earthquake. That is precisely what happened in Punjab in the decade that followed that speech. The felling of thousands of 'small' trees during Operation Blue Star and the anti-Sikh pogrom of November 1984 was bound to cause tremors in Punjab. The killings of thousands of innocent Sikhs were also bound to generate intense anger among an entire community, as getting 'very angry' over the killing of a loved one cannot be the prerogative of a single family or party.

Sikhs comprise about 1.75 per cent of India's population, and since they had hardly any voting potential outside Punjab, some politicians thought they could easily be ignored and pushed about. And that was what happened. As a result, Punjab's industrial and economic growth, already stalled due to the impact of Op-1 launched in 1978, suffered a huge setback. Earlier, the whole of India belonged to the Sikhs, and vice-versa. But following the November 1984 pogrom, an entire insecure generation of Sikh youth got bottled up in Punjab. And the next generation got busy, either enjoying life by living far beyond their means or by seeking greener pastures in countries like Canada. Many more, who were left behind in the race for life, started cutting themselves off from the realities of the world by taking refuge in drugs.

Those Sikhs, especially of the younger generation, who had to stay outside Punjab for one reason or the other, sought safety in becoming clean-shaven as they had observed or heard that both in Haryana in November 1982 during Asian Games and the anti-Sikh pogrom of 1984, it was the turban over the head of a Sikh and not the Sikh per se, which was under attack. Gradually it became a matter of convenience amongst the Sikh youth and the young Sikh mothers found it extremely difficult to raise, train and maintain a turbaned Sikh young boy in the family.

The Pakistani agenda

Pakistan had been smarting from the loss of its eastern wing ever since Bangladesh emerged as an independent nation in December 1971 with India's help. In my view, the turmoil in Punjab, set in motion by the activities of the 1 Akbar Road group, was the greatest gift India could have given to Pakistan, which it has continued to relish until today. The Inter-Services Intelligence (ISI) had always been meddling in the affairs of Punjab. But until the early 1980s this meddling was limited to small-scale operations like smuggling and intelligence collection, mainly because of an unreceptive population.

The activities of the 1 Akbar Road group created fertile ground for the ISI to make deeper inroads in Punjab, and they took full advantage of this situation. They organized training for the disgruntled young Sikh extremists by taking them across the border, or even by supplying them with the latest arms, including AK-47 rifles, within Punjab. It was generally believed by knowledgeable observers at that time that some of the killings in Punjab in the first half of the 1980s were directly or indirectly carried out by ISI-backed militants. And their interference continued for a long time after that.

Operation Blue Star and the anti-Sikh pogrom of November 1984 helped Pakistan carry forward its two-pronged agenda, planned by the wily (Jalandhar-born and St. Stephen's College-educated) President (1978–1988) Muhammad Zia-ul-Haq. In pursuit of that policy, throughout the 1980s and even later, Pakistan continued to add fuel to the fire in Punjab, to keep the Indian security forces tied up with restoring peace and stability in the state. On the other hand, the ISI upgraded the level of its covert support to separatists in Jammu and Kashmir and increased the level of cross-border infiltration of Pakistan-based terrorists.

The overstretched Indian security forces were thereafter forced to control the situation on two fronts. While Punjab was still counting its dead and looking for missing loved ones, by the time the situation stabilized in in that state, it had worsened considerably in J&K. I have always believed, and have shared my views on the subject with close friends, that the situation in J&K would not have worsened as it has, had 1 Akbar Road not fiddled with the situation in Punjab.

The outcome of Op-2 launched by the 1 Akbar Road group in the early 1980s ended in the events of 1984. It also gave birth to a hitherto non-existent issue – Khalistan – thereby providing an opportunity to certain countries, particularly Pakistan, to use that as a handle to further their respective agendas vis-a-vis India. The ISI would find one reason or another to continue destabilizing the strategically located state of Punjab. A new dimension to this situation was added when, in August 2019, the NDA government revoked Article 370 of the Indian Constitution, which had granted limited autonomy to the state of Jammu and Kashmir. The subsequent decision to divide the state into two Union Territories – J&K and Ladakh – must have come as a rude shock to Pakistani authorities. As a result, the ISI is expected to further bolster its pro-Khalistan propaganda in Punjab and in countries such as Canada, the UK and the US, which have a sizeable Sikh diaspora.

Over the years, Pakistan's ISI has created a number of organizations, assets, and built an impressive infrastructure within Pakistan, in Western countries and even among some sympathisers in Punjab to carry forward its anti-India and pro-Khalistan agenda. Out of the nine foreign-based Sikhs declared as individual terrorists under the Unlawful Activities Prevention Act (UAPA) by the Ministry of Home Affairs on 1 July 2020, four enjoy the ISI's hospitality in Pakistan. They are Paramjit Singh Panjwar, head of Khalistan Commando Force (KCF), Ranjit Singh Neeta, head of Khalistan Zindabad Force (KZF), Wadhawa Singh, leader of Babbar Khalsa International (BKI) and Lakhbir Singh, leader of International Sikh Youth Federation (ISYF). Two, namely Bhupinder Singh Bhinda and Gurmeet Singh Bagga, important members of KZF are based in Germany, Hardeep Singh Nijjar the Khalistan Tiger Force (KTF) chief is in Canada, Paramjit Singh, head of the UK branch of BKI is in the UK and Gurpatwant Singh Pannun, leader of Sikhs for Justice (SFJ), is based in the US.[1] Interestingly, the name of Dal Khalsa International (DKI) chief Gajinder Singh, who had hijacked an Indian Airlines plane in 1981, does not figure in this list. He continues to live in Lahore.

While the external ramifications of ISI-sponsored pro-Khalistan activities are dealt with in the next chapter, it will be relevant to mention here that with the opening of the Kartarpur Corridor and Pakistan's plans of promoting religious tourism to other places of interest to the Sikhs in that country, the role of the above-mentioned organizations and other 'assets' created by Pakistan could be further intensified and diversified.

In addition to generating foreign exchange for Pakistan, this is likely to expose a large number of Sikh religious tourists, both from India and abroad, to their anti-India designs. The ISI can also launch high-sounding Sikh religio-social societies or NGOs in third countries, and even in Punjab, to generate money, thereby making their pro-Khalistan and anti-India operations financially self-sustaining.

An atmosphere vitiated

It is easy to mix poison in a pond of water but very difficult to purify a pond thus poisoned. Following the November 1984 anti-Sikh pogrom, turbaned Sikhs living outside Punjab were viewed with suspicion, and snide remarks continued to be made against them by the ignorant, malicious or a certain section of an indoctrinated public for quite some time. As an example, sometime in the middle of 1985, I had gone to the Lodhi Road post office to send a letter by Speed Post. I was standing in a queue of seven to eight people and there was only one person ahead of me at the counter. A peon or an office help, who must have been not more than thirty years old, walked into the post office with a number of envelopes in his hand and stood in front me without even looking at the queue.

No sooner had I asked him to go to the end of the queue and wait for his turn than he started shouting, 'How come these people are still roaming around India? Why don't they leave this country and go to their country?' At the time, I had the physical strength to pin him to the ground in seconds and to tell him, 'Who are you to ask me to leave my country? I was born here and will die here.' But better sense prevailed when I realized that I should not give that individual the dignity of being thrashed in public by a senior Government of India official. Giving him a scornful look, I stood quietly even as the post office staff asked him to move to the end of the queue.

Even a distant state like Bihar could not remain immune to such influences. Sponsored by his elder brother, Amarjit Sohi had emigrated from Punjab to Edmonton in Canada in 1981. There he took a job as a bus driver. He also joined a local Punjabi literary society and became an actor and playwright in a Punjabi theatre group. Strictly opposed to Sikh fundamentalism, he was also opposed to state oppression. Still holding his Indian passport, Sohi returned to India in November 1988 to pursue his interest in drama as a playwright, but instead joined an activist group advocating land reforms in Bihar.

Local police arrested Sohi and his associates a day before they were to launch an agitation (for land reforms). Though clean-shaven, Sohi's Canada connection led the police to believe that they might have captured a Sikh terrorist. That led to a thorough interrogation at the local police station. To his luck, a young lady deputy commissioner with a Punjab background was convinced about his innocence and got him transferred to judicial custody to let him pursue his case in a court of law. He was charged under the Terrorist and Disruptive Activities (prevention) Act (TADA).

As he was still an Indian citizen, he was denied access to Canadian diplomatic officers.

After spending twenty-one months in prison, eighteen of them in solitary confinement, he was finally discharged in July 1990 as a result of the efforts of some Canadian journalists and activists, including members of Amnesty International. On his return to Canada he acquired Canadian citizenship. In November 2015, he was elected Member of Parliament as a Liberal Party candidate from Edmonton Mill Woods constituency. He joined Prime Minster Justin Trudeau's cabinet and served as minister for information and communities from November 2015 to July 2018. He, however, lost his seat to his Conservative Party rival in the last elections held in 2019.[2]

Fake encounter

Amongst the most shocking examples of how a vitiated atmosphere can lead to immense cruelty was a July 1991 incident in Pilibhit district of Uttar Pradesh. On 12 July 1991, a group of Sikh pilgrims from Pilibhit was returning by bus after visiting Nanakmatha, Patna Sahib, Hazur Sahib and other places of pilgrimage. Police intercepted the bus near a bridge at Kachhalghat in Pilibhit district at 11 a.m. and forced ten male Sikh passengers to get off the bus and sit in another vehicle. The rest of the passengers, including the women and children, were taken to a local gurudwara. On the intervening night of 12 and 13 July, the ten Sikhs were taken to a nearby forest and shot dead in a fake encounter by a joint team from three adjoining police stations – Bilsanda, Neuria and Pooranpur. The next day, the policemen claimed that ten Khalistan terrorists, having previous criminal records, had been killed and arms and ammunition had been recovered from them. The police got an autopsy of the dead bodies done before cremating them the same day.

On the basis of a PIL filed by Senior Advocate R.S Sodhi, the Supreme Court entrusted the investigation of the case to the CBI. Filing charges against fifty-seven policemen on 12 June 1991, the CBI described the motive behind the killings as a desire on the part of the local police to earn rewards and recognition for killing 'terrorists'. The CBI court at Lucknow framed charges on 20 January 2003 and finally sentenced forty-seven policemen to life imprisonment on 4 April 2016, twenty-five years after the incident. By that time, ten of the accused had died and twenty-seven others who had retired from service had gone underground and were not available on the day of the judgment. According to one report, the local police later located six of the missing cops, including Inspector Harpal Singh who was posted as station house officer of Neuria police station at the time of the fake encounter.[3]

During my seven-year tenure as an IPS officer in Uttar Pradesh, I had enjoyed genuine respect from my juniors. I could also observe that Sikhs were never treated as 'outsiders'. In fact, their contribution to the development of the Terai area, of which Pilibhit was a part, was duly appreciated. In an otherwise caste-ridden society, Sikhs were considered to be the sort who 'minded their own business'. In the way that viruses don't recognize territorial boundaries, it appeared that sections of the UP police too were infected by the communal virus. They might have heard stories of their Punjab police counterparts getting out-of-turn promotions, rewards, other benefits and recognition for killing 'terrorists'. But what they forgot was that Uttar Pradesh was not Punjab, where such incidents might be overlooked in the mistaken belief that

that doing so would serve the larger interest of bringing peace and stability to a troubled state.

To ascertain how the Punjab Police actually dealt with terrorism during that period, I sought out my batchmate Chaman Lal (IPS 1964 MP). What he told me at the India International Centre on 8 August 2020 is summed up below:

On DGP Punjab K.S. Dhillon's request, Chaman Lal joined Punjab Police as DIG (Administration) in January 1985 and was assigned the task of revamping the state's police in the aftermath of Operation Blue Star. In April 1986, he was appointed DIG (Border) BSF at Gurdaspur, with oversight powers over Punjab Police to deal with the problem of terrorism in the border areas. On promotion, he joined Punjab Police as IGP (Border) which post he held from April 1988 to October 1988.

As DIG (Border) BSF and later as IGP (Border) Punjab Police, he extensively toured the rural areas of the three most adversely effected districts of Punjab and found that there was no sign of communal tension between Sikhs and Hindus. He also found that the policy of ruthless suppression of Sikh militancy was taking the Punjab Police nowhere. If a terrorist was killed, his place was quickly taken by another. That convinced him to follow a policy of winning hearts and minds of the local population, as it would be a better way to isolate the hard-core and Pakistan-inspired terrorists. Chaman Lal's policy of dealing with the situation as per the law eventually helped him to win the confidence of the people of Punjab and also of DGP Julio Ribeiro (March 1986–March 1988). In recognition of the services rendered by him during that period, the Government of India bestowed upon him the national award of Padma Shri on the occasion of the 1988 Republic Day.

Following Operation Black Thunder II (May 9 to 18, 1988), as per information reaching Ribeiro (by now advisor to the governor of Punjab) the general rural population had lost all respect for the 'boys' (a term used in Punjab at the time to describe the terrorists). Keeping that in view, the rural populace's feeling was that the best way to further isolate the 'boys' would be to put a stop to the cordon and search operations launched under DGP K.P.S. Gill's instructions. When this suggestion was discussed by Ribeiro with Governor S.S. Ray in the presence of Gill, the latter's policy of consolidating the gains from Black Thunder by mopping up the collaborators of terrorists, prevailed over the policy of winning hearts and minds of the rural population as suggested by Ribeiro.

During his seven months' stay in Punjab after K.P.S. Gill took over as DGP (April 1988–1990 and again from 1991 to December 1995) Lal observed that police started wielding immense power, becoming a law unto themselves. There was rampant corruption. Lawful policing was derided as a soft policy. During cordon and search operations, Punjab police used to pick up a number of young men. Only if the parents of these men paid money to the police was a case registered. Otherwise they were eliminated without any trace. To get higher rewards in some cases, the category of a captured terrorist was deliberately raised by registering false cases against him, before he was eliminated.

On 4 March 1988, on his release from Ferozepur jail, Jasbir Singh Rode (nephew of Bhindranwale) started his march towards Golden Temple. Chaman Lal wanted to prevent him from entering the temple as he felt it would help in further fanning extremism in Punjab and it would subsequently be difficult to dislodge him and his militant followers from the temple. But he was overruled by Gill. As apprehended by Chaman Lal, after his appointment as Jathedar of Akal Takht, Rode made a fiery speech declaring he would fight for Khalistan, complete freedom and implementation of Anandpur Sahib resolution.

To register his protest, Lal held a press conference in Kotwali Amritsar and blamed K.P.S. Gill for following a wrong policy. Soon after that, Chaman Lal who had already become a 'liability' for K.P.S. Gill and his men, was asked to report to the home ministry at New Delhi in October 1988 and was finally repatriated to his cadre – Madhya Pradesh – after four months.

After a three year tenure as DGP Nagaland, Chaman Lal joined BSF Headquarters New Delhi as Additional DGP and finally retired in September 1996.

My experiences

Soon after Indira Gandhi's assassination, an unwritten decision was taken not to post any Sikh officer or staff member to the R&AW stations in west Europe and North America on the grounds that they could not be trusted. That decision also impacted the future intake of Sikhs into the Department. It was obvious that these decisions were taken at the highest level. Similar instructions might have been issued to other sensitive ministries and departments too. Even though I was privy to some of the most sensitive information the Department handled, I suddenly became ineligible for a posting to west Europe or North America, simply because I happened to be a Sikh and thus could not be fully trusted to be posted in these places. It was not the place of posting, but the procedure of selection that bothered me. That a segment of the Department's officers and staff members were not eligible for postings to certain regions because of their religious belief started to trouble me. I was upset not just for myself but on behalf of all Sikhs at the R&AW.

From January 1985 onwards, I began sending a note annually to the secretary (R) to convey that I was not available for foreign assignments during that year on account of personal reasons. The real reason behind sending the note was that I did not want my religion to become a factor in my selection or non-selection for a particular post. Throughout that period, and even much after I retired from service, nobody other than the secretaries (R) concerned would be familiar with the real reasons behind two unusual aspects of my career at the Department. First, was my transfer, in November 1983, from two highly sought-after divisions to an analysis division. The second, was my remaining at headquarters for ten years at a stretch, as against the prevailing norm of officers staying only three to four years at headquarters. It was in pursuance of this policy that in the middle of 1985, a very senior Sikh officer who had headed two 'C' classification (based on living conditions) stations earlier and should have been posted to an 'A' station in the normal course, was sent to third 'C' station.

Sometime in mid-1989, I had a one-on-one discussion with Secretary A.K. Verma in his room about the absurdity of that decision. Slightly emotionally, I told him that my family had a genealogical table, going back almost one hundred generations. Out of those, the last eighteen generations have been Sikhs. All of them were born in India and died here. Since approximately AD 1800 even the records of the immersion of ashes of my successive Sikh ancestors are available either at Haridwar, or Kiratpur in Punjab. I had myself seen the entries of the Ganga immersions in the bahi (record of immersions) maintained for our village by the Panditji at Haridwar. I had also seen the signatures of my father and great-grandfather in that bahi, as visitors who had come to immerse the ashes of their loved ones.

Thereafter, looking straight into Verma's eyes, I said, 'How come a person of my background is not to be trusted, whereas a first-generation person of foreign origin is living in 1 Safdarjung Road as the wife of the prime minister of the country? Have you personally satisfied yourself about her credentials? If not, you have failed in your duty as secretary.'

Naturally, Verma was shocked to hear what I had to say, but kept quiet. It appeared he had realized the merit of my questioning him on a fundamental issue. My sincerest apologies to Sonia Gandhi, who was obviously the subject of the above conversation. However, at the time I could think of citing no better example to defend my honour as my loyalty to the country had come into focus as a result of a decision that had obviously been taken at her husband's behest.

I finally agreed to go to Tokyo as one of the ministers in the embassy of India in November 1990. There were a number of reasons for my accepting that offer. Both my son and daughter had joined undergraduate courses, and the family was facing a sort of a financial crunch because of that. I could see that, like some of their friends, they too wanted to see more of the world, and possibly study abroad, though they never mentioned it. Also, the post was specially upgraded to the rank of minister for me.

Despite my outwardly silent satyagraha, I continued to get 'outstanding' appraisals in my annual service records. That was evident from the proceedings of the departmental promotion committee (DPC) held in December 1987, which had considered the cases of officers of four batches (1962 to1965) together for promotion from director to joint secretary rank, wherein I had superseded officers two years senior to me. As a result, I was at the top of the panel approved for appointment as joint secretary. Though all the approved officers were simultaneously promoted as joint secretaries to avoid embarrassment to the superseded officers, I was in line to head the Department, when the time came for it.

14

The Way Forward

AT THE time of writing this, forty-two years have passed since Operation Bhindranwale-Khalistan (Op-1) was conceived in 1978 by Sanjay Gandhi with the blessings of Indira Gandhi, and forty since its scope was upgraded from a state-level to a national-level operation (Op-2), with the sole purpose of winning elections due by January 1985 for the Congress. Unfortunately, India continues to grapple with the forces set in motion by the misadventure of a couple of power-wielding young men and their friends, all extra-constitutional entities.

The religious divide of gigantic proportions created over a period finally led to an ill-conceived, badly planned and horribly executed Operation Blue Star, and to a carefully planned and surgically executed pogrom against Sikhs that followed the assassination of Indira Gandhi in Delhi and some other cities of India. In Punjab, the anguish this generated amongst the Sikh youth resulted in the most dreadful decade the state had seen.

Thousands of angry young Sikhs took to militancy, lost their lives – some accounted for, but many more still missing – before peace returned to this land.

While Sikhs were awaiting justice for the horrendous crimes of November 1984 and what happened in Punjab before, during and after Operation Blue Star, other than some window-dressing in the form of the appointment of thirteen commissions, committees and SITs (see Annexure II), nobody really attempted to unravel and address the actual issues involved, as if the appointment of mere commissions and committees were good enough to settle the matter. For good measure, what happened in Punjab during the fifteen-year period since Op-1 was launched was intentionally relegated to a non-issue.

The passage of time has not diminished the need to chart a way forward. If anything, the years gone by have shown how the aftershocks of cataclysmic events can last for decades. Indeed, forces inimical to the interests of India continue to find new and creative ways to invoke these very events to their advantage. In the overall interest of the nation, these issues need to be addressed seriously and cannot simply be brushed under the carpet.

Before suggesting a way forward, I would like to examine what had been said or done in this connection by the political parties in or out of power at the Centre since 1984, and how forces arraigned against India's interests are taking advantage of these unresolved issues.

The Congress response, over time

Of the Congress governments that came to power since 1984, nothing was expected from Prime Minister Rajiv Gandhi (November 1984 to November 1989) since he was a part of the problem. P.V. Narsimha Rao, who did not succumb to the various pressures of 10 Janpath throughout his tenure (June 1991 to May 1996) as prime minister, could have done something. But his own hands were not clean. Dr Manmohan Singh's minority Congress party-led UPA (United Progressive Alliance) government had no time – or more appropriately, no intention – during its two successive five-year terms (May 2004 to May 2014).

Dr Singh, however, did tender an apology in parliament on 12 August 2005 about what happened in November 1984. But it was more in the nature of a technical apology, meant to cleanse the Congress of its subconscious guilt. That would be evident from the wording of the apology: 'I have no hesitation in apologizing to the Sikh community. I apologize not only to the Sikh community, but to the whole Indian nation because what took place in 1984 is the negation of nationhood enshrined in our Constitution.'[1] But he did not mention who the persons responsible for that 'negation of nationhood' were. Moreover, any such apology should have come directly from the president of the Congress party, rather than from a prime minister heading a coalition government, of which the Congress party was one of the many members.

Some senior Congress leaders, especially Rahul Gandhi, did make some half-hearted, unconvincing and even contradictory statements to clarify their party's role in the November 1984 anti-Sikh pogrom. In October 2013, at an election rally in the village of Kherli in Rajasthan, Rahul Gandhi recalled his association with the two guards who assassinated Indira Gandhi. He said, 'One day, in anger, my friends killed my grandmother … There was anger in me that was like a burden. That anger was throttling me. And one day I understood. This is what happened …' Further, referring to the 2013 Hindu-Muslim riots of Muzaffarnagar, Rahul said, 'As I said before, anger is planted. It does not happen, it is planted … I too am a victim of terrorism … First you plant anger, then you ask, why are you becoming a terrorist? A terrorist is born because anger is planted in him.'[2]

In January 2014, answering a question by Arnab Goswami on the television channel Times Now on the Congress party's likely involvement in the Sikh killings in November 1984, Rahul Gandhi said, 'I remember, I was a child then. I remember that the government was doing everything that it could to stop the riots, trying to stop the killings.' However, he admitted, 'Some Congressmen probably were involved. There is a legal process through which they have gone. Some Congressmen have been punished for it.'[3]

But responding to a question on the 1984 pogrom at the International Institute of Strategic Studies in London on 24 August 2018, Rahul Gandhi said, 'It was a tragedy and painful experience. I don't agree Congress was involved.' Incidentally, that function was organized by Sam Pitroda in his capacity as head of the Indian Overseas Congress, and he was also on the podium during that address.[4]

As late as 4 December 2019, an effort was made to pass the blame for the 1984 pogrom to then Home Minister P.V. Narasimha Rao. Dr Manmohan Singh, speaking at an event at New Delhi organized in the memory of former Prime Minister I.K. Gujral, said '... perhaps the massacre of the Sikhs that took place in November 1984 could have been avoided' had Rao acted on the advice of Gujral to call in the army at the earliest to control the situation.[5] It appears that Dr Singh may not have been aware that Rao had been rendered powerless by the 1 Akbar Road group by the time Gujral and others met him with the request to call the army to control the situation.

Obviously, with 10 Janpath in control of the Congress, senior Congress leaders continued to toe the party line on the issue for decades. That policy, as revealed by the statements made by senior party leaders over the years from time to time, can be summed up as 'oppose every move aimed at linking 1 Akbar Road with the anti-Sikh pogrom, launch counter-offensive by blaming others of similar crimes, continue denying any role of the Congress as long as possible'. The hope was that lies uttered repeatedly would gain currency as gospel truth and that, over a period of time, all would be forgotten or become outdated and irrelevant.

On 9 May 2019, head of the Indian Overseas Congress, Sam Pitroda, answering a question about the anti-Sikh pogrom by a television reporter at a meeting at Dharamsala, Himachal Pradesh, said in a nonchalant manner, '*Hua to hua*' (What happened, happened).[6] Though senior party leaders, including Rahul Gandhi, tried to control the damage and made Pitroda apologize for his remarks, Pitroda's inadvertent and unguarded remark had let the cat out of the bag.

The BJP perspective

As far as the Bharatiya Janata Party (BJP) was concerned, with the Akali Dal leaders forced to adopt a hard-line stance on issues of Sikh interest, and Indira Gandhi having hijacked the Hindu agenda, the BJP adopted an equally pro-Hindu hard-line position to remain relevant in Punjab politics and to protect its Hindu vote-bank. Even the RSS, which had some inkling of the Bhindranwale-Khalistan issue much earlier, continued, if not increased, their morning 'shakha' (local branch) activities to reassure the Hindus of Punjab of their presence. It was in that context that senior BJP leader Lal Krishna Advani has written in his autobiography, *My Country, My Life* (Rupa & Co, 2008), that the BJP's agitation against Sikh extremism influenced Indira Gandhi's decision to order troops into the Golden Temple in 1984.[7]

Though Atal Bihari Vajpayee's minority government remained in power from 1998 to 2004, it could not do much to address issues related to Punjab and the 1984 pogrom as a result of its coalition compulsions and the sensitivities of its Hindu vote-bank in the north, which had still not fully recovered from the lingering poisonous effects of the policy of the Hindu-Sikh divide.

The BJP's victory in the 2014 general elections appeared to have changed the situation. It came to power for the first time with a majority of its own (282 out of a total of 543 seats) in the House and improved its performance (303) in the 2019 elections. Also, its National Democratic Alliance (NDA) partners have no interest in defending the Congress's role in Punjab or 1984 pogrom.

As mentioned in the Preface, signs of change, especially since 2017, were the main reason I felt encouraged to write this book. Certain actions taken by the NDA government during the year-long celebrations of the 550th birth anniversary (on 12 November 2019) of Guru Nanak, and also the convictions of some well-known criminals linked to the 1984 pogrom, appeared to have created a favourable impression of the present government on the Sikhs of Punjab and some of those living abroad.

Decisions taken by this government related to Guru Nanak's birth anniversary celebrations included removing in September 2019 the names of 312 of the remaining 314 Sikh NRIs from the black list that barred them from travelling to India; sanction of Rs 175 crore to Guru Nanak Dev University in Amritsar for establishment of the Centre for Inter-faith Studies; development of Sultanpur Lodhi, a town associated with the life of Guru Nanak, as a heritage city; opening of the Kartarpur corridor from the Indian side; and display of the Sikh religious symbol *Ek Onkar* (there is only one God) on Air India aircraft.[8]

The speeding up of investigations and proper prosecution in some of the 1984 pogrom-related cases has resulted in the conviction of some of the accused. In November 2018, the court of the additional sessions judge, Delhi, awarded the death sentence to Yashpal Singh and a life sentence to his co-accused, Naresh Sherawat, for the murder of two Sikh brothers from the Rangpuri area. On 28 November 2018, the Delhi High Court, setting aside a twenty-two-year-old appeal, upheld the five-year sentence awarded by the trial court to seventy of the eighty-nine accused for their role in the violence in the East Delhi area of Trilokpuri in 1984. However, the Supreme Court, on 30 April 2019, acquitted seven of these persons. Finally, on 17 December 2019, in a much-awaited judgment, the Delhi High Court awarded a life sentence to Congress politician Sajjan Kumar.[9]

Pak-sponsored activities in the West

Taking advantage of the prolonged denial of justice to the Sikhs by successive governments of India, Pakistan started making concerted efforts to internationalize the Khalistan issue by using their existing and newly created assets living in Pakistan, India and the Western countries, especially the UK, Canada and the US. Of these, the US-based organization Sikhs for Justice (SFJ), led by Gurpatwant Singh Pannun, had been the most vocal in the last few years.

At a rally held in London's Trafalgar Square on 12 August 2018, in which some separatist Kashmiris also participated, it was decided to 're-establish Punjab as an independent country' and hold 'Punjab Referendum 2020' in twenty cities in India, the US, Canada, the UK, Australia, New Zealand and some other European and Asian countries, to coincide with the thirty-sixth anniversary of the anti-Sikh pogrom of November 1984.

Keeping in view the anti-national and subversive activities of Sikhs for Justice, the Government of India declared this group an 'unlawful association' in July 2019, under the Unlawful Activities (Prevention) Act (UAPA).[10] However, sensing that its agenda had little appeal among the Sikh masses in India and abroad, SFJ has since invited all communities, including Dalits, to participate in the so-called Punjab Referendum.[11]

Those involved in pro-Khalistan and anti-India activities today are doing exactly what I had predicted in my meeting with Director (R) Gary Saxena on 8 June 1984. I had also spoken about the possibility of such things happening in February-March 1990, when I told B. Raman that the R&AW white paper that he had presented was full of white lies. The gist of my prediction in both those instances was that two parallel external influences would be working in earnest to encourage pro-Khalistan persons, organizations and associations. The main force was the Pakistan's ISI, for reasons stated earlier, and the second were some Western countries such as the US, Canada and the UK.

These countries would normally not do anything to contain or curb anti-India activities in view of the growing Sikh electorates in certain constituencies where they could influence the election results at the federal or national level. And to justify their inability to restrain pro-Khalistan and anti-India activities, they would continue emphasizing their constitutionally enshrined values of freedom of speech, freedom of association and so forth. There are, however, other ways of controlling such activities, if these countries so desired. But they would only be inclined to do so if their respective commercial or collective geopolitical interests were being served in some way.

As far as the collective geopolitical interests of the Western countries led by the US are concerned, the rise of China and its increasing economic, military and political clout as a parallel superpower is causing significant concern to them. These countries will do everything possible within their means to ensure that India is on board to contain China's rise. If India chooses to join them, then it is possible that pro-Khalistan elements may be asked to remain dormant for the time being.

There are quite a few examples of such issues being shifted to the backburner by the Western countries when it suited their geopolitical interests to do so. One example is that of Tibet, which was kept on the back burner when US President Richard Nixon's February 1972 visit to China ushered in a new era of relations between the US and China, and effectively removed China as a Cold War foe to allow the US to concentrate its efforts on the disintegration of the Soviet Union. Once that objective was achieved, the Tibet issue was brought back once again on the front burner. So, the SFJ leaders and other pro-Khalistan elements should remain ready to move from the front burner to the back burner or even into cold storage, depending on the convenience of their host countries.

Pakistan is using pro-Khalistan elements in the same manner as Indira Gandhi had used Bhindranwale to further her party's prospects. However, the end result of such operations proves usually disastrous for the persons or parties who allow themselves to be used for furthering their controllers' interests. Their handlers, at the most, stand to lose a certain amount of money, time and resources spent on such operations, in the hope that the risk-reward ratio might one day turn in their favour and pay dividends on their original investment.

It is understandable, therefore, that a certain number of persons involved in pro-Khalistan activities are directly or indirectly being financially compensated by the ISI and are also drawing pecuniary and other benefits resulting from their presence in certain Western countries. Logical arguments will have no effect on such people. My advice to Sikhs who join or support such protests even if it is out of mere curiosity is to see through their game of destabilizing Punjab, which has still not fully recovered from the consequences of a disastrous decade and a half following the launch of Op-2 by Indira Gandhi.

Knowing Sikh history fairly well, I can say that no amount of ISI propaganda can shake the loyalty of the Sikhs of Punjab towards their country. Their contributions towards India's Independence cannot be written off with one stroke of the pen. India had always belonged to the Sikhs and they will continue to belong to India.

I was, however, dismayed to read a news item about the projection of a large photograph of Bhindranwale outside Gurdwara Sri Guru Singh Sabha in Southall, London, next to the image of the fifth Sikh Guru Arjan Dev, to mark the occasion of the guru's martyrdom day on 5 June 2020.[12] What a contrast. Guru Arjan Dev made major contributions towards raising the Sikh edifice over the foundation laid by Guru Nanak and gave his life for protecting the Sikh faith. Whereas Bhindranwale willingly and knowingly colluded with the Congress to further its interests, which created a chain of events that led to the destruction of the Akal Takht and the loss of thousands of innocent lives. I hope after reading my book, the management of gurdwaras such as the Southall one would think twice before eulogizinge Bhindranwale, for whatever services to the Sikh faith they believe he might have rendered.

Truth and reconciliation

A lasting solution to the activities of anti-India forces abroad lies in addressing the basic problem at home. It is clear by now that no useful purpose will be served by beating a dead horse, namely the appointments of commissions and committees or even SITs. Even if some more goons or criminals are convicted, that would not address the grave hurt the Sikh community at large has suffered, and the trauma of a bloody decade and half since the launch of Op-2 in 1980. Let justice S.N. Dhingra's SIT be the last in that series.

So how can closure be achieved? In the absence of proper enforcement of criminal procedure, at least grant the Sikhs an opportunity to understand why, how and what actually happened between 1980 and 1995 in Punjab and elsewhere in India, and who the people responsible for it were. Also, they must know how many Sikhs lost their lives, honour and property, and how many are still missing and yet to be accounted for. These issues can only be addressed by means of a very bold political decision by a leader who can carry a majority of Indians with him, to undo a historic wrong done to a particular community of India for no fault of theirs.

Let the nation not live with that guilt forever, as it cannot be brushed under the carpet as Sam Pitroda tried to with his '*hua to hua*' comment. The community and the country need closure, and the sooner the better. I am quite hopeful that if the general public is made aware of the background and origin of these problems, they would be receptive towards, if not appreciative of, such a decision. I have shared the truth as known to me through this book, and I am sure that a number of people in the know of relevant and crucial facts would not hesitate in coming forward with information they perhaps possessed all these years but did not have the courage to disclose.

I think the appointment of a truth commission, or more appropriately a truth and reconciliation commission (TRC), as was done in the case of South Africa, though on a much smaller scale, would help bring closure to this sordid episode and also pull the rug from under the feet of anti-India forces that are taking advantage of these unresolved issues.

It is widely accepted that a truth commission (i) is focused on the past, rather than on ongoing events; (ii) investigates a pattern of events that took place over a period of time; (iii) engages directly and broadly with the affected population, gathering information on their experiences; (iv) is a temporary body, with the aim of concluding with a final report; and (v) is officially authorized or empowered by the state to carry out the assigned task.

A TRC would have to be established in India through an Act of parliament or an ordnance followed by an Act. It should be headed by a retired chief justice of the Supreme Court of India, with two sitting or retired judges of the Supreme Court as its members. I am sure India has at least three such persons of unimpeachable integrity who are willing to perform their duty as a service to the nation without any expectation of being compensated for it.

Their time-bound mandate could include the following: Was there any genuine demand for Khalistan in Punjab before 1980? If so, how many people believed in that concept at that time? If not, who were the persons responsible for the seeding of such a demand and what were the reasons thereof? Why did so many rounds of negotiations between the government and Akali leaders fail to produce any result, which could have put an end to extremist activities in Punjab? Why were softer options to capture Bhindranwale from the Golden Temple complex rejected?

Was Operation Blue Star the only solution to restore peace in Punjab? How many people actually died in Operation Blue Star? Have all the people in the Golden Temple complex and the adjacent guesthouses and offices of the SGPC present on the premises on the eve of Blue Star been accounted for? Were Bhindranwale and his two associates, Amrik Singh and Thara Singh, captured alive and then tortured to death? And if so, under whose instructions? Was anyone of the members of the 1 Akbar Road group in touch with senior army officers involved in that operation, directly or indirectly? And if so, for what purpose? Did the Golden Temple library catch fire accidentally or it was a case of arson? Were some precious historical books/documents and artefacts seized by the army from the library? If so, can they be returned? How many persons died in encounters with police in Punjab till the mid-1990s and how many of those encounters were real, and how many false? How many people are still missing in Punjab and not accounted for so far?

Regarding the murders, rapes, looting and burning of Sikh properties in Delhi and other cities in India in November 1984, the first thing that needs to be decided is whether what happened was a simple riot or needs to be classified as a pogrom or even a genocide, as per Article 2 of the UN Convention on Genocide, with its related consequences for the perpetrators of such heinous crimes. Was it pre-planned? Were the controlling powers of the home minister over Delhi Police usurped by the 1 Akbar Road group?

Who were the powerful persons who planned and directed what happened during the four fateful nights and days in Delhi from 31 October to 3 November 1984? How many people actually died in Delhi and elsewhere? What was the role of the Delhi police, especially some of the officers, first in overlooking or encouraging the killers and then later in covering up the culpability of those involved? Who were the persons behind the cover-ups? Why has justice not been dispensed to the aggrieved parties for such a long time?

These are some points that I could think of as the scope for a truth and reconciliation commission. I am sure there are better informed and more knowledgeable people who could add to this list of questions. Some of the terms of the South African TRC could also be incorporated in India's TRC. Besides, the TRC could be given the mandate to form its own questions as the inquiry progresses. The general amnesty clause could encourage a number of people to reveal important information. Two or more 'reconciliation registers' could be established, so that Indians who wish to express regret for their past individual or collective failures or misdeeds can do so through this platform. One such register could be placed outside the Golden Temple at Amritsar and the other in New Delhi, at a prominent place like the outer gate of Parliament House, or at India Gate or Jantar Mantar, and the rest in other cities such as Kanpur, where Sikhs were targeted.

Along with these physical registers, arrangements should also be made for ID-based electronic registers to let people tick on one or more listed viewpoints, as per the TRC's suggestion. To avoid misuse of the right to sign the physical registers and the right to access the electronic register, only Indian citizens and persons of Indian origin should be eligible to exercise these rights.

Simultaneously, an all-party apology needs to be tendered at a joint session of the Indian parliament in a sincere and proper manner. It could be drafted along the lines of the apology tendered in the Canadian House of Commons by Prime Minister Justin Trudeau and Opposition parties on 18 May 2016 (see Chapter 1) for a comparatively minor incident like Komagata Maru.

The above measures must be implemented. It is time for Punjab, and India, to lay the past to rest.

Annexure 1

Early Years of the R&AW and Change of Designations

THE RESEARCH & Analysis Wing was created in September 1968 through the bifurcation of the Intelligence Bureau (IB). At the time, the IB headquarters were located in a high-security and well protected part of the first floor of South Block, just above the office of the director general, military operations (DGMO). Director IB (DIB) M.L. Hooja, three of his senior joint directors and some of the top-secret and sensitive divisions functioned from there. The rest of the officers, including two joint directors, R.N. Kao and K. Sankaran Nair, with their respective charges, had their offices in nearby buildings in Lutyens' Delhi. With the creation of the R&AW, DIB and the rest of the senior officers and their staff vacated this space and moved to a portion of the first floor of North Block allocated to the Ministry of Home Affairs.

The work of sensitive divisions dealing with liaison and management of stations located abroad which was earlier handled by IB was taken over by the R&AW. Newly appointed head of the R&AW Rameshwar Nath Kao (IPS 1940 Uttar Pradesh) was promoted to the rank of additional secretary, and his close confidante, Deputy Director Col. I.J.S Hasanwalia (Retd) and three newly appointed heads of sensitive divisions moved to the South Block portion just vacated by the IB. The rest of the divisions and officers, including the R&AW's number two, K. Sankaran Nair (IPS 1943 Madras), began work at the R.K. Puram government complex and some private/residential accommodations spread across nearby colonies in New Delhi.

When I joined the R&AW in February 1972, our office (establishment wing) was in a residential building in Green Park in New Delhi. Kao had by that time been promoted to secretary rank. This arrangement of offices scattered over multiple locations continued till early 1981, when the entire staff of the R&AW, including those sitting in South Block, shifted to a newly constructed building at the Central Government Offices complex off Lodhi Road. The South Block office space was handed over to the Ministry of Defence.

R.N. Kao's rank of secretary was personal to him. The rest of the officers carried IB/paramilitary forces ranks, such as director, joint director, deputy director, joint deputy director and assistant director. These ranks continued to be used till mid-1985, when pursuant to the formation of a separate dedicated cadre, for the R&AW, previous IB/paramilitary forces ranks were replaced by secretarial ranks, such as secretary, special secretary (with a secretary's pay), additional secretary, joint secretary, director, deputy secretary and undersecretary. G.C. (Gary) Saxena was the last R&AW chief to use the director rank, and he was the first secretary of the R&AW. My rank was also changed from that of deputy director to director.

This is why readers might find two designations being used for the same person at different places in the book.

The Congress lost the sixth Lok Sabha elections in March 1977, resulting in the formation of Prime Minster Morarji Desai's four-party coalition government. Kao, who should have retired in May 1976 at the age of fifty-eight but was asked by Indira Gandhi to continue, finally put in his papers after the change in government. When K. Sankaran Nair took over from Kao, Morarji Desai reduced his rank from that of secretary to director because he suspected the R&AW to have been involved in Emergency-related activities. Nair opted for early retirement in protest. Desai also considerably reduced the department's budget, and consequently its strength, which seriously affected its performance for some time to come.

Nair's successor N.F. Suntook, was originally an emergency commissioned officer of the Indian Navy and later joined the Indian Police Service and finally the Indian Frontier Administrative Service. As a young IPS officer Suntook had worked with Desai in Bombay when the latter was chief minister (of the erstwhile Bombay State) and was able to gain his confidence. Following Indira Gandhi's return to power in January 1980, he maintained a good working relationship with her on account of his professional approach and some outside help from Kao. Gradually, he was able to restore the department to its original strength.

Annexure II

1984 Pogrom: Commissions, Committees and SITs

1. **Marwah Commission**: November 1984. Ved Marwah, additional commissioner of police, Delhi, was tasked to inquire into the role of Delhi Police during the November 1984 'riots'. As he was about to complete his inquiry in mid-1985, he was asked by the commissioner of police, Delhi, not to proceed further. His records were taken over by the government. Except for his handwritten notes, the rest of his records were handed over to the Misra Commission.
2. **Misra Commission**. May 1985. Justice Ranganath Misra, a sitting judge of the Supreme Court, submitted his report in August 1986. It was made public in February 1987. In his report, he said it was not part of his terms of reference to identify any individual but he was to only determine whether any violence had happened. His report recommended the formation of three committees. While recommending no

criminal prosecution of any individual, the commission also cleared all high-level officials of the charge of directing the riots. In its findings, the commission did acknowledge that many of the victims testifying before it had received threats from the local police. While the commission noted that there had been 'widespread lapses' on the part of the police, it concluded that 'the allegations before the commission about the conduct of the police are more of indifference and negligence during the riots than of any wrongful acts'.

3. **Kapur-Mittal Committee**: February 1987. This was created following the Misra Commission recommendations. It consisted of Justice Dalip Kapur and Kusum Lata Mittal, IAS (Retd) former secretary to the government of Uttar Pradesh. In its report submitted in 1990, the committee held seventy-two police officers guilty of conspiracy or gross negligence. Although it recommended dismissal of thirty of the seventy-two officers, no one was punished.
4. **Jain-Banerjee Committee**: Formed in 1987 as a result of the Misra Commission report, it comprised former Delhi High Court judge M.L. Jain and retired inspector general of police A.K. Banerjee. Although this committee recommended registration of cases against Sajjan Kumar in August 1987, no case was registered against him. When, in November 1987, press reports criticized the government for not registering cases despite the committee's recommendations, in December 1987, one of the co-accused in Sajjan Kumar's case filed a writ petition in the Delhi High Court and obtained a stay of proceedings against the committee's recommendations, which was not opposed by the government. The Citizen's Justice Committee, an organization working for the victims of the 1984 pogrom filed an application for vacation of the stay. The

writ petition was decided in August 1989 and the high court abolished the committee. An appeal was filed by Citizen's Justice Committee in the Supreme Court of India.

5. **Poti-Rosha Committee**: Appointed in March 1990 as successor to the Jain-Banerjee Committee by Prime Minister V.P. Singh's government. In August 1990, the committee comprising retired chief justice of the Gujrat High Court, Justice P. Subramanian Poti, and retired IPS officer P.A. Rosha, recommended filing of cases based on affidavits submitted by victims of the violence, including cases against Sajjan Kumar. When a CBI team went to Sajjan Kumar's home to question him, his supporters held a demonstration and threatened them against persisting with the cases against Kumar. When the committee's term expired in September 1990, Poti-Rosha decided to end their inquiry.
6. **Jain-Aggarwal Committee**: 1990. Appointed as successor to the Poti-Rosha Committee, it consisted of Justice J.D. Jain and former DGP of Uttar Pradesh, D.K. Aggarwal. It recommended registration of cases against H.K.L. Bhagat, Sajjan Kumar, Dharam Das Shashti and Jagdish Tytler. It also suggested the establishment of two or three special investigation teams of Delhi police under a deputy commissioner of police, supervised by an additional commissioner of police answerable to the CID, and a review of the workload of the three special courts set up to deal with the riot cases. The appointment of a special prosecutor to deal with the cases was also discussed. The committee was wound up in August 1993, but the cases it recommended were not registered by the police.
7. **Ahuja Committee**:1987. It was the third committee appointed on the recommendation of the Misra Commission, to determine the total number deaths caused by the Delhi

riots. As per its report submitted in August 1987, a total of 2,733 Sikhs were killed in the city.

8. **Dhillon Committee**: 1985. Headed by Gurdial Singh Dhillon, this committee was appointed to recommend measures for rehabilitation of the surviving victims of the riots. The committee submitted its report towards the end of 1985. One major recommendation was that the businesses (which had suffered damage in the carnage) with insurance coverage whose claims had been denied should receive compensation as directed by the government. Although the committee recommended ordering the (nationalized) insurance companies to pay the claims, the government did not accept its recommendations and the claims were not paid.
9. **Narula Committee**: 1993. Appointed by Madan Lal Khurana's BJP government in Delhi. The committee submitted its report in January 1994, recommending registration of cases against H.K.L Bhagat, Sajjan Kumar and Jagdish Tytler.
10. **The Nanavati Commission**: 2000. Appointed through a unanimous resolution passed by the Rajya Sabha following dissatisfaction expressed by some members on the outcome of the previous commissions. Headed by a retired judge of the Supreme Court, Justice J.T. Nanavati, the commission submitted its report in February 2004. The report indicated 'that the local Congress leaders and workers had either incited or helped the mob in attacking the Sikhs'. The commission issued notices to H.K.L. Bhagat, Sajjan Kumar, Dharam Das Shastri and Jagdish Tytler, and also added a new name to the list, former Union minister and Congress party leader Kamal Nath. In its report submitted in May 2005 it specifically mentions that 'the systematic manner in which the Sikhs were thus killed indicate[s] that the attacks on them were organized.'. But the

report dismissed allegations against Rajiv Gandhi. However, it recommended the reopening of four cases previously closed by the police.

11. **Mathur Committee**: 2014. Headed by a retired judge of the Supreme Court, G.P. Mathur. In its report, the committee noted that 'a proper investigation of the offences committed was not conducted' and that 'some kind of sham effort had been made to give it the shape of investigation.' It recommended the creation of an SIT to examine whether other cases that had been closed by the police needed to be reopened. The SIT comprised senior IPS officer Pramod Asthana, a retired district and sessions court judge, Rakesh Kapoor, and then deputy commissioner of Delhi police, Kumar Gyanesh.
12. **Central Government SIT**: 2015. Constituted as a result of the Mathur Committee recommendations. Comprising the above-mentioned persons, it opened a number of cases. As a result, two persons – Naresh Sherawat and Yashpal Singh – were convicted. But on December 2017, the SIT closed 186 cases without investigation. Thereafter, in a hearing on 10 January 2018, the Supreme Court decided to set up its own SIT to investigate these 186 cases.
13. **SIT headed by Justice S.N. Dhingra**: Details given in Chapter 11.

Timeline

1977	March. Indira Gandhi loses the sixth Lok Sabha elections. Morarji takes over as the PM. Congress loses Punjab state elections. P.S. Badal becomes the CM.
1978	Sanjay Gandhi and Zail Singh enlist Bhindranwale's support for Op-1.
1978	13 April, Amritsar Nirankari Convention. Thirteen Sikhs and three Nirankaris killed.
1978	August. Dal Khalsa created by Zail Singh and other Punjab Congress leaders.
1980	January. Indira Gandhi wins seventh Lok Sabha elections. Becomes the PM. Op-1 converted to Op-2.
1980	24 April. Nirankari head Gurbachan Singh shot dead.
1980	23 June: Sanjay Gandhi dies in an air crash. Replaced by Rajiv Gandhi as Indira Gandhi's main advisor.

1980	December. New division in the R&AW to look after Sikh extremism, etc.
1981	March. Sikh Education Conference, Chandigarh. Ganga Singh Dhillon presides.
1981	August. R.N. Kao appointed Senior Advisor.
1981	9 September. Lala Jagat Narain shot dead. Bhindranwale arrested on 20 September.
1981	29 September. Dal Khalsa highjacks IAC flight. Demands Bhindranwale's release.
1981	16 October. First of the twenty-six rounds of talks for a negotiated solution.
1982	April. Bhindranwale visits Delhi with his gunmen.
1982	19 July. Bhindranwale shifts to Guru Nanak Niwas.
1982	1 August. Indira Gandhi visits Richmond Hill Gurudwara, Queens, New York.
1982	4 August. Dharam Yudh Morcha launched.
1982	3 November. Swaran Singh formula for peaceful solution first approved and then sabotaged overnight by Indira Gandhi.
1982	4 November. SAD announces plan to disrupt Asian Games at New Delhi.
1982	December. Meeting of 5,000 ex-servicemen at the Golden Temple.
1983	April: SAD announces Rasta Roko Morcha.
1983	25 April: DIG of police A.S. Atwal shot dead while exiting the Golden Temple complex.
1983	5 October. Six Hindus dragged out of a bus and shot dead in Kapurthala District.
1983	6 October. Darbara Singh government dismissed. Governor replaced.

1983 15 December. Bhindranwale shifts from Guru Nanak Niwas to Akal Takht.

1984 February. Balwant Singh sabotages withdrawal of Akali morcha.

1984 26 May. Last round of talks with SAD leaders at secret location. Home Minister Rao not available to Kuldip Nayar after having tasked him to convince SAD leaders on division of Chandigarh.

1984 June. Longowal calls for stoppage of grain movement out of state and non-payment of taxes from 3 June.

1984 4–7 June. Operation Blue Star.

1984 July. Central government white paper on Punjab tabled in parliament.

31 October. Indira Gandhi's assassination by her two Sikh security guards.

Rajiv Gandhi administered oath of office as the PM by President Zail Singh.

1984 31 October–3 November. Anti-Sikh pogrom in Delhi and other cities of India.

Notes

Preface

1 G.S. Chawla, *Bloodshed in Punjab: Untold Saga of Deceit and Sabotage*, New Delhi: Har-Anand Publication Pvt Ltd, 2016, pp. 7–8.

2 Kuldip Nayar, *Beyond the Lines: An Autobiography*, Delhi: Roli Books, 2012.

1: Introduction

1 *The Emergency – A Personal History* by Coomi Kapoor. See also *Indian Express* news report by Manoj C.G. Updated June 13, 2015.

2 Pranab Mukherjee, *The Dramatic Decade: The Indira Gandhi Years,* New Delhi: Rupa Publications India, 2014.
See also, http://www.millenniumpost.in/ss-ray-pushed-clueless-indira-to-decalre-emergency-48157, accessed on 27 March 2020.

3 B. Raman, *The Kaoboys of R&AW:Down Memory Lane,* New Delhi: Lancer Publishers, 2012, p. 87.

4 William Dalrymple and Anita Anand, *Kohinoor: The Story of the World's Most Infamous Diamond, New Delhi:* Juggernaut, 2016.

2: Canada and the Sikh Diaspora in the Late Seventies

1 Narinder Singh, *Canadian Sikhs: History, religion, and culture of Sikhs in North America*, Ottawa: Canadian Sikh Studies Institute, 1994, pp. 32–33.
2 Ibid., pp. 44–45.
3 Ibid., p. 56.
4 Ibid., pp. 72–73.
5 Harish K. Puri, *Making of Ghadar Movement*, Part I: A Compilation on the Ghadar Movement, Patiala: Publication Bureau, Punjabi University, 2013, pp. 145, 155.
6 *The Ghadar Movement: Background, Ideology, Action & Legacies*, Part II: A Compilation on the Ghadar Movement, Patiala: Publication Bureau, Punjabi University; Darshan S. Tatla, *Komagata Maru Voyage and the Ghadar Uprising, Part III (2):* A Compilation on the Ghadar Movement, Patiala: Publication Bureau, Punjabi University, pp. 198-199.
7 Harish K. Puri, *Making of the Ghadar Movement*, p. 123.
8 Darshan S. Tatla, *Komagata Maru Voyage and the Ghadar Uprising*, p. 200.
9 Ibid., p. 213.
10 CBC News, 18 May 2016.
11 Ontario Council of Sikhs, *Sikhs in Ontario*, Toronto: Ontario Council of Sikhs, 1993, pp. 34–36.
12 Uday Singh's obituary in Sikh24.com in its issue dated 23 November 2013.

3: Punjab in the Late Seventies and My Return to Headquarters

1 G.S. Chawla, *Bloodshed in Punjab: Untold Saga of Deceit and Sabotage*, New Delhi: Har-Anand Publication Pvt Ltd, 2016, pp. 5–7.
2 Kuldip Nayar, *Beyond the Lines. An Autobiography,* New Delhi: Roli Books, 2012), p.282.
3 https://theprint.in/politics/rivalry-between-sikhs-nirankaris-is-almost-a-century-old/151853/, accessed in June 2020.
4 Mark Tully and Satish Jacob, *Amritsar: Mrs Gandhi's Last Battle*, New Delhi: Rupa Publications, 2006, p. 60.
5 Kuldip Nayar: *Beyond the Lines. An Autobiography*, p. 282.
6 G.S. Chawla, *Bloodshed in Punjab: Untold Saga of Deceit and Sabotage*, New Delhi: Har-Anand Publications, 2016, p. 69.

7 Mark Tully and Satish Jacob, *Amritsar: Mrs Gandhi's Last Battle*, p. 60.
8 B.G. Deshmukh, *From Poona To Prime Minister's Office: A Cabinet Secretary Looks Back*, New Delhi: HarperCollins Publishers, 2004, p. 359.
9 Ibid.
10 Ibid., p. 97.
11 Mark Tully and Satish Jacob, *Amritsar: Mrs Gandhi's Last Battle,* p. 61.
12 Ibid.
13 Ibid.
14 Ibid., p. 62.

4: The Rise of Bhindranwale (1980–81)

1 Mark Tully and Satish Jacob, *Amritsar: Mrs Gandhi's Last Battle*, New Delhi: Rupa Publications, 2006, pp. 65–66.
2 G.S. Chawla, *Bloodshed in Punjab: Untold Saga of Deceit and Sabotage*, New Delhi: Har-Anand Publications, 2016, p. 102.
3 Ibid., p. 103.
4 Mark Tully and Satish Jacob, *Amritsar: Mrs Gandhi's Last Battle,* p. 66.
5 Ibid., p. 67.
6 Kanwar Sandhu, interview of Lt Gen. S.K. Sinha, 26 June 2011, https://www.youtube.com/watch?v=db5GX0LLN-4, accessed on 6 April 2020.
7 G.S. Chawla, *Bloodshed in Punjab: Untold Saga of Deceit and Sabotage,* p. 73.
8 Ibid., p. 74.
9 Mark Tully and Satish Jacob, *Amritsar: Mrs Gandhi's Last Battle,* p. 70.
10 Ibid., p. 71.
11 Ibid., p. 71.
12 Ibid., p. 72.

5: Negotiated Solution: A Prolonged Charade?

1 G.S. Chawla, *Bloodshed in Punjab: Untold Saga of Deceit and Sabotage*, New Delhi: Har-Anand Publications, 2016, p. 74.
2 P.C. Alexander, *Through The Corridors of Power: An Insider's Story*, New Delhi: HarperCollins India, 2004, p. 241.
3 Ibid., p. 244.
4 Mark Tully and Satish Jacob, *Amritsar: Mrs Gandhi's Last Battle*, New Delhi: Rupa Publications, 13th Impression, 2018, p. 69.
5 P.C. Alexander, *Through the Corridors of Power: An Insider's Story,* p. 247.

6 Ibid., p. 248; and G.S. Chawla, *Bloodshed in Punjab: Untold Saga of Deceit and Sabotage*, p. 97.
7 P.C. Alexander, *Through the Corridors of Power: An Insider's Story,* p. 249.
8 Mark Tully and Satish Jacob, *Amritsar: Mrs Gandhi's Last Battle*, 2006, pp. 79–80.
9 Kuldip Nayar, *Beyond the Lines: An Autobiography*, New Delhi: Roli Books, 2012, p. 284.
10 Ibid., p. 284.
11 Ibid., p. 284.
12 Ibid., p. 285.
13 Ibid., p. 281.
14 Ibid., p. 28.
15 G.S. Chawla, *Bloodshed in Punjab: Untold Saga of Deceit and Sabotage*, p. 26.
16 Ibid., p. 38.
17 Ibid., p. 26.
18 Ibid.
19 Ibid.
20 Ibid., p. 39.
21 Mark Tully and Satish Jacob, *Amritsar: Mrs Gandhi's Last Battle*, p. 83.
22 https://www.nytimes.com/1982/11/19/world/under-threat-new-delhi-braces-for-sikh-protests.html
23 G.S. Chawla, *Bloodshed in Punjab: Untold Saga of Deceit and Sabotage*, p. 134.
24 P.C. Alexander, *Through the Corridors of Power: An Insider's Story,* p. 258.
25 Ibid., p. 258.
26 Mark Tully and Satish Jacob, *Amritsar: Mrs Gandhi's Last Battle*, p. 90.
27 Ibid., p. 92.
28 G.S. Chawla, *Bloodshed in Punjab: Untold Saga of Deceit and Sabotage*, p. 90.
29 P.C. Alexander, *Through the Corridors of Power: An Insider's Story,* pp. 291–92.
30 Kuldip Nayar, *Beyond The Lines: An Autobiography*, p. 291.

6: Indira Gandhi's 1982 US State Visit

1 *India Today,* 31 August 1982; *New York Times,* 28 July 1982.
2 *New York Times,* 1 August 1982.
3 *India Today,* 28 February 1983.

7: A State of Controlled Chaos

1 Mark Tully and Satish Jacob, *Amritsar: Mrs Gandhi's Last Battle*, New Delhi: Rupa Publications, 2006, p. 94.
2 Ibid., p. 95.
3 *India Today*, 30 April 1983.
4 Mark Tully and Satish Jacob, *Amritsar: Mrs Gandhi's Last Battle*, p. 95.
5 Ibid., p. 92.
6 *India Today*, 31 May 1983.
7 Ibid.
8 Mark Tully and Satish Jacob, *Amritsar: Mrs Gandhi's Last Battle*, p. 98.
9 Ibid., p. 100.
10 Ibid, p. 121.
11 Ibid., p. 103.
12 Ibid., p. 105.
13 Ibid., p. 117.
14 G.S. Chawla, *Bloodshed in Punjab: Untold Saga of Deceit and Sabotage*, New Delhi: Har-Anand Publications, 2016, p. 29.
15 Mark Tully and Satish Jacob, *Amritsar: Mrs Gandhi's Last Battle*, p. 117.
16 Ibid., p. 137.

8: My Third Visit to the US and Canada

1 *India Today,* 31 October 1983.
2 Based on a telephonic conversation with Ambassador K.C. Singh (Retd) on 26 May 2020.

9: The Aborted Heliborne Commando Operation

1 B. Raman, *The Kaoboys of R&AW: Down Memory Lane*, New Delhi: Lancer Publications, 2007, p. 96.
2 https://philmiller.info/2014/01/15/margaret-thatcher-gave-full-support-over-golden-temple-raid-letter-shows, accessed on 15 June 2020.
3 *The Guardian*, 4 February 2014.
4 BBC World News, 7 June 2014.
5 *The Guardian*, 4 February 2014
6 https://www.rediff.com/news/special/helicopter-deal-indias-dubious-westland-saga/20130220.htm, accessed on 15 June 2020.

7 PTI report in *The Economic Times*, 12 July 2018.
8 *India Today*, 31 January 2014.
9 Based on my conversations with R.T. Nagrani, IPS (Retd). Used with permission.
10 Based on my discussions with M.P.S Aulakh, IPS (retd). Used with permission.
11 Navdeep Gupta, interview by Global CPN TV, Punjab. https://www.youtube.com/watch?v=ypzsNfvlG28, accessed on 5 June 2019.

10: P.C. Alexander, R.N. Kao and B. Raman

1 https://www.outlookindia.com/newswire/story/p-c-alexander-a-man-for-all-seasons/730806, accessed on 30 June 2020.
2 https://www.nytimes.com/1985/04/16/world/19-are-charged-in-indian-espionage-scandal.html, accessed on 30 June 2020.
3 P.C. Alexander, *Through the Corridors of Power: An Insider's Story*, New Delhi: HarperCollins India, 2004, p. 292.
4 G.S. Chawla, *Bloodshed in Punjab: Untold Saga of Deceit and Sabotage*, New Delhi: Har-Anand Publications, 2016, p. 28.
5 P.C. Alexander, *Through the Corridors of Power: An Insider's Story*, p. 293.
6 A.B. Vajpayee, *State of the Nation: Four Decades in Parliament*, New Delhi: Shipra Books, 1996, p. 504.
7 B. Raman, *The Kaoboys of R&AW: Down Memory Lane*, New Delhi: Lancer Publications, 2007, p. 117.
8 Ibid., p. 95.
9 Ibid., p. 105.
10 Ibid., p. 105.
11 Ibid., p. 107.
12 *The Economic Times*, 10 June 2020.
13 B. Raman, *The Kaoboys of R&AW: Down Memory Lane*, p. 114.
14 Ibid., p. 110.

11: Operation Blue Star

1 Mark Tully and Satish Jacob, *Amritsar: Mrs Gandhi's Last Battle*, New Delhi: Rupa Publications, 2006, p. 147.
2 P.C. Alexander, *Through the Corridors of Power: An Insider's Story,* New Delhi: HarperCollins India, 2004, p. 294.

3 Ibid., p. 294.
4 Ibid., pp. 295–298.
5 Mark Tully and Satish Jacob, *Amritsar: Mrs Gandhi's Last Battle*, p. 144.
6 P.C. Alexander, *Through the Corridors of Power: An Insider's Story*, pp. 298–99.
7 Mark Tully and Satish Jacob, *Amritsar: Mrs Gandhi's Last Battle*, p. 142.
8 Ibid., p. 145.
9 Kanwar Sandhu, interview of Lt Gen. S.K. Sinha. https://www.youtube.com/watch?v=db5GX0LLN-4&t=2s, accessed on 30 June 2020.
10 Based on my meetings and conversations with G.S. Pandher, and email from him dated 12 February 2020.
11 P.C. Alexander, *Through the Corridors of Power: An Insider's Story*, p. 300.
12 Ibid.
13 Mark Tully and Satish Jacob, *Amritsar: Mrs Gandhi's Last Battle*, pp. 152–53.
14 Ibid., p. 168.
15 Ibid., p. 170.
16 Ibid., p. 171.
17 Ibid., p. 172.
18 Ibid., p. 171.
19 Ibid., p. 151.
20 Ibid., p. 167.
21 Ibid., p. 176.
22 Ibid., p. 177.
23 P.C. Alexander, *Through the Corridors of Power: An Insider's Story*, p. 302.
24 Mark Tully and Satish Jacob, *Amritsar: Mrs Gandhi's Last Battle*, p. 182.
25 Ibid., pp. 182–83.
26 Ibid., p. 183.
27 *Mint*, updated on 6 June 2014; *India Today*, 15 November 1984.
28 Mark Tully and Satish Jacob, *Amritsar: Mrs Gandhi's Last Battle*, pp. 197–98.
29 Sanjay Suri, *1984: The Anti-Sikh Violence and After*, Noida: HarperCollins India, 2015, pp. 181–85.

12: Indira Gandhi's Assassination and the Anti-Sikh Pogrom

1 *The Washington Post*, 5 September 1985. See also Sanjay Suri, *1984: The Anti-Sikh Violence and After*, Noida: HarperCollins India, 2015, p. 208.

2 A Joint report by Rao, Amiya Ghosh, Aurobindo Pancholi quoted in *The Economic Times* ePaper, 17 December 2018.
3 https://economictimes.indiatimes.com/opinion/interviews/vinay-sitapati-on-congress-betrayal-of-pv-narasimha-rao-and-bjps-attempts-at-reviving-his-legacy/articleshow/52918738.cms, accessed on 30 June 2020.
4 Sanjay Suri, *1984: The Anti-Sikh Violence and After*, p. 27.
5 Justice Ranganath Misra Commission report (available on the Internet).
6 Sanjay Suri, *1984: The Anti-Sikh Violence and After*, pp. 46–53.
7 Ibid., pp. 211–212.
8 *Outlook*, 18 January 2020.
9 *The Times of India*, 16 January 2020.
10 *Outlook*, 18 January 2020.
11 My telephonic discussion with Amar Bhushan, IPS (Retd), former special secretary, cabinet secretariat, Government of India, New Delhi, on 6 June 2019.

13: The Aftermath

1 *The Tribune*, 2 July 2020; and *The Hindu*, 1 July 2020.
2 *Edmonton Journal*, 4 February 2015; Sohi's interview with Hamdard TV, 11 March 2016 and *Global News*, Canada, 19 September 2019.
3 *The Economic Times*, 4 & 5 April 2016; *Live Mint*, 5 April 2016 and *Deccan Chronicle*, 5 April 2016.

14: The Way Forward

1 https://www.thehindu.com/news/the-india-cables/Manmohan-Singhs-apology-for-anti-Sikh-riots-a-lsquoGandhian-moment-of-moral-clarity-says-2005-cable/article14692805.ece, accessed on 30 June 2020.
2 https://www.youtube.com/watch?v=lv0lfj85oMA, accessed on 30 June 2020.
3 Sanjay Suri, *1984: The Anti-Sikh Violence and After,* Noida: HarperCollins India, 2015, pp. 36–37.
4 *The Times of India*, 27 August 2018.
5 *The Times of India* and *The Economic Times*, 6 December 2019.
6 *The Times of India*, 10 May 2019.

7 *Hindustan Times*, 8 April 2008.

8 *Hindustan Times*, 13 September 2019; *The Times of India*, 28 September 2019; *India Today*, 28 October 2019; *Pioneer*, 8 November 2019.

9 *The Times of India*, 21 November 2018; *The Times of India* and *The Economic Times,* 29 November 2018.

10 *The Times of India*, 11 July 2019, 6 August 2019; 13 August 2018.

11 *The Tribune*, 30 January 2020.

12 *The Times of India*, 5 June 2020.

www.ingramcontent.com/pod-product-compliance
Lightning Source LLC
LaVergne TN
LVHW101636100826
845155LV00011B/25/J
* 9 7 8 9 3 9 0 3 2 7 7 2 0 *